Emblems of Pluralism

THE CULTURAL LIVES OF LAW

AUSTIN SARAT

SERIES EDITOR

Emblems of Pluralism: Cultural Differences and the State
by Carol Weisbrod

Emblems of Pluralism

CULTURAL DIFFERENCES AND THE STATE

Carol Weisbrod

PRINCETON UNIVERSITY PRESS
PRINCETON AND OXFORD

ISBN (cl.): 0-691-08924-8
ISBN (pbk.): 0-691-08925-6

British Library Cataloging-in-Publication Data is available

This book has been composed in Sabon and Futura

Printed on acid-free paper. ∞

www.pupress.princeton.edu

Printed in the United States of America

10 9 8 7 6 5 4 3 2 1

All of us then are living within numberless, more or less compactly, occasionally quite loosely, organized associations, and our fate in life will, in the main, be conditioned by the kind of position we are able to achieve within them.

—EUGEN EHRLICH, *Fundamental Principles of the Sociology of Law*

Contents

Acknowledgments

✦ *EMBLEMS OF PLURALISM* is the development of material that has engaged me for a very long time. Inevitably, the book is built on past and present work and association.

Many people have provided assistance at some point in the project. Family, friends, and participants in the meetings at which this work was first presented have all made contributions. Among those to be particularly thanked are Milner Ball, Mark Janis, Carolyn Jones, Richard Kay, Martha Minow, Carl Schneider, and Steven Wilf. Thanks are also due to the Centre for Studies of Religion and Society at the University of Victoria, where I was a fellow in January 1998.

Aviam Soifer deserves special thanks for his consistent willingness to read and comment on drafts. References to art and art history show my debt to Pamela Sheingorn.

I would like to thank Austin Sarat for his general encouragement of interdisciplinary writing on law and for his specific suggestions concerning the manuscript. And I am grateful also for the comments made by anonymous reviewers for Princeton University Press.

I continue to be grateful for institutional support from the Law School and the Law Library of the University of Connecticut.

Finally, I would like to acknowledge helpful exchanges over many years with the late Leon Lipson and the late Henry Schwarzschild.

This book is based in substantial part on reworking of the following publications:

"Towards a History of Essential Federalism: Another Look at Owen in America." *Connecticut Law Review* 21 (1989): 979.

"The Law and Reconstituted Christianity: The Case of the Mormons." Reprinted by permission from *Religious Conscience, the State, and the Law: Historical Contexts and Contemporary Significance,* by John McLaren and Harold Coward (eds.), the State University of New York Press. © 1999 State University of New York. (All Rights Reserved.)

"Minorities and Diversities: The Remarkable Experiment of the League of Nations." Originally published in the *Connecticut Journal of International Law* 8 (1993): 359.

"Emblems of Federalism." *Michigan Journal of Law Reform* 25 (1992): 795.

Other related work is also used, and cited as appropriate.

Introduction

✦ "TODAY we take the state for granted," writes Joseph Strayer. "We grumble about its demands; we complain that it is encroaching more and more on what used to be our private concerns."[1] At the same time, he says, we can hardly conceive of life without the state. "The old forms of social identification are no longer absolutely necessary. A man can lead a reasonably full life without a family, a fixed local residence, or a religious affiliation, but if he is stateless he is nothing." Such a person has "no rights, no security, and little opportunity for a useful career." The conclusion is there "is no salvation on earth outside the framework of an organized state."

We shape our experiences as citizens of the state. At the same time we are members of other groups. The norms to which we are subject as citizens are called law. The norms of groups other than the state are, at least initially, often called roles or frames. When these solidify, when the group is identified and the relationship between the individual and the group is seen as structural, we call these normative systems group codes or rules.

This book consists of essays on the subject of individuals, groups, and the state, focusing on the state's response to cultural difference, a response that often takes the form of law.

There is no attempt here to define culture. A useful starting point for discussion is Raymond Williams's *Keywords,* which notes that *culture* is one of the most complicated words in the language.[2] Clearly, the term can be defined from within a discipline or a usage. A familiar anthropological definition, for example, is "[that] complex whole which includes knowledge, belief, art, morals, law, custom, and any other capabilities and habits acquired by man as a member of society."[3] As Terry Eagleton notes, this seems to mean that "[c]ulture is just everything which is not genetically transmissible."[4] The idea of culture adds to the scholarly conversation about law and society an opportunity to invoke materials beyond the

---

[1] Joseph Strayer, *On the Medieval Origins of the Modern State* (Princeton: Princeton University Press, 1970), 3; cf. W. H. Auden, "September 1, 1939," in *Selected Poems,* ed. Edward Mendelson (New York: Vintage Books, 1979), 88: "There is no such thing as the State / And no one exists alone."

[2] Raymond Williams, *Keywords: A Vocabulary of Culture and Society,* rev. ed. (Oxford: Oxford University Press, 1985).

[3] Terry Eagleton, *The Idea of Culture* (Oxford: Blackwell, 2000), 34.

[4] Eagleton, *The Idea of Culture.*

social science familiar to the sociologist, or the literature, however defined, used by law-and-literature scholars. In effect, the idea of culture
allows a connection between law and anything that people do.

The effort to relate law and culture looks at official law, state law, from
a stance outside law and its personnel. It uses *culture* to invoke literary,
artistic, and journalistic worlds. To the extent that the effort relates law
to "cultural studies," a question arises beyond those ordinarily associated
with interdisciplinary work in law: Current work in cultural studies often
identifies itself with a particularly intense form of boundary breaking, a
challenge to givens that regularly invokes the transgressive. How could
law, often taken to express all that is orderly, authoritative, and powerful,
have anything to contribute to the destabilizing agendas and strategies
associated with cultural studies?

Various answers are possible here. One relates to the point that law to
some degree creates the conditions of culture. Another notes that law, as
a cultural product, has something in common with other cultural products.[5] In the anthropologist's definition, laws are part of culture. Still another focuses on the point that while law is to some extent a mandarin
text, it is itself a subject of popular culture.[6]

This book builds on another answer, however, to the effect that the
familiar description of law posited originally—those norms emanating
from and enforced by the state—while a view of law that is certainly
common, is not the only characterization available to us. In the same way
that cultural studies tries to break open the concept of culture, this book
tries to open some ideas relating to law and the state.[7]

Although the book uses an idea of difference illustrated largely by ethnic and religious difference, it also discusses other sorts of difference and
stresses that what counts as difference is not constant. The social (or attributed) meanings of difference change, as do individuals' and groups'
ideas about the meanings and importance of differences. The book assumes that representations of group life can be found in judicial opinions
as well as in television programs or novels, and these representations are
not independent of each other. Moreover, relations between law and cul-

---

[5] See Carol Weisbrod, "Fusion Folk: A Comment on Law and Music," *Cardozo Law Review* 1999:1439.

[6] Lawrence Friedman, "Lawyers and Popular Culture," *Yale Law Journal* 98 (1989): 1579.

[7] This effort may be seen as writing "against law," in the sense that it writes against a particular idea of law. On law/culture and the idea of writing against, see Austin Sarat and Thomas R. Kearns, eds., *Law in the Domains of Culture* (Ann Arbor: University of Michigan Press, 1998), intro. See also the comment of Rosemary Coombe, "Contingent Articulations," in the same volume, p. 22 n. 1.

ture exist over time, so that the same legal event may have a first life and then a second and a third.

The book argues that the ideas of individual identities, groups, and states are not fixed, either in themselves or in relation to each other. A "state" may be stronger or weaker than internal groups, and groups may be internal or external to states—or both, existing as subgroup and as supranational organization. The relative distribution of power differs in different contexts and is not determined a priori. So too the "self."

For Ludwig von Mises, writing in 1944, the American and the German views of government and state were radically different. "To the American mind the notion of an *Obrigkeit,* a government the authority of which was not derived from the people, was and is unknown. It is extremely difficult to explain to a man to whom the writings of Milton, Paine, the Declaration of Independence, the Constitution and the Gettysburg Address are the fountain springs of political education what is meant by this German term *obrigkeit.*" Mises illustrates with a Prussian quotation from 1838: "[I]t is not seemly for a subject to apply the yardstick of his wretched intellect to the acts of the chief of state and arrogate to himself, in haughty insolence, a public judgment about their fairness."[8]

State, in short, is not a word with one meaning. At the same time, we moderns are committed to the importance of the state, just as we are committed to law. In fact, according to one view the state and the law are basically one thing. If we look for the state, we find officials: "For the jurist, the State can be nothing other than the body of laws in force at a given time and place. The State itself is created by the law. State and law coincide: the State *is* the legal system."[9]

The emphasis on the state is parallel to the historical tendency of American law toward centralization. "One basic, critical fact of 19th century law," Lawrence Friedman writes, "was that the official legal system began to penetrate deeper into society."[10] The master trend is "to create one legal culture out of many; to reduce legal pluralism; . . . to increase the proportion of persons, relative to the whole population, who are consumers or objects of that law. This master trend continues, and accelerates."

[8] Ludwig von Mises, *Bureaucracy* (Grove City, Pa.: Libertarian Press, 1944), iv. He also uses material from 1891: "Our officials . . . will never tolerate anybody's wresting the power from their hands, certainly not parliamentary majorities whom we know how to deal with in a masterly way. No kind of rule is endured so easily or accepted so gratefully as that of high-minded and highly educated civil servants. The German state is a State of the supremacy of officialdom--let us hope, that it will remain so."

[9] Alessandro D'Entreves, *The Notion of the State: An Introduction to Political Theory* (Oxford: Oxford University Press, 1967), 5. In effect, there is no state other than officials. And for the jurist, these officials are created by and act under the law.

[10] Lawrence M. Friedman, *A History of American Law* (New York: Simon and Schuster, 1973), 99.

As part of this master trend and the corresponding emphasis on the state, we can see official law as uniquely important. Thus, Ronald Dworkin begins *Law's Empire* by saying that "[w]e live in and by the law. It makes us what we are: citizens and employees and doctors and spouses and people who own things."[11] Given this view of law's importance, it is no wonder that much legal theory has focused on issues of official adjudication.

But there are other views, in which, for example, state law itself is bounded by other rulers and other "law." We have the familiar and opaque statement of John Chipman Gray: "[T]he real rulers of a political society are undiscoverable."[12] And pluralist tendencies continue. In America, Lawrence Friedman tells us, the struggle between centralism and decentralism is persistent and continuing. "[D]ecentralization does not vanish," he says, "even in the teeth of the master trend of American legal history."[13]

In his discussion of America as a "plastic" and "malleable" society, Merle Curti refers to a "widespread commitment to anti-statism and voluntary associations."[14] Thus, there is a tension between the lawyer's story of American history (in the beginning, America was founded under the Constitution, Blackstone was important,[15] and the Marshall Court undertook national consolidation) and that told by others (in the beginning, America had little sense of the state[16] and did not follow Blackstone).[17] For lawyers, the master trend of centralization and vertical relationships almost entirely ignores, if it does not conceal, the pluralist or horizontal counterstory.

[11] Preface to Ronald Dworkin, *Law's Empire* (Cambridge: Belknap Press of Harvard University Press, 1986), vii; see also Alexander M. Bickel, *The Morality of Consent* (New Haven: Yale University Press, 1975), 5 (discussing law as the value of values).

[12] John Chipman Gray, *Nature and Sources of the Law* (New York: Columbia University Press, 1909), 77.

[13] Friedman, *History of American Law,* 572.

[14] Merle Curti, "Robert Owen in American Thought," in *Robert Owen's American Legacy: Proceedings of the Robert Owen Bicentennial Conference,* ed. D. Pitzer (Indianapolis: Indiana Historical Society, 1972), 57.

[15] But what did Blackstone represent? For the ambiguity of Blackstone on significant issues, e.g., natural law and legislative sovereignty, see Robert Cover, *Justice Accused: Antislavery and the Judicial Process* (New Haven: Yale University Press, 1975), 25.

[16] See, e.g., Samuel Huntington, *American Politics: The Promise of Disharmony* (Cambridge: Belknap Press of Harvard University Press, 1981), 35. Huntington indicates that the idea of the state "never took hold among the English North American colonists," despite "fulminations of Blackstone." The state, he says, appears in American political thought only at the end of the nineteenth century. See also S. Skowponek, *Building a New American State: The Expansion of National Administrative Capacities, 1877–1920* (New York: Cambridge University Press, 1982) (Early America had little idea of the state, but, instead, a sense of "courts and parties" (28)).

[17] Huntington, *American Politics.*

By contrast, the pluralist story would not surprise a legal anthropologist. In a review article on work in legal anthropology, Sally Engle Merry describes two orientations as to pluralism, the first beginning with research derived from the colonial situation and focused on the interaction between the indigenous legal system and the law brought by the colonial power, the second, more recent, centered on work acknowledging that the phenomenon of legal pluralism is more generalized.[18]

One might say that legal anthropology stands to pluralism as Freud stood to the unconscious. Responding to the idea that he had discovered the unconscious, Freud noted that philosophers and poets had been well aware of the unconscious; what he had contributed was a way of studying it scientifically.[19]

Those in political theory or law who have studied pluralism and written on the question have ordinarily addressed others who approached the question in a comparable way, focusing on the literatures familiar in those particular conversations. But, of course, there are various ways of studying things scientifically, and even ways of thinking about things that may not qualify as "scientific."

Conversations about pluralism go on within many fields and even, quite generally, in forums that are not in "fields" (or "disciplines") at all, but simply discussions among people who think about their environments. Montaigne, in assessing the sovereignty of custom, was thinking about pluralism, as was Montesquieu in thinking about law in different settings and climates.

The idea that legal pluralism is ubiquitous was reinforced by another source of legal pluralist thinking that derives from studies in legal history, and particularly the work of F. W. Maitland on Gierke. This material was linked to historical studies in the field of church and state, a field that, as Marc Galanter once commented, is the locus classicus of pluralist thinking. Political theory, and particularly the work of the English pluralists in the 1930s, was also built on an exploration of the relationship between individuals, groups, and states. Yet another set of ideas rejecting the state as sole source of normative thinking and power comes from Foucault, who argued generally for a diffuse sense of the sources of power and coercion, some public, some private.

Montesquieu much earlier noted that "many things govern men," "Climate, religion, laws, the maxims of the government, examples of past things, mores and manner." These formed the general spirit. He believed

---

[18] Sally Engle Merry, "Legal Pluralism," *Law and Society Review* 22 (1988): 869–96.

[19] Freud quoted in Lionel Trilling, "Freud and Literature," in *The Liberal Imagination: Essays on Literature and Society* (New York: Viking Press, 1951), 34.

that to the extent that any one of these dominated, the others would yield. In some places it would be one thing, in some another.[20]

This book draws widely on these different discussions, stressing that the questions treated here are understood as important in many different contexts, and that debates over these universal questions are conducted in different vocabularies.

A central issue in many discussions is the idea of state sovereignty. Austinian positivism, with its emphasis on the command of the sovereign, and the idea of law as founded in the state, took hold in the modern world. In America, for example, legal pluralist tendencies within the state system itself are presented as minimized by rules of priority. These rules appear on the surface to resolve conflicts by reference to the differing degrees of "rank formality" of the competing laws. Thus in America we say that the federal Constitution is supreme and stands over all contrary law, that federal statutes stand over state law, and so on.[21] Leon Lipson has offered a conventional map of a legal system.

> According to that map, the accuracy of which need not yet concern us, law is prescribed by a single, known official organ, or by two or more of them in compliance with a process that itself has been officially prescribed; law is interpreted and applied to disputes by a court or a set of courts, or by sets of courts linked through secondary rules that are calculated to reconcile or harmonize conflicts; the statutes and regulations emanate from agencies coordinated closely or loosely under central authority.

And finally, "compliance is known to be enforced where necessary by official authority whose physical power is in general adequate to the purpose."[22]

If we do raise questions about the accuracy of the map, we find that it is highly idealized. There are irregularities in the legal system itself that have been flattened out, and the people, individuals and groups who are the objects of the official gaze, who observe it as it is observing them, are not yet in the picture.

---

[20] Montesquieu, *Spirit of the Laws,* trans. and ed. Anne M. Cohler, Basia Carolyn Miller, and Harold Samuel Stone (Cambridge: Cambridge University Press, 1989), bk. 19, chap. 4, p. 310; see also p. 494. As Isaiah Berlin pointed out, this idea underlies historical jurisprudence and modern sociology of law. Isaiah Berlin, "Montesquieu," in *Against the Current: Essays in the History of Ideas* (London: Hogarth Press, 1980), 130–61, 154.

[21] See Patrick Atiyah and Robert Summers, *Form and Substance in American Law: A Comparative Study of Legal Reasoning* (Oxford: Oxford University Press, 1987), 56.

[22] Leon Lipson, "International Law," in *Handbook of Political Science,* ed. F. Greenstein and N. Polsby (Reading, Mass.: Addison-Wesley, 1975), 415–16.

This book is an attempt to offer a more complete account of certain phases of the relations between individuals, groups, and the state, with a continuing emphasis on cultural resonances of those relationships and with a focus on the American experience as an illustration of certain ideas.

The discussion here is offered in two parts, each part represented by a nineteenth-century American folk painting, the emblems referred to in the book's title. The first painting is the *Historical Monument of the American Republic,* by Erastus Field. It is used to introduce state-centered hierarchical versions of the relationship between groups and the state. The second is the more familiar *Peaceable Kingdom,* by the Quaker Edward Hicks, used here (as it has been used by others) to represent a more horizontal relation between groups and the state, one in which groups are accorded more recognition and more autonomy but in which the state still has a role, sometimes larger, sometimes smaller.

Part 1 begins with a short essay on Field's *Historical Monument* that serves as an introduction to the first four chapters, which focus on American material and describe aspects of relations between groups and the state within a hierarchical, state-centered theory of state and government. Each of the first four chapters tries to go into or behind a reification, whether it is the "state" (chap. 1) or "sovereignty" (chap. 2) or the representation by the state of a particular religious group (Mormons, Amish in chapters 3 and 4). The description of the Field painting emphasizes the preoccupation with height and the stress on political events, conventionally understood. In effect, the individuals are "flat-affect" units in the structure, which is the dominant thing. The first chapters comment on this political architecture.

Chapter 1 describes the visit to the United States of the English utopian Robert Owen in 1825. Owen's address to the American Congress is particularly stressed to make the point that the encounter strikes us today as odd—our utopian theorists do not have that much to do with our politicians. It seems that we are much more accustomed to interaction between reformers and politicians.[23] But a conversation between politician and utopian was not so odd then, and the United States was an experiment almost as innovative as Owen's New Harmony. The lines between public and private were not so fixed, and the meaning of federalism was still very much being explored.

The second chapter deals broadly with the early history of sovereignty in the United States and suggests that in nineteenth-century America it was attached to other groups; to the individual states, in Calhoun's theo-

---

[23] On the distinction, see Russell Jacoby, *The End of Utopia: Politics and Culture in an Age of Apathy* (New York: Basic Books, 1999), 25–27. "Over the years and against the conventional wisdom, utopians sustained a vision of life beyond the market" (27).

ries of sectionalism; to such groups as the Indian tribes; and even to individuals in the theories of radical individualists. Chapter 2 concludes a description of a short American case in which again the idea of groups and the issues of overlapping identities and memberships are presented historically as having complexities that are often lost in discussions that focus on a single membership.

The third chapter explores the idea that groups are a threat, as an *imperium in imperio*. The idea that there can be only one undivided sovereignty is most obviously challenged, in the history of Western political organization, by the claims of the church. Chapter 3 treats the Mormon Church in America as a particularly complicated example of how a modern state deals with the issue of an *imperium in imperio*. It opens with an overview of the field of church and state against which the history of the Latter-day Saints in America is described. An analytical framework that was used in earlier work of mine[24] (which resonates most obviously with the church-sect distinction offered by Troeltsch) is used here to trace the history of the Mormons from persecuted group, an overgrown utopia in effect, to a state within a federal system of states. A part of that story is an account of law's direct intervention in the life of an internal group, shaping its inner life, its religion and practice. Another part concerns the limits of law, demonstrated by the point that among fundamentalist Mormons polygamy was not wiped out, even though the practice was denounced by the federal government, the government of Utah, and the Mormon Church. The chapter concludes with a treatment of two films, used to evoke a continuing discomfort over the Mormon polygamous past.

Another aspect of the group-state problem is reviewed in the fourth chapter; this time the focus is on the dissenting individual within the group and the problem of the role of the state, which because it is there has an important voice in the story, whatever it does or does not do. One stress here is again on the images of the Amish in American culture, including films, and in judicial opinions. The general point is that law is not freestanding and inevitably triumphant but is in fact limited in what it can do, at least in some instances. The chapter uses a particularly tragic legal encounter from the 1940s in which an individual Amishman sued his community and then, from an entirely formal point of view, "won" his case. The uncertain meaning of that victory is made plain in the newspaper coverage of the case.

---

[24] Weisbrod, "Family, Church, and State: An Essay on Constitutionalism and Religious Authority," *Journal of Family Law* 26 (1987–88): 741.

Chapter 5 opens with a discussion of the Mennonites in Germany to introduce the theme of corporatism.[25] The chapter moves from a description of the privileges of the Mennonites to the issue of the pariah people. The legal status of the Jewish community of czarist Russia is used as an example here. The chapter concludes with a discussion of group issues in early-twentieth-century New York City as these related to Catholics. The chapter creates the background to the theoretical discussions of part 2, which introduce ideas of state power and group power as less hierarchically related.

The description of the Hicks painting of *The Peaceable Kingdom* that opens part 2 makes the point that more horizontal relations can be envisioned between groups (including the state as a kind of group). Horizontal discussions have often invoked the biblical images of Isaiah and the idea of harmony in the *Peaceable Kingdom*. But one must see that even in the peaceable kingdom as imagined by Hicks, the lion is a central commanding figure that, in some versions of the painting, is so dominant as to threaten the peace of the peaceable kingdom. The earlier chapters of part 2 consider some of the theories and some of the structures that address the problem of the lion. Later chapters relate the lion to the human figures in the painting, children—future adult selves.

Chapter 6 opens with a review of philosophical and political theories of sovereignty and proceeds to a description of theories that both challenge the monist idea of sovereignty and respond to the liberal lack of interest in group or associational life. The chapter describes the ideas of two pluralist theorists who were visitors to the United States in the late nineteenth century (the Dutch prime minister Kuyper and the anarchist prince Peter Kropotkin) as well as the English pluralists. The chapter then moves to a discussion of Alexander Pekelis. Born in Odessa in 1902, and an Italian law professor when he emigrated to the United States in 1941, Pekelis drew on his early experience in czarist Russia in describing his understandings of the American position on religious liberty and on the place of group autonomy in a liberal state.

The effort of the League of Nations to protect minority rights through treaties is described in chapter 7, along with the problems left open by the system. Here the state is both the League of Nations, considered as a kind of international state, and smaller sovereignties, the states under the treaties and the minorities that are also typically linked to national states. The chapter includes a discussion of the ways in which groups were identi-

[25] An issue that haunts discussions of group rights. See Elizabeth B. Clark, "Breaking the Mold of Citizenship: The Natural Person as Citizen in Nineteenth Century America (a Fragment)," in *Cultural Pluralism, Identity Politics, and the Law,* ed. Austin Sarat and Thomas R. Kearns (Ann Arbor: University of Michigan Press, 1999).

fied under the treaties and a review of problems that the treaties did not resolve. Most important among the treaties' weaknesses was an assumption that identities were clear and self-evident, and that certain identities could be used as the basis of the pluralist structure. The argument here is that identities are overlapping and shifting, and that the institutionalizing of a pluralism based on one form of identity freezes one moment of social and cultural history. The chapter ends with one of the most important cases to be adjudicated under the Minorities Treaties system, upholding the right of minority schools to exist and rejecting a state monopoly on education. This idea, that the state must be the sole educational voice, did not die, however, and we see a version of it again in the next chapter in the arguments of Julian Huxley.

Law, as has been observed, works not exclusively or even primarily through direct sanctioning of deviant behavior but through orienting or reorienting thought and consciousness, accomplished in large part through education. The largest form of the lion is represented in chapter 8 by Julian Huxley, who as director of UNESCO was interested in an internationally agreed-upon educational structure. This approach is juxtaposed with two other theoretical perspectives, that of Ludwig von Mises, who urged a minimal role for the state, and that of Hannah Arendt, who on the basis of her own distinctions between public and private realms considered certain actions inappropriate for state systems. Arendt's controversial piece on school segregation is the prime text for the discussion, which focuses on racial groups particularly. The chapter concludes with a treatment of *Pierce v. Society of Sisters*, a case from the 1920s that is foundational for the rights of religious and private schools.

The discussion of education makes plain that issues of identity and group life within larger states are centrally involved with the issues of children and the formation of identity and values in children. Schools are one aspect of this process, but not the only one. Chapter 9 discusses the involvement of the state in early identity formation when it removes a child from the family of origin and places the child with a second family. This may be done in the context of divorce, or death, or child neglect proceedings, or international upheaval. It may be done out of religious conviction (as in the Mortara episode in the nineteen-century Papal States) or out of what is perceived as simple necessity, as in the case of the Dutch Jewish orphans after the Second World War. The issues involved here are highly complex, resting on not only different memberships but also different ideas of membership.

Chapter 10 brings together two kinds of relations among the individual, the state, and the group. The first sees the individual at the center of various affiliations and offers a discussion of how an individual orders these group memberships and norms. This question is illustrated by the story of Susanna and the Elders. The second sees the individual self as having a social or plural interior. The groups that the individual creates or joins (according to liberal theory) might then be seen as participants in interior dialogues within each individual. A discussion of names and naming practices illustrates this idea. The chapter concludes with a discussion of the complex self and law, suggesting that this is one of the points at which law invokes a critical fiction.

Although it is organized around two paintings and although other pictures are from time to time described, this is not an emblem book in the technical sense.[26] To begin with, there are not enough pictures. And there are no mottos providing a reading of the pictures. One reason for the absence of such mottos may be suggested here: mottos relating to the meaning of the emblems are inevitably limiting, while pictures here are used to evoke rather than define. The treatment of the specific interactions and frameworks should open and not close the discussion.

---

[26] Rosemary Freeman, *English Emblem Books* (New York: Octagon, 1970). Certain characteristics are "commonly agreed to be essential by the emblem writers themselves." "1. An emblem book should be a collection of moral symbols. 2. It should have pictures, or . . . should postulate the existence of pictures. 3. Attached to each picture should be a motto or brief *sententia* . . . 4. there should be an explanatory poem or passage of prose in which the picture and motto are interpreted and a moral . . . is drawn" (238–39).

PART ONE

Monumental Federalism

Erastus Field's *Historical Monument of the American Republic* is a painting about history, not about theories of federalism, but to the extent that it invokes political (rather than social) history, it implies a hierarchical understanding of American federalism.[1] It is a representation of vertical relations between groups.

The painting was begun in the 1860s, and Field finished most of the piece by 1867. In 1876, Field added the Philadelphia Centennial Exhibition Hall to the top of what was called the Central Tower, and, in 1888, he added the two end towers.[2] Mary Black recorded that Field saw the painting as "the culmination and chief work of his long career."[3]

Frank Jenkins described the painting as follows:

From a formal garden, reminiscent of the brand-new park of an industrial town, rise ten great towers, circular and polygonal in plan, made up of sections diminishing as they rise. These are encrusted with an incredible array of architectural bric-a-brac. Almost every style is represented—Egyptian, Greek, Roman, even medieval machicolations are introduced. Seven of the telescope-like towers are joined near their summits by delicate iron suspension bridges, across which steam-trains puff.[4]

Mary Black noted in her catalog of Field's work, "Every level of every tower in Field's Monument is keyed to an incident in American history."[5] Apparently, the "idea of an historical painting on a grand theme had been with Field since the beginning of his career. The evolution of his plan followed a long progress likely to have been conceived as early as November 1824 when he entered Samuel Morse's studio as an apprentice student."[6]

---

[1] The painting is on exhibit at the Museum of Fine Arts in Springfield, Massachusetts, as part of the Morgan Wesson Memorial Collection.

[2] Mary C. Black, *Erastus Salisbury Field: 1805–1900* (Springfield, Mass.: Museum of Fine Arts, 1984), 41.

[3] Black, *Erastus Salisbury Field*. Field was an itinerant painter who spent most of his career in the Northeast. Mary C. Black, "Erastus Salisbury Field and the Sources of His Inspiration," *Antiques*, February 1963, 201–4. Black writes that in 1933 the painting was found rolled up in the attic of a relative's home and "rescued by Madeline Ball Wright, Field's grand-niece, from ignominious storage in a shed behind a pig sty in Plumtrees in the mid-1940's" (47).

[4] Frank I. Jenkins, "Some Nineteenth-Century Towers," *Journal of the Royal Institute of British Architects*, February 1958, 124, 126.

[5] Black, *Erastus Salisbury Field*, 41.

[6] Ibid., 42. Black notes that "Field was as violently opposed to slavery as Morse was for it. While both men opposed secession, their divergent views made the interpretation of the *Monument* as it came from Field a far different painting than anything Morse might have created" (42).

Field himself published a descriptive catalog of the *Historical Monument of the American Republic* that predates the addition of the two final towers.[7] The catalog begins with a paragraph explaining Field's ultimate intention: he wanted a real structure to be built. Following the plan depicted in the painting, the structure would have a central tower surrounded by other large and elaborate towers.[8] The various human figures in the painting would be statues with "[t]he dark figures . . . represented in bronze to denote the colored race."[9]

The Field catalog contains a statement of his limits and purpose. "I am not a professed architect," Field writes, "and some things about it may be faulty. Be that as it may, my aim has been to get up a brief history of our country or epitome, in a monumental form."[10] Field explains that the columns represent the colonies and the states. He also describes not only each of the towers, but each of the small pictures on the towers, beginning with the settlement of Jamestown by the English in 1607.[11] The figures on the first or central tower consist of armies, presidents, and the Forty-Fourth Congress.[12] The other towers have elaborate representations of various battles and incidents in American history, placing considerable emphasis on the Civil War. Outside the towers we see ladies and gentlemen out for a walk and troops "marching around the monument which illustrates the centennial anniversary of the American Independence."[13] The *Monument* includes text from the Declaration of Independence[14] and a long essay on the critical importance of the Bible. The platform of the main towers carries the letters "T. T. B.," meaning "The True Base."[15] Although conceived as a plan for an architectural work, Field's monument remains a painting. No structure based on it has ever existed.

We can view Erastus Field's folk painting as representing a federal scheme focused on political units (states and colonies), imbedded in huge towers, which are connected in various ways to the whole. It emphasizes public officials, armies, and great political controversies. It seems to represent a conception of federalism

---

[7] Erastus Salisbury Field, "Descriptive Catalogue of the Historical Monument of the American Republic" (Amherst, Mass.: H. M. McCloud, 1876), reprinted and included in Black, *Erastus Salisbury Field.*

[8] Ibid., 1.

[9] Ibid.

[10] Ibid.

[11] Ibid., 1, 4. Field's description of a portion of the eighth tower in the center of the painting indicates the level of his detail: "Above the constitution are seen individuals watching for a chance to assassinate the heads of the government. Seward is on his bed. Above on the great platform the assassin Booth is shooting the President. Washington is near by expressing astonishment at such a deed. Under the canopies on the pillars, people are weeping. Above is seen the funeral procession of the President. Above is his tomb. On the top of the eighth tower President Lincoln is ascending in a fiery chariot and an angel is in the act of crowning him" (10).

Frederick B. Robinson observed that while the painting "cannot be called great art, it is outstanding in the field of folk-art. And of even greater importance it provides still further insight into the philosophy and thought of 19th century America." "Erastus Salisbury Field," *Art in America,* October 1942, 244, 253.

[12] Field, "Descriptive Catalogue," 10–11.

[13] Ibid., 11.

[14] Ibid., 6.

[15] Robinson, "Erastus Salisbury Field," 253.

involving the federal government and the states—hierarchical, integrated, and titanic—that is dominant in American history. Field's painting was said to be preoccupied with height.[16] And so, one might say, is political federalism. The federalist position from the start focused on central authority. This tendency is generally seen to have strengthened over time, perhaps along the lines of the structurally integrated model used by Erastus Field. But there is a counterstory. There are challenges, repeatedly, to the main story.

[16] See Jenkins, "Some Nineteenth-Century Towers," 126. Perhaps it also has a subtext of violence.

CHAPTER 1

Owen in America: Ambiguities in the Concept of the Federal System

> In dealing with the State we ought to remember that its institutions are not aboriginal, though they existed before we were born; that they are not superior to the citizen; that every one of them was once the act of a single man; every law and usage was man's expedient to meet a particular case; that they all are imitable, all alterable; we may make as good, we may make better.
>
> —RALPH WALDO EMERSON, "Politics"

✦ IT is conventional in work on groups and associations in America to turn to early commentators on our institutions and, particularly, to the observations of Alexis de Tocqueville, whose reflections on the structure of American society went far beyond the description of governmental institutions. "Better use has been made of association and this powerful instrument of action has been applied to more varied aims in America than anywhere else in the world."[1] Tocqueville's observations on the importance of voluntary associations in the American political system are so substantial that, writing in 1970, Hannah Arendt could still refer to Tocqueville's chapters on this subject as "still by far the best in the not very large literature on the subject."[2]

For all the strength of Tocqueville's work, there is reason to begin a preliminary consideration of these subjects, not with the observer-sociologist, but with the reformer-practitioner, Robert Owen. Justice Joseph Story met Robert Owen on his American trip and wrote to his wife that Owen was "so visionary an enthusiast that he talks like an inhabitant of Utopia."[3] Yet Owen, like all practicing communitarians, had to be realis-

[1] Alexis de Tocqueville, *Democracy in America,* trans. George Lawrence (New York: Harper and Row, 1960), 1:198.

[2] Hannah Arendt, "Civil Disobedience," in *Is Law Dead?* ed. Eugene V. Rostow (New York: Simon and Schuster, 1971), 238.

[3] Arthur Eugene Bestor, "Letter from Joseph Story to his wife (Feb. 9, 1825)," in *Backwoods Utopias: The Sectarian Origins of the Owenite Phase of Communitarian Socialism in America, 1663–1829,* 2d ed. (Philadelphia: University of Pennsylvania Press, 1970), 106.

tic. Owen came to America with a political commitment to the idea of communities that would become a worldwide network of communities, and he connected this plan to American political federalism.

As to American federalism, our sense of the inevitability of the present adjustment is doubtless ahistorical: "To us of the present day it seems that the Constitution framed in 1787 gave birth in 1789 to a national government such as that which now constitutes an indestructible bond of union for the states; but the men of that time would certainly have laughed at any such idea."[4] Thus, Kenneth Stampp has said that "[b]y the end of the 1820s, after the government under the federal Constitution had been in operation for forty years, the prevailing view of the Union in the political rhetoric of the time still remained that of an experiment."[5] He argues that "a substantial case for perpetual Union was not devised until several decades after the adoption of the Constitution."[6] This chapter attempts to recapture that sense of openness and experiment in political structure by telling the story of Robert Owen's visit to America in 1825.

Owen, a reformer, philanthropist, and communitarian, left Wales at the age of ten and, by the age of twenty, was the manager of a mill in Manchester. In a short time he established himself as one of the wealthier cotton spinners of his age. He managed the cotton mills at New Lanark, Scotland, from 1800 to 1829, establishing a model system for the training of workers and children on the basis of ideas outlined in his books. It was in New Lanark that he made his name as the archetype of the benevolent entrepreneur. In educating the factory children, diminishing the hours of labor, and quite spectacularly improving conditions, his main concern, as he explained it, was to make the workpeople "rational" and thus to bring "harmony" to the community, to make it a place where social peace would reign, as he believed it had reigned in the rural community he had known as a boy in Wales.[7]

Owen's work at New Lanark turned him to communitarianism, and a number of American utopian experiments were based broadly on Owenism). The focus here is on his visit to America and, particularly, his addresses to the American Congress.

See also *Life and Letters of Joseph Story,* ed. William Wetmore Story (Boston: C. C. Little and J. Brown, 1851), 485–86.

[4] Woodrow Wilson, *The State: Elements of Historical and Practical Politics,* rev. ed. (Boston: D. C. Heath, 1900), 463.

[5] Kenneth Milton Stampp, *The Imperiled Union: Essays on the Background of the Civil War* (Oxford: Oxford University Press, 1980), 29.

[6] Ibid., viii. On the idea of experimentation, see generally Paul C. Nagel, *One Nation Indivisible: The Union in American Thought, 1776–1881* (repr., New York: Greenwood Press, 1964), 13–31.

[7] Robert Owen, *A New View of Society and Report to the County of Lanark,* ed. V. A. C. Gatrell (Harmondsworth: Penguin, 1970), 9.

That picture—the utopian lecturing to the politicians—is one to which we do not know how to react. We see a marginal figure speaking to central figures, an exotic addressing the mainstream. (Perhaps, however, he was an important exotic? Comparable, in some sense, to Gandhi meeting with the British?) We hardly know how to think about Owen in America because our sense that politicians are important and utopians are not blinds us to their position in their own time, as two points on an experimental spectrum. Specifically, utopian theorists and practitioners, as much as politicians,[8] must deal with questions relating to their ideas of the ideal world and the existing world, the future, as they envision it, and the present.[9]

A lawyer comes now to the issues of decentralization and pluralism with strong preconceptions in favor of the importance of official law and the central state.[10] This idea informs our historical narrative, and we may view with surprise and even amusement the image of Robert Owen, the "gentle bore,"[11] lecturing the American Congress. Yet Owen's concerns were closer to those of the Congress than we presently appreciate, and the distance between the utopian and the legislators was not so great as presently appears.

While one may emphasize substantive values in dealing with utopian communitarianism (cooperation or community, for example), nineteenth-century American utopianism also typically contains a structural or political value in its commitment to the small-scale political unit.[12] This idea

---

[8] Herbert Simon, *Administrative Behavior* (New York: Macmillan, 1947), 101. Simon writes, "The highest level of integration that man achieves consists in taking an existing set of institutions as one alternative and comparing it with other sets. . . . Thought at this comprehensive level has not been common to all cultures. In our Western civilization it has perhaps been confined to (1) the writings of Utopian political theorists and (2) the thought and writings surrounding modern legislative processes."

[9] "Owen was quite clear that he was the practical, realistic reformer who had demonstrated a workable future and that it was those who promoted illusions of a religious or political economic nature who were the really dangerous fantasists." Vincent Geoghegan, *Utopianism and Marxism* (London: Methuen, 1987), 13.

[10] In part, this is because local community values are not always good. "An appealing, albeit somewhat utopian, vision of participatory democracy informs [states rights arguments]. Yet the underlying reality of a long and largely successful history of exclusion, discrimination, and economic domination in local government remains a bit sobering." Aviam Soifer, "Truisms That Never Will Be True: The Tenth Amendment and the Spending Power," *University of Colorado Law Review* 57 (1986): 793, 797.

[11] Harriet Martineau, *Biographical Sketches* (London: Macmillan, 1869), 313, quoted in G. D. H. Cole, *Robert Owen* (London: E. Benn, 1925), 241.

[12] Not all utopians are communitarians. Bellamy's ideas, for example, are statist. See Arthur Lipow, *Authoritarian Socialism in America: Edward Bellamy and the Nationalist Movement* (Berkeley and Los Angeles: University of California Press, 1982). See the discussion of Bellamy in Krishan Kumar, *Utopia and Anti-utopia in Modern Times* (Oxford: Blackwell, 1987), 132–67. Nonetheless, the Kaweah community in California is sometimes described as Bellamist. See Yaacov Oved, *Two Hundred Years of American Communes*

has certain affinities with the concept of federalism. Communitarianism can also be seen in relation to concepts of political and legal pluralism, which stresses not merely single experiments (an emphasis in American federalist discussion), but also continuing experiments and a permanent diversity within the society. Issues of size, experimentation, and diversity were discussed by state politicians, as well as by utopians, and were strikingly in evidence in antebellum America.

Owen visited the United States in 1824–25.[13] This chapter outlines his views on pluralism and federalism and compares them with the political theories of some of the Americans with whom Owen met. A utopian/political encounter seems particularly useful in this inquiry for two reasons. Because utopian theorists and practitioners conceive of themselves as an alternative to the existing social order, they are forced to confront the issue of their relation to the outside world and, particularly, to the state more directly than, for example, the founders of limited-purpose internal associations, whose functions are not usually conceived so broadly. Moreover, the utopian community is a form of voluntary association (or even corporation) that bridges the categories of public and private or governmental and nongovernmental. Thus, we can fit voluntary associations into our treatment of federalism.[14]

The parallel between Owen's ideas and the propositions of American political federalism are well known to scholars of utopianism. Thus, in his work on Owenism, Bestor quotes the familiar observation of Holmes, dissenting in *Truax v. Corrigan*,[15] that the law should not "prevent the making of social experiments that an important part of the community desires, in the insulated chambers afforded by the several States, even though the experiments may seem futile or even noxious."[16]

(New Brunswick, N.J.: Transaction, 1988), 240. On the Kaweah Cooperative Commonwealth, see Robert Hine, *California's Utopian Colonies* (San Marino, Calif.: Huntington Library, 1953; repr., New Haven: Yale University Press, 1966), 78. Bellamy's ideas apparently drew people to the colony, though Bellamy himself thought that such enterprises could succeed only on a national scale.

[13] For an account of the visit, see Bestor, *Backwoods Utopias*. On Owen in general, see John F. C. Harrison, *Quest for the New Moral World: Robert Owen and the Owenites in Britain and America* (New York: Scribner, 1969), and more recently, Anne Taylor, *Visions of Harmony: A Study in Nineteenth Century Millenarianism* (Oxford: Oxford University Press, 1987).

[14] See, e.g., Alexander Pekelis, "Private Governments and the Federal Constitution," in *Law and Social Action: Selected Essays of Alexander Pekelis,* ed. Milton R. Konvitz (Ithaca, N.Y.: Cornell University Press, 1950), 91, discussed in chap. 6, below.

[15] 257 U.S. 312, 344 (1921) (Holmes, J., dissenting).

[16] Ibid., quoted by Bestor, *Backwoods Utopias*, 18; see also *New State Ice Co. v. Liebmann,* 285 U.S. 262, 311 (1932) (Brandeis, J., dissenting) ("It is one of the happy incidents of the federal system that a single courageous State may, if its citizens choose, serve as a laboratory; and try novel social and economic experiments without risk to the rest of the

Owen came to America as a leading exponent of a tradition in which enterprises were founded that are today called utopian. They were often known in their own time as *communitarian*. Bestor writes: "What these enterprises had in common was the idea of employing the small experimental community as a lever to exert upon society the force necessary to produce reform and change. The ends might differ, with economic, religious, ethical and educational purposes mingled in varying proportions. But the means were uniform, consistent and well defined. These enterprises constitute a communitarian movement because each made the community the heart of its plan."[17]

Not only was membership in a community a matter of individual choice, but the whole process by which communitarianism was expected to spread and remake the world was conceived in noncoercive terms. Voluntary imitation, the communitarian believed, would suffice. Small communities having succeeded, many nations would gradually harmonize with them.

As Bestor indicates, "[T]he group procedure that was the heart of the communitarian program corresponded to a like tendency that ramified through many American institutions and many fields of American thought."[18] Citing Gierke, Maitland, and Tocqueville on political associations, Bestor is explicit on the connections to federalism:

Federalism, in the sense opposed to consolidated nationalism, is an important complement of this respect for, and encouragement of autonomous groups. It is therefore no accident that many close parallels to the communitarian argument may be found in the classic expositions of the role of states in the American federal system. . . . [So] ingrained in American experience was the idea of group procedure—of trying political and social experiments upon units of society less than the whole— that communitarians found little difficulty in winning a hearing for their own proposals, couched as they were in familiar terms.[19]

Probably no one received a better hearing than Robert Owen. Oneida's founder, John Humphrey Noyes,[20] said in 1870 that Owen "stirred the very life of the nation with his appeals to Kings and Congresses, and his

---

country"). See generally Gregory Claeys, "Paternalism and Democracy in the Politics of Robert Owen," *International Review of Social History* 27 (1982): 160, 161–207.

[17] Bestor, *Backwoods Utopias*, 3.

[18] Ibid., 16.

[19] Ibid., 18–19.

[20] On Oneida, see Carol Weisbrod, *The Boundaries of Utopia* (New York: Pantheon Books, 1980); see also Carol Weisbrod, "On the Breakup of Oneida," *Connecticut Law Review* 14 (1982): 717.

vast experiments at New Harmony."[21] New Harmony was founded in 1825 and collapsed in 1827, in part, some suggested, because Owen himself did not stay in America to guide the community. Thus, the Owenite paper *New Moral World* explained that, while "families of all descriptions" were gathering at New Harmony, Owen had to leave for a year. During this period, differences arose among the different nationalities, and "this absence of Mr. Owen, at this critical period, was unfavorable for the immediate harmony and quiet settlement of the colony into one family, with one interest."[22] As Noyes saw it, New Harmony had "for its antecedent the vast reputation that Owen had gained by his success at New Lanark."[23] Owen "came to this country with the prestige of a reformer who had the confidence and patronage of Lords, Dukes and Sovereigns in the old world."[24]

Arthur Bestor has offered a detailed account of Owen's American trip, which lasted from January 3 to April 13, 1825.[25] Bestor records that, on November 26, 1824, Owen was received by John Quincy Adams, secretary of state (whom Owen had already met when Adams was in England).[26] He also saw President James Monroe and John C. Calhoun, among many others.[27] And, Bestor writes, while there were "other conversations as well . . . surely none [was] so remarkable as the council ring in the Dennison Hotel, where Owen sat down with a group of Choctaw and Chickasaw Chiefs and gravely explained his new view of society through an interpreter."[28]

Bestor describes Owen's American tour as "one of the greatest triumphs of his career."[29] Before this, Owen "had discussed his plans in

[21] John Humphrey Noyes, *Strange Cults and Utopias of the Nineteenth Century America* (Philadelphia: J. P. Lippincott, 1870; repr. New York: Dover, 1966), 22.

[22] *The New Moral World,* September 12, 1835, 363. For an assessment of the significance of New Harmony, see George Lockwood, *The New Harmony Movement* (New York: Appleton, 1905; repr. New York: Dover, 1971), 1–6.

[23] Noyes, *Strange Cults and Utopias,* 44.

[24] Ibid.

[25] Bestor, *Backwoods Utopias,* 106–14. I have relied heavily on this account.

[26] Ibid., 108.

[27] Ibid.

[28] Ibid., 108–9. See generally, Rezin Welch McAdam, *Chickasaws and Choctaws: A Pamphlet of Information Concerning Their History, Treaties, Government, Country, Laws, Politics and Affairs* (1891; repr. Wilmington, Del.: Scholarly Resources, 1975); Angie Debo, *The Rise and Fall of the Choctaw Republic* (Norman: University of Oklahoma Press, 1934); Arthur H. Derosier Jr., *The Removal of the Choctaw Indians* (Knoxville: University of Tennessee Press, 1970); Grant Foreman, *The Five Civilized Tribes* (Norman: University of Oklahoma Press, 1934). Owen also met on his trip a southerner (a brother of Jefferson Davis, later president of the Confederacy) who was interested in Owenite ideas for his plantation. See Janet Sharp Hermann, *The Pursuit of a Dream* (Oxford: Oxford University Press, 1981), 3–7.

[29] Bestor, *Backwoods Utopias,* 110.

small select groups, but from the beginning he had contemplated a great public campaign . . . that would culminate in the presentation of his plans to Congress."[30] Bestor continues: "Owen reached Washington just as the House of Representatives brought the long presidential canvass to a close by choosing John Quincy Adams as the next occupant of the White House." It was a particularly good time for the visit.

> The electoral excitement was over, yet the Capital was crowded with the leading figures of American public life. Owen's prospective visit had been announced long before in the papers, and at that time the *National Intelligencer* had welcomed Owen as one of those "who seem to have had no thought but how to lessen the sufferings of the unfortunate and better the conditions of the human race in every quarter of the world."[31]

Bestor notes that an even more extraordinary tribute to Owen was the fact that he was "readily granted the use of the Hall of Representatives in the Capitol for two addresses. The first time by arrangement with Henry Clay, the second time through the good offices of John Quincy Adams."[32]

Bestor reports that Adams heard Owen, as did James Monroe, several members of the Cabinet, the Supreme Court, and the Congress.[33] Owen then visited Jefferson and Madison. Bestor concludes that "in every outward respect, Owen's 100 days in the east—it was precisely that—had been a triumphant success."[34] The general attention paid to Robert Owen, when he visited the United States in 1824–1825, was extraordinary. Even taken by itself, it might be enough to prove the nonmarginality of the utopian tradition in America. Owen was a man of some importance, and this may be adequate as an explanation for his American triumph. But one may also agree with Bestor that some of Owen's preoccupations were shared by the Americans with whom he spoke. This shared concern may have provided additional reason for their interest in Owenism. Owen was committed to the small community as the basic unit of society, a family of from three hundred to two thousand forming a link in a system of such families.[35] His advocacy of federated small units had deep resonances with certain ideas in American political life. New Harmony itself died after a few years. But discussion of the images that Owen put forward, which

---

[30] Ibid.

[31] Ibid., 111.

[32] Ibid.

[33] The text of Owen's speeches appeared in the *National Intelligencer* and were then printed as pamphlets (ibid., 112).

[34] Ibid., 113.

[35] See discussion in Owen, *New View*, 226.

inevitably raised issues of the relations between federated units, small groups and larger structures, minorities and majorities, continued.

Robert Owen's thinking may be explored in a variety of ways in the American setting. In 1972, for example, Merle Curti suggested that one could consider the influence of Owen and the Owenite community, New Harmony, on the "American career" of such ideas as communitarianism, cooperation, and socialism.[36] One could also, he said, consider such things as "family, education, sex relations and religion."[37] It is in the history of communitarianism or utopian socialism that Owen is remembered and known today, and this was also largely true in the early 1820s. But, as Bestor notes, by the "end of the 1820's Owenism was identified in the public mind less with communitarianism, than with free thought."[38]

Bestor writes that the memory of speeches at the Capitol in 1825 was largely obliterated in 1829 by Owen's debate with Alexander Campbell in Cincinnati. This debate was designed, as Owen stated, "to prove that the principles of all religions are erroneous, and that their practice is injurious to the human race."[39] Another approach would be to identify the relationships between the main tenets of Owenism and the "basic traditions and values in the American experience."[40] One such relationship would be Owen's secular millennialism and the sort of millennialism found in America. Another relationship would be the issue of Owenism and the general American belief in "the feasibility of nonviolent social change" and "a related belief in the possibility of an easily achievable social harmony."[41] As to the expectation of a nonviolent social change, Curti adds that it would come "through the contagious influence of successful small social experiments and demonstrations."[42] This belief in the inevitable spread of the (successful) social experiment marks Owenite thought.

While the nature of the transition itself is not detailed, the before-and-after pictures are clear in Owenite writing. Thus:

> IN THE OLD IMMORAL WORLD . . . The governments have been formed by the necessities of the periods when they were respectively established, when men were ignorant and inexperienced, and when the animal propensities alone directed and governed the human race.

[36] Curti, "Owen in American Thought," 56.

[37] Ibid.

[38] Bestor, *Backwoods Utopias*, 228.

[39] Ibid.; see Martin E. Marty, *The Infidel* (Cleveland: Meridian, 1961); Edward Madden and Dennis Madden, "The Great Debate: Alexander Campbell vs. Robert Owen," *Transactions of the Charles S. Peirce Society* 18 (1982): 207–26.

[40] Curti, "Owen in American Thought," 56.

[41] Ibid., 57.

[42] Ibid.

IN THE NEW MORAL WORLD ... The governments will be formed to proceed in the most open and direct course to give a new and highly superior character to the population of the world, and to surround the population in all climates, with new and highly superior external circumstances or arrangements; by which health of body and mind will be insured, and thereby, the gradual improvement of the race; by which the injurious distinctions of color and form shall be made to cease; by which one interest shall be made evident to, and be pursued by all; by which one language will, of necessity, soon be desired, written, and spoken; by which wars will cease, and national revenues will become useless or be easily obtained; by which the continuance of private property will be seen to be an evil of enormous magnitude, and will be, in consequence, eagerly relinquished by all; by which the various opposing religions of faith, which make men irrational, will die a natural death, and be succeeded by the simple religion of pure charity, which will cover the earth as the waters cover the sea, and induce all men to adopt the system of public property; by which falsehood shall be forever abandoned, and truth shall be universally established; and by which this earth shall, indeed, become a terrestrial paradise, and all its inhabitants a race of highly intelligent, moral, and superior beings.[43]

Owen's speech to the Congress illustrates his belief that, since only persuasion was required, the road to success lay in gaining the commitment of men in power. A wise leader would be the agent of social change.

To the extent that Owen's thought was federalist, it is likely that he was influenced by the ideas of his associate, the scientist William Maclure.[44] As Bestor has noted, the success of the federal system in the United States encouraged Maclure to hope that "thousands, or hundreds of thousands of small societies" might exist, separate yet federated, and might "traffic and deal with each other in the true spirit of equality, . . . exchanging labor for labor, without permitting avarice to introduce its poison in the form of coin."[45] Moreover, those societies would not counteract or injure one another.[46]

---

[43] *New Moral World* 28 (May 9, 1835): 222.

[44] William Maclure (1763–1840) was a Scottish-born scientist who, like Owen, created his own fortune early and became interested in educational theory. He was one of those in the "boatload of knowledge," which was organized to join Owen in 1825. Maclure later broke with Owen over Owen's handling of the community and established his school as an independent entity (Bestor, *Backwoods Utopias,* 190–91). "As Owen's project withered away, Maclure's was coming into flower" (ibid., 200). Maclure's school and the school press, which published a number of scientific volumes, as well as Maclure's *Opinions on Various Subjects,* continued for some time.

[45] Bestor, *Backwoods Utopias,* 152 (quoting Maclure).

[46] Ibid., 152.

Maclure was particularly impressed with a traditional federalist justification, the possibility of experimentation in local groups. Maclure noted that "[e]ach township might experiment on every thing that could conduce to their comfort and happiness, without interfering with the interests of their neighbors."[47] If a failure resulted, it "could only hurt the contrivers and executors of the speculation, forcing them to nullify their mistakes, and guaranteeing them against a perseverance in error."[48] Maclure included several short discussions of representation and small size in his *Opinions on Various Subjects*—discussions echoing familiar themes in American political discourse.

But there are differences, it seems, between Owen's emphasis and Maclure's. While based on small groups, Owen's federalism does not stress experiment.[49] Whereas Maclure's conception is dynamic—including the possibility of failure and error—Owen's "federalism," greatly tempered by paternalism and centralism, is not.[50] Owen was, in general, considerably more certain of the universal applicability of his own vision than pluralists characteristically are.[51]

These points can be illustrated by Owen's presentation to the American Congress.[52] Announcing the establishment of his new community at New Harmony, Owen said that those who saw it would, of necessity, be converted to his approach instantly and without conflict. "I have been asked," he said, "what would be the effect upon the neighborhood and surrounding country, where one or more of these societies of union, cooperation, and common property, should be established?"[53] Owen's answer was the following:

[47] Ibid., 14.

[48] Ibid.

[49] Owen did make some references to experiments in his talk to the American Congress, particularly to his own experiments (leading to his particular result) and to the "imperfect experiments of the Moravians, Shakers, and Harmonites." Address by Robert Owen, February 25, 1825, reprinted in Oakley C. Johnson, *Robert Owen in the United States* (New York: Humanities Press, 1970), 32. His view of his own system was that it was an experiment that could not fail itself and could not fail to be the basis of a new system, "unless we can imagine that there are human beings who prefer sin and misery to virtue and happiness" (35).

[50] See Richard Adamiak, "State and Society in Early Socialist Thought," *Survey* 1 (1982): 26; Claeys, "Paternalism and Democracy." See generally Bestor, *Backwoods Utopias;* Harrison, *Quest;* and George Lockwood, "New Harmony's Place in History," in *The New Harmony Movement.*

[51] Owen's temperamental predisposition is captured in the comment of his father-in-law: "Thou needest to be very right for thou art very positive." Robert Owen, *The Life of Robert Owen by Himself* (London: Bell, 1920), 99.

[52] Address of February 25, 1825; address of March 7, 1825, in Johnson, *Robert Owen,* 21–64.

[53] Address of March 7, 1825, 52.

My conviction is, that, from necessity and inclination, the individual or old system of society, would break up, and soon terminate; from necessity, because the new societies would undersell all individual producers . . . [and] from inclination, because it is scarcely to be supposed that anyone would continue to live under the miserable, anxious, individual system of opposition and counteraction, when they could with ease form themselves into, or become members of, one of these associations of union, intelligence, and kind feeling.[54]

The communities would create an environment in which this result would be inevitable. As Owen explained to the legislators:

Having discovered that individuals were always formed by the circumstances, whatever they might be, which were allowed to exist around them, my practice was to *govern* the circumstances; and thus by means imperceptible and unknown to the individuals, I formed them, to the extent I could control the circumstances, into what I wished them to become; and in this manner were the beneficial changes effected in the population under my care.[55]

Owen was asked about the effects of these communities on the government, and answered:

[The communities] are in complete union with the principles on which the constitution of this country is founded. The constitution is essentially a government of the union of independent states, acting together for their mutual benefit. The new communities would stand in the same relation to their respective State Governments, that the States do now to the General Government.[56]

Two observations are worth stressing about Owen's view of the relationship between his communities and the outside government. First, Owen envisions what we would call a private form, the voluntary association or corporation, turning into a unit within a governmental hierarchy,

[54] Ibid. The Noyes chapter "Inquest on New Harmony," in *Strange Cults and Utopias*, includes some comments of members of the Oneida community who read the chapter and then discussed it at an evening meeting. One said, "The people Mr. Owen had to deal with in Scotland were of the servile class, employees in his cotton-factories, and were easily managed, compared with those he collected here in the United States. When he went to Indiana, and undertook to manage a family of a thousand democrats, he began to realize that he did not understand human nature, or the principles of Association" (53, quoting S. R. Leonard). Along similar lines, Maclure suggested that "the materials in this country are not the same as in the cotton spinners at New Lanark, nor does the advice of a patron go so far" (quoted in Harrison, *Quest,* 37).

[55] Address of February 25, 1825, 27.

[56] Address of March 7, 1825, 53.

rather in the tradition of the Massachusetts Bay Company. John Winthrop and others met somewhere in Cambridge University, of which most of them were alumni, in August 1629 and signed an agreement to emigrate to New England within seven months, provided they could carry over the government and charter of the Massachusetts Bay Company. This important proviso protected them from the king, who otherwise might confiscate their charter, as had happened to the Virginia Company only five years earlier. And it so happened, whether by chance or design, that the Massachusetts Bay Charter did not require the stockholders to meet in any particular place. The stockholders voted for the transfer and elected John Winthrop governor.[57] Owen's suggestion evokes the early history of the corporation with its emphasis on the public or quasi-governmental aspects of the form.[58] Second, while Owen referred to American political federalism, no one at the time was certain what the relation of the central government to the states really was. When Owen said that he wanted the communities to be as states in their relations to a larger unit, he raised more issues than he perhaps appreciated. The nature of the federal union itself was far from clear, and the United States was, in a sense, as much an experiment as any utopian community.

Owen noted of his visit that "[t]he men most active in promoting the adoption of the New American constitution, and who wrote and perfected their 'Declaration of Rights' acknowledged to the Founder of the Rational System, that they were, in 1825, after a trial of half a century, greatly disappointed in the result of the work."[59] They were, of course, speaking to someone whose experiment was even more uncertain than their own.

Owen visited the United States some years after New England federalists expressed their disaffection with the central government at the Hartford Convention and some years before the major American controversies over slavery and secession reached their climax. Perhaps because of those special historical concerns—like the slavery issue, which would finally

---

[57] Samuel Elliot Morison, *The Oxford History of the American People* (Oxford: Oxford University Press, 1965), 65.

[58] Owen's description of the New Harmony enterprise makes plain that, at one level, it is conceived as a private undertaking, a corporation, or a voluntary association: "I am prepared to commence the system on my own private responsibility, or with partners having the same principles and feelings with myself; or by joint stock companies, under an act of incorporation from the state governments of Indiana and Illinois, in which the new properties which I have purchased, with a view to these establishments, are situated—or, by a general incorporated company, formed of the leading persons in each state, who could easily form arrangements by which the benefit of the system might be obtained, with the least loss of time, by all the inhabitants within each Government, belonging to the Union" (address of February 25, 1825, 33).

[59] Robert Owen, *The Book of the New World* (New York, 1845), 149.

threaten the nation itself—others in America had a more sophisticated vision, making up, at certain points, for something Owen himself lacked. At least one of the Americans Owen spoke with on his early visit, John C. Calhoun, was to arrive at a full-scale commitment to the importance of the veto power of the small group and to an attack on a monistic theory of sovereignty in a central state. Others, whom we may represent by Owen's meeting with Indian tribal leaders, became concerned with the problem of locating sovereignties within the larger state. A comparison between Owen's ideas and those of the Americans he met reveals that others, more concerned with diversity—or perhaps with maintaining their own differences—were also more systematic in attempting to solve the structural problems of permanent internal communities. Some of these attempts are reviewed in the next chapter.

CHAPTER 2

Indians and Individualists: A Multiplicity of Sovereignties

> The decisions on Indian title can hardly be understood unless it is recognized that dealings between the Federal Government and the Indian tribes have regularly been handled as part of our international relations.
>
> —FELIX COHEN, "Original Indian Title"

✦ PROFESSOR JOHN BURGESS in *Political Science and Constitutional Law* defined sovereignty as the "original, absolute, unlimited universal power over the individual subject and over all associations of subjects." This definition has been disputed in theory and is not altogether consistent with certain social facts.[1]

Conceptions of pluralism and federalism can take several forms. Some versions rely on the idea of sovereignty, noting that it can be located in groups other than the state. These versions fit well with the way we view Indian tribes, religious groups, and other organizations whose functioning can be seen in terms of nonstate but statelike authority and law. In these versions of federalism, an individual seems to belong to two sovereign groups: state and church or state and tribe.

Another version of pluralism or federalism sees the individual as belonging to many different kinds of groups—some voluntary and others not—only some of which can comfortably be called sovereign. On some views it is individuals themselves who must be considered sovereign.

The problem of minorities can exist no matter how small the relevant community. Pushed to its extreme, it becomes the problem of individual sovereignty, since the individual can be the minority in relation to the tiny community or to anything larger. The voluntary association—or nonstate "interest group"—can be the minority in relation to some part of government, and the individual federated state can be the minority in relation

---

[1] Burgess, *Political Science and Comparative Constitutional Law* (Boston: Ginn and Co., 1890), 1:52.

to the central government. We can use language of sovereignty with reference to individual sovereignty as much as to nation-state sovereignty.

Viewing the matter broadly, one sees that Owen and others concerned
with groups are flanked on both sides by those concerned with either the
state or the individual. Of those concerned with either groups or individuals, only some are centrally focused on questions of minorities, differences, or pluralism. Owen, as noted, was not. But Calhoun and the Indians are well known among those whom we now associate with pluralist
concerns.

We have some record of the conversation between Owen and Calhoun
in a brief account of Calhoun's response to Owen from Owen's companion, Donald MacDonald. (When MacDonald met Harrison and Calhoun,
the latter "remarked that he felt great interest in Mr. Owen's proceedings & thought that there were now at work in the world some active
principles which gave assurance of important improvements in society
being very near at hand.")[2] The discussion that follows is, therefore, not
found in any narrative record of interaction between Owen and Calhoun;
in effect, what is provided is the other half of the imaginary conversations
that began with Owen's presentation of his new view of society. Calhoun's thought leads us to a pluralism that sees a group interest—in his
case, a proslavery interest—as fundamentally important.[3]

Calhoun's version of localism, found in the *South Carolina Exposition
and Protest,* was first addressed to the Tariff Act of 1828.[4] The exposition

[2] *The Diaries of Donald MacDonald, 1824–1826,* ed. Caroline Snedeker (Indianapolis:
Indiana Historical Society, 1942), 329; see also Arthur Bestor, "Book Review," *New York
History,* January 1943, 80–86.

[3] Calhoun (1782–1850) studied at Yale and the Litchfield School of Law, served in Congress until 1817, was then appointed secretary of war by Monroe, and was secretary of war
when he met Owen. Calhoun was vice president from 1825 to 1832 under John Quincy
Adams and Andrew Jackson and finally became a senator from South Carolina. He is largely
remembered as having devoted his career to the cause of state's rights and the defense of
slavery. See generally Louis Hartz, *The Liberal Tradition in America* (New York: Harcourt
Brace and World, 1955); Richard Hofstadter, *The American Political Tradition and the Men
Who Made It* (New York: Vintage, 1948); Charles Merriam, *A History of American Politi-
cal Theories* (New York: Macmillan, 1906), 267–304; August Spain, *The Political Theory
of John C. Calhoun* (New York: Bookman Associates, 1951); George Kateb, "The Majority
Principle: Calhoun and His Antecedents," *Political Science Quarterly* 84 (1969): 583;
Charles Merriam, "The Political Philosophy of John C. Calhoun," in *Studies in Southern
History and Politics,* 2d ed. (New York: Kennikat Press, 1964), 319–64.

[4] Tocqueville discussed the tariff controversy: "The French Revolution and the War of
1812 had created "manufacturing establishments in the North of the Union," by inhibiting
communication between America and Europe (*Democracy in America,* 1:389). Tocqueville
comments that the doctrine of nullification, which had come out of that controversy,
"would, in principle, destroy the federal bond and actually bring back that anarchy from

argued that the state had a legal right to "refuse obedience to a national act when the state deemed the act to be contrary to the Constitution."[5] Calhoun's argument was directed essentially against the tyranny of the majority and was designed to protect the minority interest of the southern states—without secession.[6]

Calhoun's developed doctrine for reconciling majority and minority interests, often referred to as a doctrine of the "concurrent majority," has been summarized this way.

> The numerical majority consisting of men subject to self-centeredness . . . can be tyrannical and oppressive in the area of a self-centered minority's rights and interests. . . . Therefore each sectional majority or each major-interest majority should have the constitutional power to veto acts of the federal government, which represented the numerical majority, when those acts were deemed, by a majority of the people comprising the section or interest, to be adverse to the welfare of the section or interest.[7]

The emphasis on state, sectional, or interest-group difference, in fact on difference, is clear. But, of course, Calhoun remains a problem. Theodore Woolsey began his discussions of Calhoun's views on representation with

---

which the Constitution of 1789 delivered Americans" (1:391). Tocqueville had earlier noted that "[i]n America the liberty of association for political purposes is unlimited," using the tariff-free trade controversy as an example. "It must be admitted," he wrote, "that unlimited freedom of association has not yet produced in America the fatal results that one might anticipate from it elsewhere" (1:192). He concluded that "freedom of association has become a necessary guarantee against the tyranny of the majority" (1:192).

[5] Calhoun, quoted in C. Gordon Post, ed., *A Disquisition on Government*, by John Calhoun (Indianapolis: Bobbs-Merrill, 1953), xiv.

[6] The idea of the "tyranny of majority" (see generally Tocqueville, *Democracy in America*, vol. 1, chap. 8) was familiar earlier to readers of *The Federalist*. "It is of great importance in a republic, not only to guard the society against the oppression of its rulers, but to guard one part of society against the injustice of the other part." *The Federalist* No. 51 (James Madison), quoted in Tocqueville, *Democracy in America*, 1:260. One can speculate on the impact of Connecticut politics—and the feelings that resulted in the Hartford Convention—on Calhoun's later work. See Anna Ella Carroll, "Calhoun and His Nullification Doctrine," *Living Age* 70 (1861): 444–46. "Calhoun derived his first treasonable ideas of nullification and secession from the Hartford Convention" (444). Thus, it has been said that "[n]ot the South, not slavery, but Yale College and Litchfield Law School made Calhoun a nullifier." Margaret Coit, *John C. Calhoun: American Portrait* (Boston: Houghton Mifflin, 1950), 42. Gordon Post notes that Calhoun studied with the federalist Timothy Dwight at Yale and that Dwight "along with many other New Englanders in the early nineteenth century proposed secession as a solution for sectional conflict" (introduction to Calhoun, *A Disquisition on Government*, viii).

[7] Post, introduction to Calhoun, *A Disquisition on Government*, xxii.

a kind of apology: "What weight ought to be attached, then, to the views of the late John C. Calhoun, whose consecration of his life to the defense of slavery should not blind his countrymen to his great ability?"[8]

One reading of Calhoun in American history puts him and his concerns clearly in the past.[9] Yet for those interested in groups and associations, Calhoun becomes an important figure. Thus, Alexander Pekelis wrote that, while "[t]he monistic conception has under various forms proclaimed that there has been but one law, the law of the state, and that there is but one government, the government of the state," still "there has been no generation and no country which did not count among its best legal minds one or more opponents to this monistic theory."[10] Pekelis listed Calhoun among the thinkers who "approached the problem from different angles," but were all essentially pluralistic.[11] The different angles Pekelis named included the idea of concurrent majority.[12]

The Chickasaw and Choctaw chiefs were in Washington in the fall and early winter of 1824–25 to negotiate the terms of their removal from Mississippi to Oklahoma.[13] As secretary of war, Calhoun was directly concerned with this enterprise. As in the case of Owen and Calhoun, we have no transcript of the conversation between Owen and the Indians. But again we have an account from a companion of Owen's, this time, his son. According to William Owen, his father cautioned the chiefs against adopting what had been found to be injurious in civilized life.

> [He] said that he had come more than three thousand miles to promote plans, by which he hoped to make the red brethren superior to the whites. He said the Indians taken when young amongst white, would become like whites, and vice versa and he concluded that it would be

[8] Theodore Woolsey, *Political Science: Or the State Theoretically and Practically Considered* (New York: Scribner, 1877), 2:292.

[9] See Ralph Henry Gabriel, *The Course of American Democratic Thought* (New York: Greenwood, 1940), 103–10. Richard Hofstadter included a chapter on Calhoun entitled "John C. Calhoun: The Marx of the Master Class" in *The American Political Tradition*, 67–91. Hofstadter believed that Calhoun's concepts of nullification and the concurrent voice "have little more than antiquarian interest for the twentieth-century mind" (68). For him, the point is that "[b]efore Karl Marx published The *Communist Manifesto*, Calhoun laid down an analysis of American politics and the sectional struggle which foreshadowed some of the seminal ideas of the Marx's system" (ibid.). Robert Dahl cites Calhoun as someone whose ideas anticipated modern consociationalism. See *Democracy and Its Critics* (New Haven: Yale University Press, 1989), 260.

[10] Pekelis, "Private Governments," 104.

[11] Ibid.

[12] Ibid.

[13] Derosier, *Removal of the Choctaw*, 80–84 n. 28.

possible to unite the good in the Indian and in the civilized lives, so as to make a being superior to both.[14]

Robert Owen specifically addressed the Indians on the issue of separatism, but, on the basis of William Owen's account, the answer was not entirely responsive.

> He was desirous of knowing whether the Indians would prefer amalgamating with the whites, or forming a separate body quite distinct from them. The Indian replied that he was aware that the whites were so superior to them that they could only cope with them by imitating them, which they were endeavoring to do as well as possible, tho' still a great way behind.[15]

The conversation that we imagine between Calhoun and Owen uses the language of concurrent majorities and rests on the empirical point that the local forms will not be identical or committed to the same values.[16] The conversation that we imagine between the Indians and Owen in which Owen expounds his new view, and the Indians stress the autonomy of the Indian nation,[17] rests on the same point.

There is no discussion here of the history of government and the Indians. Nor does this piece do more than acknowledge John Calhoun's role as secretary of war in the Indian removal.[18] The Indian tribes are consid-

---

[14] William Owen, *Diary of William Owen,* ed. Joel W. Hiatt (Indianapolis: Bobbs-Merrill, 1906), 43–44.

[15] *Diary of William Owen,* 43.

[16] Calhoun did not work out the problems of minorities within the sectional minorities. Kariel concludes that Calhoun "was wrong in attributing homogeneity to the sections." Henry Kariel, *The Decline of American Pluralism* (Stanford: Stanford University Press, 1961), 152. See generally Hartz, *Liberal Tradition in America,* 145–77 (discussion of tensions in Calhoun's ideas). Calhoun sees that the case of the individual as the source of the veto is the extreme case. For a discussion of this system in Poland, see Calhoun, *A Disquisition on Government,* 54–55. It is not clear what Calhoun thought the role of different voices within the section, interest, or community should be. For a linkage of Thoreau and Calhoun, see Ralph Gabriel: "Calhoun enlarged Thoreau's individual into a section, an interest group" (*American Democratic Thought,* 110); cf. Andrew Vincent, *Theories of the State* (Oxford: Blackwell, 1987), 23 (Vincent sees group theory as a variation of individualist theory).

[17] This is not the place to review the history of the Indians and the law in America. Perhaps it is enough to say that their status over time has been anomalous and difficult. At the same time, they have represented a leading example of the continuation of ideas of group authority, at least over group members. For current treatments, see Milner S. Ball, "Constitution, Court, Indian Tribes," *American Bar Foundation Journal* 1987:1; see also Charles Wilkinson, *American Indians, Time, and the Law* (New Haven: Yale University Press, 1987); Judith Resnik, "Dependent Sovereigns: Indian Tribes, States and the Federal Courts," *University of Chicago Law Review* 56 (1989): 671.

[18] Of course, as in the case of slavery, Calhoun's policies in relation to the Indians were not consonant with his ideas of minority interest to the extent that he argued against preser-

ered, not because their history may or may not reveal effective poweror self-governance in the early nineteenth century in relation to the American government, but because they can be seen as representing the permanent (or at least indefinite) existence of the small group within the larger one. The emphasis is on the concession by the formal governmental structure of the special status of the Indians. As in the case of Calhoun, Owen met with people who are associated with pluralist ideas in American history. If Owen had explained his new view of a (uniform) society to the Indian tribal leaders, they might well have responded by presenting a world in which a small semiautonomous[19] community was functioning under the protection of a larger political unit with possibly different values.[20]

This emphasis on permanent diversity is not Owenite, nor is it a characteristic of Enlightenment thinking, a major source of Owenite views. As Harrison notes, there are pronounced intellectual rigidities in Owenism, derived from the Enlightenment: "Men and their beliefs would become simplified and standardized by the application of rational principles, and diversity—far from being a mark of excellence—would be greatly reduced."[21]

America, before the Civil War, also exhibited a number of examples of radical individualism, which were not focused on communitarianism or politics at all. A digression into this material is needed to make the point that political theory that focused more on individual rights than Owen did was not necessarily more attentive to the problem of difference.

"Seen from a lower point of view, the Constitution, with all its faults, is very good,"[22] Thoreau writes.

> [T]he law and the courts are very respectable; even this State and this American government are, in many respects, very admirable, and rare things, to be thankful for, such as a great many have described them;

---

ving the Indians as separate legal nations. He believed that "[b]y a proper combination of force and persuasion of punishments and rewards, they ought to be brought within the pales of law and civilization" (quoted in Derosier, *Removal of the Choctaw,* 41). Like the proposal to replace the manners and customs of the Indians with the Constitution and laws of the United States, this is the language of assimilation, not pluralism (ibid., 42).

[19] On semiautonomous groups, see Sally Falk Moore, *Law as Process* (Boston: Routledge and Kegan Paul, 1978).

[20] For one approach, see Robert Nozick, *Anarchy, State, and Utopia* (New York: Basic Books, 1974), 297–334 (chapter 10 entitled "A Framework for Utopia").

[21] Harrison, *Quest,* 188. However, Harrison also noted, "On the surface, Owenite communities seemed to be very tolerant" (188); see also Louis Hartz, *Liberal Tradition in America* (on the difference issue in Locke): "Locke has a hidden conformitarian germ to begin with, since natural law tells equal people equal things" (11).

[22] Henry David Thoreau, "Civil Disobedience" (1849), in *Walden and Other Writings of Henry David Thoreau* (New York: Modern Library, 1950), 656.

but seen from a point of view a little higher, they are what I have described them; seen from a higher still, and the highest, who shall say what they are, or that they are worth looking at or thinking of at all?[23]

And Thoreau expressed his views on reform:

As for adopting the ways which the state has provided for remedying the evil, I know not of such ways. They take too much time, and a man's life will be gone. I have other affairs to attend to. I came into this world, not chiefly to make this a good place to live in, but to live in it, be it good or bad.[24]

But Thoreau's was not the only individualism nineteenth-century America had to offer. We can illustrate with Josiah Warren and Lysander Spooner.[25]

Josiah Warren, once of New Harmony,[26] was once described as a "musician, inventor, and all round genius . . . perhaps the brightest mind in the community."[27] He was interested in communitarian anarchism based on individual sovereignty. One can, in this case, offer material indicating that Warren was interested in diversity and individualism in the sense of serious differences between people.[28]

[23] Ibid. "[T]he government does not concern me much," Thoreau continued. "It is not many moments that I live under a government, even in this world" (656).

[24] Ibid., 644–45. Thoreau's Walden can be seen as either a fictional or a practical experimental utopia. For a discussion of Walden as a fictional utopia, see Northrop Frye, "Varieties of Literary Utopias," in Utopias and Utopian Thought, ed. Frank E. Manuel (Boston: Houghton Mifflin, 1966), 46–47; for a reference to Walden as a practical experimental utopia, see Eduard Batalov, The American Utopia (Moscow: Progress Publishers, 1985), 84. On Walden and Thoreau's travel reading—he had "traveled a good deal in Concord"—see John Aldrich Christie, Thoreau as World Traveler (New York: Columbia University Press, 1965), 215.

[25] On Lysander Spooner (1808–1887), see Charles Shively, Biography, in The Collected Works of Lysander Spooner, vol. 2 (Wenton, Mass.: M and S Press, 1971), 15–62; Dumas Malone, ed., Dictionary of American Biography (New York: Charles Scribner's Sons, 1935), 17:466–67; The National Cyclopedia of American Biography (New York: James T. White, 1922), 419–20. Spooner's natural law position included an attack on the state licensing of lawyers in 1835.

[26] Josiah Warren (1789–1874) joined the Owenite community at New Harmony after hearing Owen speak in Ohio. Later, he formed his own anarchist communities. For a comparison of Owenite ideas and those of Warren, see William Bailie, Josiah Warren (New York: Arno Press, 1906), 6–7, 123–26; and Eunice Shuster, "Native American Anarchism," Smith College Studies in History 17 (October 1931–July 1932): 94–97. For a discussion of federalist ideas in the anarchist tradition, see George Woodcock, "Anarchism: A Historical Introduction," in The Anarchist Reader, ed. Woodcock (Hassocks, Eng.: Harvester Press, 1977), 25–26. For a general treatment, see Alan Ritter, Anarchism: A Theoretical Analysis (New York: Cambridge University Press, 1980).

[27] Jacob Dunn, quoted in James J. Martin, Men against the State: The Expositors of Individualist Anarchism in America, 1827–1908, 3d ed. (Colorado Springs: Ralph Myles, 1970), 8 n. 23.

[28] See John Humphrey Noyes, History of American Socialism (Philadelphia: J. B. Lippincott, 1870), 98, on Warren's utopianism; see also Josiah Warren, True Civilization: An Im-

But the repeated references to music, and the notion of admissible discord, suggest not only Warren as a musician, band leader of New Harmony, but also Warren who believed fundamentally that, given the right sort of education, most people would make disciplined, correct choices and that conflict would be radically minimized through education.[29]

While Warren is remembered as part of the American utopian or communitarian tradition, Lysander Spooner is cited as part of an indigenous anarchist or libertarian tradition in America.[30] He is also occasionally recalled in relation to his operation of a private mail service in competition with the federal post office.[31] Lysander Spooner's position on sovereignty is elaborated in his late work, *A Letter to Grover Cleveland:*

> The only real "sovereignty," or right of "sovereignty," in this or any other country, is that right of sovereignty which each and every human being has over his or her own person and property, so long as he or she obeys the one law of justice towards the person and property of every other human being. This is the only *natural* right of sovereignty, that was ever known among men. All other so-called rights of sovereignty are simply the usurpations of impostors, conspirators, robbers, tyrants, and murderers.[32]

---

mediate Necessity and the Last Ground of Hope for Mankind, ed. Burt Franklin (New York: B. Franklin, 1967), 18 ("No subordination can be more perfect than that of an Orchestra; but it is all *voluntary*").

[29] Lockwood, *The New Harmony Movement,* 295. The present suggestion is that some thinkers, like Owen, Spooner, or Warren, whose ideas are rooted in natural law or enlightenment approaches, are concerned with variety, rather than difference. Issues of "interests" go deeper and overlap questions of "difference" that are now discussed often in the context of feminism. See the work of Martha Minow, e.g., "Pluralisms," *Connecticut Law Review* 21 (1989): 965.

[30] George Woodcock, *Anarchism: A History of Libertarian Ideas and Movements* (Cleveland: Meridian Books, 1962), 459–60. On anarchist and antinomian traditions from Anne Hutchinson through Noyes, Warren, Benjamin Tucker, Lysander Spooner, and the immigrant radicals, see David De Leon, *The American as Anarchist* (Baltimore: Johns Hopkins University Press, 1978). See also Martin, *Men against the State.*

Note that "undesirables" of Warren's community, Modern Times, were "let alone," and they "usually" left (Martin, *Men against the State,* 85). In short, the structure assumed a certain consensus.

[31] See *United States Postal Serv. v. Brennan,* 574 F.2d 712, 717 n. 11 (1978), cert. denied, 439 U.S. 1115 (1979) ("In reaching our conclusion, we do not overlook the paper of Lysander Spooner on 'The Unconstitutionality of the Laws of Congress Prohibiting Private Mails,' published in 1844").

[32] Lysander Spooner, *A Letter to Grover Cleveland* (Boston: Benj. R. Tucker Publishers, 1886), 86; cf. Blaise Pascal, *Pensées,* ed. W. Thayer (New York: Pantheon, 1965), No. 294 ("On what shall man found the order of the world which he would govern? . . . Shall it be on justice? Man is ignorant of it"). As to John Marshall, Spooner said that "he has the

Law meant natural, universal, unalterable law. This was Spooner's argument for some decades, reflected in pamphlets, books, and encounters with government agencies.[33] Spooner argued that "law is an intelligible principle of right, necessarily resulting from the nature of man; and not an arbitrary rule, that can be established by mere will, numbers or power,"[34] and that law is "simply *the rule, principle, obligation or requirement of natural justice*." He believed that judges should declare slavery illegal on the basis of natural law.

Wendell Phillips responded with a *Review of Lysander Spooner's Essay on the Unconstitutionality of Slavery*. In a section called "What Is Law?" Phillips quoted a number of positivist definitions of law as emanating from state authority. Phillips rejected Spooner's view of the world, emphasizing the association of law and government, law and officials, law and the state, as part of an activist (abolitionist) position. Phillips was afraid that Spooner's abstract (or utopian?) natural law theories would mislead people. In short, his argument suggests that someone might have been paying attention to Spooner's arguments in the abolitionist context.

By the time that E. V. Zenker did his research on anarchism at the end of the nineteenth century, he reported that he was "quite unable to procure any book or essay by [the anarchist] Tucker, or a copy of his journal *Liberty*."[35] It is difficult to say anything specific about the influence of anarchist ideas. Atiyah and Summers suggest that Spooner was not alone.[36] "[W]hatever may have been the position of classical natural law theorists such as Aristotle and Aquinas, many American natural law thinkers did believe in a 'higher law' version of natural law, according to which positive law contrary to natural law was simply invalid as law or, even if valid, imposed no duty of obedience; indeed, in extreme cases, government action contrary to natural law gave rise to the right of rebellion or revolution."[37]

---

reputation of having been the greatest jurist the country has ever had. And he unquestionably would have been a great jurist, if the two fundamental propositions, on which all his legal, political, and constitutional ideas were based, had been true. These propositions were, first, that government has all power; and, secondly, that the people have no rights" (*Letter to Grover Cleveland*, 87).

[33] Spooner's position on law and natural law elicited a strong response and critique from Wendell Phillips on the nature of law. See *Review of Lysander Spooner's Essay on the Unconstitutionality of Slavery* (Boston: Andrews and Prentiss, 1847).

[34] Lysander Spooner, *The Unconstitutionality of Slavery*, ed. Burt Franklin (New York: Burt Franklin, 1965), 5.

[35] Ernest Viktor Zenker, *Anarchism: A Criticism and History of the Anarchist Theory* (New York: G. P. Putnam's Sons, 1897), vi–vii.

[36] Atiyah and Summers, *Form and Substance*, 237.

[37] Ibid. For Phillips's discussion of the problems with Blackstone's definition of law, see *Review of Spooner's Essay*, 8n. "If the reader asks why we do not cite Blackstone's definition—'Municipal law is a rule of civil conduct, prescribed by the Supreme power in a State,

On the general problem, Phillips argued that "[t]he Constitution will never be amended by persuading men that it does not need amendment."[38] Here we see a position, like Owen's, that is not focused on pluralism, though it stresses individual rights.[39]

Josiah Warren and Lysander Spooner remained committed to the same eighteenth-century understanding of right results through right reason (and, in Spooner's case, a self-evident natural law) that marks so much of Owen's thinking. It was not those who are associated with the utopian or anarchist tradition in America who best represent the possible pluralist implications of communitarian doctrine, but rather the slaveholder Calhoun, committed to the defense of his section, and the Indian tribes, who would for two hundred years represent a special and anomalous case in American jurisprudence, a concededly autonomous (or semiautonomous) internal group.

As A. V. Dicey remarked, federalism requires a special state of mind on the part of the inhabitants. "They must desire union, and must not desire unity."[40] The subject has been of absorbing interest to political theorists for some centuries and of particular interest to those countries like the United States whose structure is federal. Often the issue is the relative balance of power between the several parts of the federal structure and, particularly, the relative power of the national state and the internal, federated states. The issue of federalism has also been of interest to jurisprudence, particularly because of its implications for the doctrine of a single sovereignty. Thus, even John Austin was compelled to consider the case of federations, including the United States, in his work on jurisprudence.[41]

In the United States, the meaning of federalism, in theory or practice, or historically, is not easily described. We see various definitions of federalism attributed to leading figures. Hamilton is cited for an idea that em-

---

commanding what is right, and prohibiting what is wrong' . . . we think the last clause equivocal and superfluous, and, if taken in its obvious sense, false."

[38] Phillips, *Review of Spooner's Essay*, 4; see also Cover, *Justice Accused*.

[39] Spooner's arguments, thus, refer to "general principles of law and reason" and the "general sense of mankind." See, e.g., Lysander Spooner, *No Treason the Constitution of No Authority* (Boston: Lysander Spooner, 1870), 29. Spooner opposed women's suffrage on the theory that no one, male or female, had the right to make laws. Spooner, *Liberty*, June 10, 1882, 4 (reprinting an article appearing in the February 24, 1877, edition of the defunct *New Age*). In *Justice Accused*, Cover notes that Spooner was not seriously concerned with the method of the judge in any real sense (157). Indeed, he was not operating in the positivist legal tradition at all.

[40] Albert Venn Dicey, "Federal Government," *Law Quarterly Review* 1 (1885): 80, 81; cf. Daniel Elazar, "The Role of Federalism in Political Integration," in *Federalism and Political Integration*, ed. Daniel Elazar (Ramat Gan, Israel: Turtledove, 1979), 13.

[41] John Austin, "Lecture VI," in *Lectures on Jurisprudence or the Philosophy of Positive Laws*, ed. Robert Campbell, 5th ed. (London: John Murray, 1885), 1:261.

phasizes a strong national government. Jefferson and Madison are cited for the idea of a weak central government with the power basically retained by the states. As presented by lawyers, federalism becomes a federal structure in which the national government and its expositor of law, the Supreme Court, sits on top of all the internal structures.[42] Official governmental law is seen as the only law. Federalism is taken to refer to governmental agencies.

Other ideas were, however, real to the nineteenth century. A school of "no government" anarchist-individualists (including Lysander Spooner) was active in the abolitionist movement. Thoreau rejected the state as a matter not worthy of much concern. Even governmental matters relatively clear to us were quite open. The highest level of the legal hierarchy could be flatly ignored by a president: "John Marshall has made his decision: *now let him enforce it!*"[43] The comment, attributed to President Andrew Jackson, reflects the tension between law and politics, and the uncertainty in the role of the Supreme Court as the expositor of the federal Constitution as against other parts of the federal structure.

In America, the debate over the meaning of federalism has had a long and sometimes bloody history. "Down to the time of the Civil War," Charles Merriam wrote, "the centers of political activity and interest had

---

[42] For a discussion and review of the continuing debate over centralized and decentralized power in fact and legal theory, see Harry N. Scheiber, "Federalism and Legal Process: Historical and Contemporary Analysis of the American System," *Law and Society Review* 14 (1980): 663. See also Aviam Soifer and Hugh Macgill, "The Younger Doctrine: Reconstructing Reconstruction," *Texas Law Review* 55 (1977): 1141, 1168 ("Federal and state powers ebb and flow relative to one another in response to messy and mutable social, political, and economic conditions").

As has been noted, the images of the United States and its federalism have changed over time. See Gerald Frug, "The City as a Legal Concept," *Harvard Law Review* 93 (1980): 1059. The nineteenth-century idea was that there were powerful states that somehow came together for certain purposes to form a national union, whose powers were defined and limited. The concept of federalism went along with an idea of demarcation. To a contemporary mind, the federated states are internal governing structures of a larger state, not private, for they too, after all, are governmental, but still lesser. "To the modern reader, American states seem to be, like cities, entities that are intermediate between the central (federal) government and the individual" (ibid., 1105 n. 188).

[43] See Horace Greeley, *The American Conflict* (Hartford: O. D. Case, 1877), 1:106; see also Edwin Miles, "After John Marshall's Decision: *Worcester v. Georgia* and the Nullification Crisis," *Journal of History* 39 (1973): 519. As is well known, the comment is said to have been made as a response to Marshall's decision in *Worcester v. Georgia*, 31 U.S. (6 Pet.) 515 (1832), holding that the State of Georgia could not imprison missionaries who were working with the Cherokee Indians in Georgia because Indian land was not under the jurisdiction of the state. Marshall's decision, however, was not enforced. The missionaries stayed in jail. See Ulrich Phillips, *Georgia and States Rights* (Washington, D.C.: Government Printing Office, 1968), 264–65; see also William G. McLoughlin, *Cherokees and Missionaries, 1789–1839* (New Haven: Yale University Press, 1984).

been the state and the nation, rivals in the contest for supremacy which finally resulted in armed conflict."[44] But, Merriam adds, "[b]ack of this struggle lay an intense interest and devotion to the units and agencies of rural government, which had played so large and vital a part in the early days of the colonies and of the Republic."[45] These units and agencies of government, the town, the county, had been the concern of the anti-federalists and the republicans, who focused on shared values, small communities, small units. The alternatives, posed by the Hamiltonians, were associated with centralist development and the commitment to sovereignty in the federal government. This version of centralism was opposed by many, including Thomas Jefferson, who became, if anything, more concerned with small units as he became older. He wrote in 1824: "As Cato concluded every speech with the words, *Carthago delenda est,* so do I every opinion, with the injunction, 'divide the counties into wards.' "[46]

Thus, underneath many of the historical discussions of federalism and republicanism was a question about the correct size of the political unit. It has been recently said: "Lost today in the legitimate characterization of the Constitution as bent on setting limits to the power exercised by less than angelic men is the extent to which the Constitution is a grant of power to a centralized nation-state."[47] Thus, Isaac Kramnick suggests that among the paradigms being used in the political discourse of 1787 was one that involved "the state-centered language of power."[48] Some of the debate over the Constitution dealt with this issue in terms of size. How large should the republic be? The school, known now as anti-federalist,[49] urged that the size should be small and, some add, about the size of the existing states. Late in his life, Jefferson was urging a size smaller than that. This emphasis on the small unit overlaps the interest, then and now, in voluntary associations.

Faction and *voluntary association, mediating structure* and *interest group,* although they seem to be related and even, sometimes, the same thing, are often discussed in a way that fails to clarify whether the entities

[44] Charles Merriam, *American Political Ideas* (New York: Macmillan, 1920), 228.

[45] Ibid., 229.

[46] Letter from Thomas Jefferson to John Cartwright, June 5, 1824, quoted in Hannah Arendt, *On Revolution* (New York: Viking Press, 1963), 252. Arendt comments that this emphasis on wards is found in writing at the end of Jefferson's life and at a time when he had withdrawn from affairs of state (253–54).

[47] Isaac Kramnick, "The 'Great National Discussion': The Discourse of Politics in 1787," *William and Mary Quarterly* 45 (1988): 3, 23.

[48] Ibid., 24.

[49] The distrust of legislative majorities and concern with small units and issues of cultural diversity marked the arguments of the anti-federalists. See Cecelia M. Kenyon, "Men of Little Faith: The Anti-Federalists on the Nature of Representative Government," *William and Mary Quarterly* 12 (1955): 3, 10, 35–37.

are different or whether only the values or adjectives attached to the entities are different. *Faction,* for example, seems to be a negative term. *Voluntary associations* and *mediating structures* seem positive.

We can start with the discussion of republicanism offered by Gordon Wood,[50] who describes an approach in which division itself is perceived as bad. The public good is for everyone. "Since everyone in the community was linked organically to everyone else, what was good for the whole community was ultimately good for all the parts.[51] The "common interest" is carefully defined by Wood as follows: It is not, "as we might today think of it, simply the sum or consensus of the particular interests that made up the community. It was rather an entity in itself, prior to and distinct from the various private interests of groups and individuals."[52] Wood goes on to explain that this is not to say that private or competing interests were denied, they were simply to be ignored. "[A]part from the basic conflict between governors and people these were not to be dignified by their incorporation into formal political theory or into any serious discussion of what ought to be.[53] The state was "to be considered as one moral whole," and "interests and parties were regarded as aberrations or perversions, indeed signs of sickness in the body politic."[54]

The Federalist Papers present a more complicated picture. In the essay "Factions" in *Federalist* No. 10, Madison offered a now famous definition.

> By a faction, I understand a number of citizens, whether amounting to a majority or a minority of the whole, who are united and actuated by some common impulse of passion, or of interest, adverse to the rights of other citizens, or to the permanent and aggregate interests of the community.[55]

Reading the sentence with an emphasis on the word *adverse,* one might suspect that the point is ultimately substantive. Some groups and associations are fine, but "factions" are working toward bad ends. This reading is reinforced by the examples, which include "[a] rage for paper money, for an abolition of debts, for an equal division or property, or for any other improper or wicked project" (note also the reference to "sinister

---

[50] Gordon Wood, *The Creation of the American Republic, 1776–1787* (Chapel Hill: University of North Carolina Press, 1969), 58–59.

[51] Ibid., 58.

[52] Ibid.

[53] Ibid.

[54] Ibid., 58–59. Wood notes that some nineteenth-century thinkers did, however, conceive of factions as not only inevitable, but even desirable (59).

[55] *The Federalist* No. 10 (James Madison), ed. Roy Fairfield (Baltimore: Johns Hopkins University Press, 1961), 17.

views").[56] In short, *factions* may be seen as groups, associations, parties, and sects that are doing the wrong things on the merits or as groups inherently adverse to the public interest.[57] Other groups, for example, those described in *Federalist* No. 51, are much less troublesome. There will be so many of them (groups, interests, sects) that they will not be dangerous. "Whilst all authority in it will be derived from and dependent on the society, the society itself will be broken into so many parts, interests and classes of citizens, that the rights of individuals or of the minority will be in little danger from interested combinations of the majority."[58]

And finally we reach the well-known discussion by Tocqueville in which groups become the voluntary associations, which, while not without their negative side, are on the whole valuable and necessary.[59] Several features of Tocqueville's discussion are initially striking. The first is the range of groups that he saw, political associations as against civil associations, governmental associations (townships, counties) as against other forms of association, and private fraternal groups. The second is the range of characteristics of these groups, from those that are single purpose and limited in duration to those that finally become internal states.

---

[56] Ibid., 23.

[57] Cf. David Epstein, *The Political Theory of the Federalist* (Chicago: University of Chicago Press, 1984), 65 ("Even if a particular interest is part of the aggregate of interests, that interest as an impulse uniting and actuating a group is indifferent to the aggregate. . . . Madison's definition seems to detect a factious impulse at the heart of even a respectable lobby").

[58] *The Federalist* No. 51 (James Madison), 162. James Luther Adams attempted to reconcile these two essays by suggesting that the emphasis in No. 10 was on economic groups, while in No. 51, Madison focused on noneconomic and religious groups. He also suggested that "[m]isconceptions have arisen regarding Madison's view of mediating structures because of his somewhat pejorative definition of factions in *Federalist,* No. 10. . . . But Madison also saw in factions 'a salutary dispersion of power, a protection for freedom in society against potentially tyrannical intentions of the majority.'" Adams goes on to connect this problem with issues of church and state. See "Mediating Structures and the Separation of Powers," in *Voluntary Associations* (Chicago: Exploration Press, 1986), 236; see also John Madison, *Memorial and Remonstrance Against Religious Assessments,* in *Writings of James Madison* (New York: G. P. Putnam's Sons, 1900), 2:183–91 appended to *Everson v. Board of Educ.,* 330 U.S. 1, 63–72 (1946).

For a discussion of federalism and republicanism, see Mark Tushnet, "Federalism and the Traditions of American Political Theory," *Georgia Law Review* 981 (1985): 19. See also Cass Sunstein, "Interest Groups in American Public Law," *Stanford Law Review* 38 (1985): 29, 32 (describing republican and pluralist conceptions of government and noting that "[t]he pluralist conception treats the republican notion of a separate common good as incoherent, potentially totalitarian, or both"); Daniel Elazar, *The American Partnership: Intergovernmental Co-operation in the Nineteenth-Century United States* (Chicago: University of Chicago Press, 1962), 21–24.

[59] Tocqueville, *Democracy in America,* 1:189 ff., 2:513 ff.

But for all this early discussion of group life in America, one is tempted to say that there was, there must have been, a clear and universal sense of the official state as the final arbiter, setter of the limits, creator and keeper of boundaries. As to this, let us consider a Mississippi case of 1837.[60]

Fisher v. Allen upheld a married woman's capacity to own and transfer her assets—in this case, a slave. The married woman was a Chickasaw Indian, married according to the custom of the tribe. The slave was given to a daughter. A year after the gift, the legislature passed a law abolishing the tribal character of the Indians, abolishing tribal laws and customs, and conferring on the Indians the rights of citizenship. Marriages between Indians were validated. The court held that the slave could not be seized to satisfy the debts of the husband, since the slave belonged to the wife, and the gift to the daughter was good. Under the Chickasaw tribal law, a wife had property rights not generally available in Mississippi, including a "right to own separate property, to dispose of it at pleasure, to create debts and in most things act as a *feme sole*."[61] The court found that the statute could not "be construed to extend so far as to interfere with the rights to property previously acquired."[62] Shortly after, as Judith Younger puts it, "the Mississippi legislature extended *Fisher v. Allen* to include all Mississippi wives by enacting a Married Woman's Property Act."[63]

The case is a part of a story of groups and government, outsiders and insiders, society and state. We see Indians, slaves, mothers, daughters, legislatures, and courts.[64] Yet the configurations are not quite what we

---

[60] *Fisher v. Allen*, 3 Miss. (2 Howard) 611 (1837). The case is described (with an emphasis on the history of married women's property issues in Mississippi) by Judith Younger in "Marital Regimes: A Story of Compromise and Demoralization, together with Criticism and Suggestions for Reform," *Cornell Law Review* 67 (1981): 45, 60–61; see also Comment, "Husband and Wife: Memorandum on the Mississippi Woman's Law of 1839," *Michigan Law Review* 42 (1944): 1110, 1117–18 (discussion of the case): "[I]t is a hypothesis worthy of consideration that from Chickasaw custom was derived the first law giving a married woman in a common-law state any rights in her own property" (1117) (also considering the possibility that a woman who visited Louisiana and brought community property ideas back to Mississippi with her was a source of the law). On the later history of the slaves of the Chickasaw, see *United States v. Choctaw Nation*, 193 U.S. 115 (1904). The tribes were on the side of the Confederacy. The litigation concerned the provisions of the treaty of 1866 regarding the Chickasaw freedmen, ignored by both the Indians and the government. For a discussion of this case, see Aviam Soifer, "The Paradox of Paternalism and Laissez-Faire Constitutionalism: The U.S. Supreme Court, 1888–1921," in *Corporations and Society: Power and Responsibility*, ed. Warren J. Samuels and Arthur S. Miller (New York: Greenwood Press, 1987), 170–71.

[61] *Fisher*, 3 Miss. (2 Howard), 615.

[62] Ibid., 616.

[63] Younger, "Marital Regimes," 61.

[64] For an argument that some Indian tribes provide social and economic autonomy to women, see Eleanor Leacock, *Myths of Male Dominance* (New York: Monthly Review Press, 1981), 236 (mentioning Choctaw Indians specifically.)

expect. We have slaveholding Indians who are married women. Among possible readings is an open-textured history in which a legislature voids tribal law, while simultaneously recognizing its marriages. A court limits the act of the legislature to sustain tribal law on property theories. A legislature generalizes the ruling of the court (incidentally supporting tribal law) so as to benefit all married women and perhaps to clarify the situation for creditors.[65] Indian law (primitive? outsider?) sustains rights not recognized by official law (civilized? insider?) that recognizes Indian laws, nonetheless, and builds on them. It is not a clear story either of the triumph of group interest or of state hierarchy. It is a story of interactions and interpretations.

Whatever shape that history has or is given, it cannot, I assume, be the same as the shape of the history of the state or of the law, and the story does not begin with the Constitution, or the public/private distinction in particular courts. "We should look to the phenomena themselves for their proper periods," Marc Bloch suggests, noting that we would not write a diplomatic history from Newton to Einstein.[66] We shape the story to the subject, and if we use official state materials, we view them, as part of a narrative in this context, differently from the way we would view them as part of a history of the law's approach to a particular problem.

---

[65] Friedman makes the point that the litigation involving married women's property typically involved issues of creditors rights. Lawrence Friedman, *A History of American Law*, 2d ed. (New York: Simon and Schuster, 1985), 211.

[66] Marc Bloch, *The Historian's Craft* (New York: Knopf, 1962), 183.

CHAPTER 3

An *Imperium in Imperio*: The Mormon Empire and Later Developments

[This is an] exodus of the nation of the only true Israel from these United States to a far distant region of the west.

—BRIGHAM YOUNG, 1845

✦ APPROACHING the subject of religion and law from the point of view of Western liberal ideas of church and state, one sees two separate boxes. One is labeled *secular,* linked to official law and the modern Western state. The other is called *religious,* associated with private groups within the state that may have their own norms and customs but are located primarily in the private consciences of individuals.

It has been apparent to some of those who write about law and religion that these boxes are better conceived as interpenetrating units, whose areas of influence and ideologies reveal considerable overlap. This chapter opens with a brief historical sketch of the relations between law and religion and then concentrates on the history of the Mormon Church in America, used as the vehicle for a discussion of adjustments of the situation—basically the conflict between church and state—in which there are two powerful claims to priority.

Religion in this view has a collective and institutional form. This collective aspect may be based on a shared history or on the memory of historical events. These are sometimes invoked and even recalled directly and immediately by believers centuries after the historical facts may have been called into question by new criticism of ancient texts or by contemporary standards of probability and improbability.

It is useful initially to consider religion as if it existed in a world without the state. If we do this, we can see that religions tend to function in ways that are quite statelike. Canon law and Jewish law, for example, are recognizable as legal systems, involving officials, courts, processes. (Other systems may be more informal, involving adjudication by someone who is in effect a wise man, instructed in the tradition.)

Within religious legal systems, the teaching of the religion is not merely a statement of general moral command. Rather, that teaching can be quite specific about the ways in which one is supposed to live. What to those outside the tradition may be simply ritual—and meaningless or only curious—often appears crucial to the believer, if only because it is embedded in a structure that is all of a piece. (Other reasons, however, may also be invoked. The ritual can be justified as useful—or healthy—for the individual believer, or, in another framework, it may protected and defended as useful to the group to the extent that it helps to maintain group boundaries.)

Religions claim jurisdiction over their members. The question of who is a member of a religious group is seldom simple, because religions tend to define their own membership in ways that may be different from both state and individual definitions. Religions can monitor the behavior of their members through a range of sanctions, though in the modern world certain punishments are reserved to the state. Religions often have as an important part of their goal the reintegration of the backslider with the community, and particular sanctions may function with this purpose in mind. Membership questions may at times be relevant to state law issues (because religions in fact exist within states), and the state may regulate the religion (declaring certain practices illegal, for example) and also protects the members of the religious group.

Some aspects of religious legal systems are clearly not consonant with Western liberal ideals of individual liberty. The degree to which it is possible to intervene in those religious legal systems to change these aspects of religious law will depend on whether the state's foundational ideas include some concept of the autonomy of religious groups and the autonomy of religious development of doctrine. To the extent that autonomy is respected in principle—or even reluctantly acknowledged in fact, on the theory that religious groups may be a hot potato[1]—the state will aggressively intervene only in unusual instances. This does not mean that the state will be without influence. Rather, the state's influence will show itself mainly through indirection, perhaps through the activities of individual members of the religious group, trying to change religious law from the inside.

Religious groups respond to the modern secular state by trying to influence or even co-opt it to enforce religious norms universally, or by trying to separate themselves from the state so that they can operate (quasi) autonomously. This distinction may be made by labeling the former pattern a *mode 1* interaction, in which a religion hopes to universalize its

---

[1] Zechariah Chafee Jr., "Internal Affairs of Associations Not for Profit," *Harvard Law Review* 43 (1930): 993.

values, acting through the state, and the latter a *mode 2* interaction, in which a religion seeks room for its practices, preserving its own singularity without attempting a universal application of them.[2] Modes 1 and 2 may work in combination. Religious groups when conceived as standing apart from the state, can be as powerful, at least in theory, as the state itself. Their general effort may be to reduce the areas of conflict with the state by changing the state. Thus, some images of religion and the state involve political activism, and one can see self-immolation of monks and the participation by religious leaders in campaigns for political change as attempts to change state policy and law as these relate to everyone. This way state policy and law will operate more consonantly with religious policy and law.

Globally, we have seen long traditions in which rulers committed their states to a particular religion, or the populace was for a long period of time dominantly of one religion. Issues of religion and the state then overlap substantially with the nature of national identity. Specifically, does one nation mean one ethnicity and one religion, or is it possible to accommodate nation-states in which there are different ethnicities and religions? The issue still persists today.

Where relations between religion and the state are traditionally close, for example Islamic states and Israel, governments enforce religious law explicitly, particularly in relation to personal status, marriage, and divorce.

The American approach to church and state is founded on ideas inscribed in the constitutional principles of "free exercise" and "no establishment," referred to as the separation of church and state.[3]

The American experiment was based on the idea that the nation itself would not be committed to a particular religion. The rejection of religious tests for public office in Article 6 of the Constitution was an explicit statement of what we would come to refer to as First Amendment ideas as they concerned the federal government. This did not mean that the states, which sometimes had established churches, automatically ended such of-

---

[2] See generally Weisbrod, "Family, Church and State," where this approach is described in more detail.

[3] This idea is not accepted in many countries and is not part of the international commitment to religious toleration or freedom of religion. See Arcot Krishnaswami, "Study of Discrimination in the Matter of Religious Rights and Practices. Sub-commission on Prevention of Discrimination and Protection of Minorities," *U.N. Doc. E/CN.4/Sub.2/200/Rev. 1*, U.N. Sales No. 60XIV.2 (1960), 12, reprinted in *New York University Journal of International Law and Politics* 11 (1978): 227–96. Krishnaswami, working on the problem of religious minority rights for the United Nations, revealed a notable familiarity with a wide range of church-state arrangements in different countries, but he did not suggest that formal structural disestablishment was a necessary part of religious liberty.

ficial linkages. The First Amendment spoke directly only to issues of the national government, and state establishments survived for some time. Even after the last formal state disestablishment of the churches in Connecticut and Massachusetts the United States experienced a long period of identification as a Christian nation that continued after the formal incorporation of the First Amendment in the Fourteenth Amendment and made the First Amendment applicable to the states.

In the case of Utah, the story begins with an attempt by a religious group to reduce conflict with the state by leaving the state itself—the exodus of the Mormons to what in 1850 became the Territory of Utah. Some decades later, an enabling act passed by Congress in 1894,[4] authorizing Utah's constitutional convention and mandating certain constitutional provisions, resulted in a constitution approved by Utah voters in 1895. On January 4, 1896, the Mormon-dominated territory was proclaimed a state by President Grover Cleveland.

Utah was admitted to membership in the Union under a state constitution providing for religious freedom and the rejection of polygamy. The polygamy language read, "[P]erfect toleration of religious sentiment shall be secured, and . . . no inhabitant of said State shall ever be molested in person or property on account of his or her mode of religious worship: *Provided,* That polygamous or plural marriages are forever prohibited."[5] The state constitution also provided that no church would ever take control of the state: "There shall be no union of church and state, nor shall any church dominate the state or interfere with its functions."[6]

These two provisions highlight those aspects of the domestic and political aspects of the doctrine and culture of the Latter-day Saints that troubled its neighbors.[7]

These textual provisions reconstituted Mormonism in its relation to the State of Utah and to the larger federal state, the United States. The first

---

[4] Enabling Act, chap. 138, 28 Stat. 107 (1894).

[5] Utah Const., art. 1, sec. 4. Enabling Act, chap. 138, 28 Stat. 107, sec. 3 (1894).

[6] Utah Const., art. 1, sec. 4. On the history of church-state separation in Utah see *Society of Separationists v. Whitehead,* 870 P.2d 916 (Utah 1993).

The American Constitution contains both an antiestablishment and a free exercise clause. Some constitutions create religious liberty with only a free exercise clause in effect. On such an approach, see Richard Kay, "The Canadian Constitution and the Dangers of Establishment," *DePaul Law Review* 42 (1992): 361.

[7] We can also see the official solution adopted in the form of constitutional provisions, words on parchment that, as Walton H. Hamilton wrote long ago, we trust to bind government. See Richard S. Kay's discussion of Hamilton's line in "American Constitutionalism," in *Constitutionalism: Philosophical Foundations,* ed. Larry Alexander (Cambridge: Cambridge University Press, 1998). Also see Hamilton's distrust of the words-on-parchment approach in "The Path of Due Process of Law," in *The Constitution Reconsidered,* ed. Conyers Read (New York: Columbia University Press, 1938), 167–90.

part of this chapter reviews the unsuccessful efforts of nineteenth-century Mormons to reach an accommodation with the U.S. government on the issue of polygamy (through an argument based on the free exercise clause, litigated and rejected in *Reynolds v. United States*) and concludes with the new constitution. The second part of the chapter considers the twentieth-century history of polygamy and the modern association of the Mormon Church with traditional family structures. The third part discusses reconstitution of church-state relations in a situation of disestablishment, under an approach to constitutionalism that moves beyond the idea of the Constitution as text to the idea of a working framework of religious groups in the modern state.

The major nineteenth-century narrative of the Mormon encounters with the American legal system over the issue of polygamy begins in 1852, when the Mormons announced publicly that they were practicing plural marriage,[8] and ends in 1890, when the triumph of the federal government was formally acknowledged by the Mormon Church. It includes the trek to the Great Salt Lake Basin, described by George Bernard Shaw as "one of the most extraordinary episodes in the white settlement of the world."[9] The move to the West was, as Brigham Young made plain, an escape from the United States.[10]

This history remains central to the Mormons' understanding of their relationship to the American story. Elder Dallin H. Oaks, representing the Church of Jesus Christ of Latter-day Saints, recalled that history in testimony submitted to the U.S. Congress in 1992. "I know of no other major religious group in America that has endured anything comparable to the officially sanctioned persecution that was imposed upon members of my church by Federal, State and local government officials," he said. "In the 19th century our members were literally driven from State to State, sometimes by direct Government action, and finally expelled from the existing borders of the United States." In fact, he noted, "[T]he experience of the Mormon pioneers is analogous to the compelled migration of many of this country's founding settlers—the Pilgrims, Separatists, Quakers, Catholics, and Puritans, who fled England and Holland to escape

---

[8] The revelation of polygamy to Joseph Smith is dated 1843. Smith was murdered in Carthage, Illinois, in 1844. On America as Israel, see Conrad C. Cherry, *God's New Israel: Religious Interpretations of American Destiny* (Englewood Cliffs, N.J.: Prentice-Hall, 1971).

[9] George Bernard Shaw, *The Political Madhouse in America and Nearer Home: A Lecture by Bernard Shaw* (London: Constable, 1939), 32.

[10] See Brigham Young's "Exodus Announced, October 8, 1845," in Edwin S. Gaustad, *A Documentary History of Religion in America* (Grand Rapids, Mich.: W. B. Eerdmans, 1982–83), 1:359–60.

religious persecution and to seek a sanctuary where they could practice their religion free from persecution."[11]

But the federal presence was not to be eliminated. In 1850, Utah became a territory, subject to the authority of the American Congress. The Republican Party platform of 1856 included a reference to polygamy as one of twin relics of barbarism; slavery, of course, the other.[12] The campaign against polygamy waited for the end of the Civil War, and then it began in earnest.

A critical moment in the narrative occurred in 1879, when the Supreme Court in *Reynolds v. United States,* which litigated a federal statute, the Morrill Act,[13] passed in 1862 to deal with bigamy in the territories. Sixteen years later a test case involving George Reynolds of Utah, secretary to Brigham Young, finally reached the Supreme Court. Reynolds's central argument in the Supreme Court was that his conviction for bigamy could not stand because polygamy was an exercise of rights protected under the religious liberty guarantees of the First Amendment, directly operative in the territories. His rights, he said, were violated by the congressional action.[14] Reynolds requested the trial court to instruct the jury that if it

---

[11] Dallin Oaks, Testimony on Religious Freedom Restoration Act, Hearings before the Subcommittee on Civil and Constitutional Rights of the Committee on the Judiciary, House of Representatives, 102nd Congress, 2d Sess. on H.R. 2797 (Religious Freedom Restoration Act of 1991), May 13–14, 1992, 23. "I am privileged to appear before you today to testify in behalf of the Church of Jesus Christ of Latter-day Saints in support of congressional enactment of H.R. 2797. I am here to represent the official position of our 8-million-member church at the request of its highest governing bodies, the first presidency and the Quorum of the Twelve Apostles, of which I am a member" (23). He continued: "As a general rule, our church does not take positions on specific legislative initiatives pending in Congress or State legislatures. Our action in this matter is an exception to this rule. It underscores the importance we attach to this congressional initiative to restore to the free exercise of religion what a divided Supreme Court took away in *Employment Division v. Smith*" (23).

"It is not that LDS Church is uninterested in changing society but only that it is generally uninterested in devoting its resources to effecting such change through political activism. For the LDS Church, political change, if it is to come about at all, will occur indirectly, as the result of the world's gradual embrace of the fullness of the gospel, and the Church is for the most part content to effect that embrace within existing political and governmental structures." Frederick Mark Gedicks, " 'No Man's Land': The Place of the Latter Day Saints in the Culture Wave," *BYU Studies* 38, no. 3 (1999): 155.

[12] For discussions of the nineteenth-century Mormonism and anti-Mormonism see Lawrence Foster, *Religion and Sexuality: The Shakers, the Mormons, and the Oneida Community* (Oxford: Oxford University Press, 1981).

[13] Morrill Act, chap. 126, 12 Stat. 501 (1862). The act provided that "every person having a husband or wife living, who shall marry any other person, whether married or single, in a territory of the United States, or other place over which the United States [has] jurisdiction . . . shall . . . be adjudged guilty of bigamy."

[14] The fact that Utah was a territory was critical to the litigation, since Congress, and not the states, was bound by the First Amendment. It was only much later that the First

found from the evidence that he was married "in pursuance of and in conformity with what he believed at the time to be a religious duty, that the verdict must be 'not guilty.'"[15] This request was refused. The judge instructed the jury that

> if the defendant, under the influence of a religious belief that it was right—under an inspiration, if you please, that it was right,—deliberately married a second time, having a first wife living, the want of consciousness of evil intent—the want of understanding on his part that he was committing a crime—did not excuse him; but the law inexorably in such case implies the criminal intent.[16]

Chief Justice Waite, writing for the Supreme Court, considered the jury instruction on the subsequent appeal. The issue was whether religious belief could justify an act made criminal by federal statute.[17] The Court rejected Reynolds's claim that the religious practice of polygamy was constitutionally protected. Congress, the Court said, could not pass a law for the territories that would prohibit the free exercise of religion, but the antibigamy act was not within the congressional prohibition. The Court found the Morrill Act within the legislative power of Congress, since Congress was "left free to reach actions which were in violation of social duties or subversive of good order."[18] The Court then asked whether those who made the practice of polygamy a part of their religious belief were excepted from the operation of the statute,[19] and concluded that they were not. "To permit this would be to make the professed doctrines of religious belief superior to the law of the land, and in effect to permit every citizen to become a law unto himself. Government could exist only in name under such circumstances."

The statute was upheld by the Supreme Court. Reynolds himself served nineteen months in jail and upon his release married a third time.[20]

In 1865, Francis Lieber suggested that it might be appropriate to consider, among various amendments to the American Constitution, one declaring polygamy and polyandry a crime.[21] Presumably, he did this in part because he understood that if Utah, then a territory, were to be admitted

---

Amendment was understood to bind the states through "incorporation" in the Fourteenth Amendment.

[15] *Reynolds v. United States,* 98 U.S. 145, 162 (1878).
[16] Ibid.
[17] Ibid.
[18] Ibid., 164.
[19] Ibid., 166.
[20] Ray Jay Davis, "Plural Marriage and Religious Freedom: The Impact of *Reynolds v. United States,*" *Arizona Law Review* 15 (1973): 287, 291.
[21] See Weisbrod, "Breakup of Oneida," 14.

to the union as a state, it would be very difficult to move legally against the alternative marriage form of the Latter-day Saints. Marriage and divorce were in the control of the states, and not the federal government.[22] Without a constitutional provision to limit the behavior of the new state, Utah was free to adopt such provisions as it would regarding marriage and divorce.[23] Like many in his time, Lieber saw polygamy and theocracy as linked.

Polygamy was legally defeated in nineteenth-century America at roughly the same time that a large-scale pattern based on divorce and subsequent remarriage—"serial" polygamy, as its opponents called it, was becoming familiar. It is almost as though Mormon polygamy, the clear case, the one on which everyone could agree, was handled with particular harshness exactly because the issue of divorce, equally an attack on the basic conception of monogamous marriage for life, was a case on which a widespread societal consensus no longer existed.[24] But whether or not one accepts this relationship between the two issues, another relationship, a contrast, seems beyond dispute. While the forces of organized religion would have counted their campaign against Mormon polygamy a success, their campaign against lax divorce laws was, with a few exceptions, a failure.

The difficulty of proving plural marriage in Utah—because of the secrecy of the ceremony—was behind a second case under the 1862 statute, *Miles v. United States* (1880), reversing a bigamy conviction based on testimony of an (admitted) second wife on the grounds that under Utah law, until the first marriage was shown, the second wife was the lawful wife and could not testify against her husband. Partly because polygamy was so difficult to prove, several other congressional enactments followed the original antibigamy statutes. The last of these, which involved a disincorporation of the Mormon Church and confiscation of its property, resulted in a formal declaration (September 25, 1890) under which the Mormon Church officially abandoned polygamy. The manifesto, issued by Wilford Woodruff, the president of the Mormon Church, stated,

> We are not teaching polygamy or plural marriage, nor permitting any person to enter into its practice. . . . Inasmuch as laws have been enacted by Congress forbidding plural marriages, which laws have been pronounced constitutional by the court of last resort, I hereby declare

---

[22] See Anne C. Dailey, "Federalism and Families," *University of Pennsylvania Law Review* 143 (1995): 1787.

[23] On federalization of family law, see Judith Resnik, "'Naturally' without Gender: Women, Jurisdiction, and the Federal Courts," *New York University Law Review* 66 (1991): 1682.

[24] That consensus of course has broken down still further.

my intention to submit to those laws, and to use my influence with the members of the Church over which I preside to have them do like-wise. . . . And I now publicly declare that my advice to the Latter-day Saints is to refrain from contracting any marriage forbidden by the law of the land.[25]

Outside of Utah, hostility to the Mormon institution continued. In *Church of Jesus Christ of Latter-Day Saints v. United States* (1889) the Supreme Court said that polygamy was "a return to barbarism."[26] Justice Stephen J. Field in *Davis v. Beason* (1890) stated that bigamy and polyg-amy are crimes, tending "to destroy the purity of the marriage relation, to disturb the peace of families, to degrade woman and to debase man." By contrast to *Davis v. Beason,* the rhetoric of *Reynolds* may be seen as moderate.[27]

The Mormon attempt to defend the group in constitutional litigation was, thus, not successful. Perhaps, however, one should stress the signifi-cance of the fact that the attempt was made at all. It is not to be assumed that religious groups will feel free under their own rules to invoke rights under the state system. They may refuse to interact in this way with state legal systems and insist that such an interaction would corrupt their own institutions. But the Mormons' sense that they were also a part of the larger system was revealed not only by their use of test case litigation as a defense strategy but also by their repeated applications for statehood and their general approach to the American Constitution as divinely in-spired.[28]

The campaign against polygamy was, of course, directed at perceived immorality.[29] But it was also directed at an institution whose importance

---

[25] See Edwin Firmage and R. Collin Mangrum, *Zion in the Courts: A Legal History of the Church of Jesus Christ of Latter Day Saints, 1830–1900* (Urbana: University of Illinois Press, 1988). Carmon Hardy in *Solemn Covenant: The Mormon Polygamous Passage* (Ur-bana: University of Illinois Press, 1992) argues that, even after the Woodruff manifesto, leaders of the Mormon Church continued to sanction polygamous marriages while publicly denying their existence.

[26] This case as been viewed by several as the closest thing to a federal disestablishment of a religion that the United States has seen. See B. D. Williams, "Separation of Church and State: Mormon Theory and Practice," *Dialogue* 1, no. 2 (1946): 38.

[27] See Leo Pfeffer, *Church, State, and Freedom,* rev. ed. (Boston: Beacon Press, 1967) noting that the conflict was between Old Testament and New Testament forms of marriage.

[28] "What is the proper role of the Latter Day Saint with respect to the Constitution?" Richard Bushman, "Inspired Constitution," *Brigham Young University Studies* 4 (1962): 151–77.

[29] In litigation over the conviction of a polygamist under the Mann Act in the 1940s, the issue of polygamy was again discussed by a justice of the U.S. Supreme Court. Justice Wil-liam O. Douglas, writing the majority opinion in *Cleveland v. United States,* 329 U.S. 14 (1946), upheld the application of the Mann Act to the interstate transportation of a plural

went beyond the sins of individuals. The real point was that marriage and the family were linked to an understanding of the state. The Court in the *Reynolds* case presented a discussion of marriage as a foundation of society that continues to be of considerable importance.

> Marriage, while from its very nature a sacred obligation, is nevertheless, in most civilized nations, a civil contract, and usually regulated by law. Upon it society may be said to be built, and out of its fruits spring social relations and social obligations and duties, with which government is necessarily required to deal. In fact, according as monogamous or polygamous marriages are allowed, do we find the principles on which the government of the people, to a greater or less extent, rests. Professor Lieber says, polygamy leads to the patriarchal principle, and [*sic*] which, when applied to large communities, fetters the people in stationary despotism, while that principle cannot long exist in connection with monogamy.

The decision in the *Reynolds* case was read in the twentieth century as a statement that "found in polygamy the seed of destruction of a democratic society" and that viewed polygamy as "highly injurious to its female adherents."[30] *Reynolds* sustained a lower-court instruction to the jury referring to "pure-minded women," "innocent children," and "innocent victims of this delusion."[31] But while the decision refers to the odiousness of polygamy, the *Reynolds* opinion does not detail the injuries to the innocent victims or other evils of the institution. Rather, the court was content to leave the issue with the observation that "[p]olygamy has always been odious among the northern and western nations of Europe, and, until the establishment of the Mormon Church, was almost exclusively a feature of the life of Asiatic and African People."

Chief Justice Waite referred to the opinion as his "sermon on the religion of polygamy."[32] John Noonan has suggested that Waite "sounded precisely like his contemporary, Pope Leo XIII."[33] When he noted that the forms of marriage are basic to society and of critical significance to governmental institutions, Justice Waite cited Professor Francis Lieber's thesis that polygamy leads to the patriarchal principle. Francis Lieber

---

wife. Douglas said that "[t]he establishment or maintenance of polygamous households is a notorious example of promiscuity" (19).

[30] *People v. Woody,* 61 Cal.2d 716, 724–25 (1964).

[31] *Reynolds,* 167–68.

[32] B. Trimble, *Chief Justice Waite: Defender of the Public Interest* (Princeton: Princeton University Press, 1938), 244 n. 18.

[33] John Noonan, "The Family and the Supreme Court," *Catholic University Law Review* 23 (1973): 255. The "wall of separation," language Jefferson used in the opinion, became a part of the conventional rhetoric in the field of church and state.

(d. 1872), a German emigré who achieved considerable distinction as a publicist in America,[34] was deeply interested in the forms of marriage and in the connections between the state and marriage. *Reynolds v. United States* constitutes an endorsement of Lieber's views on marriage. It was an invocation of one of the serious intellectual names of the age in connection with a cause he had long defended, and it is possible that Chief Justice Waite did not detail the dangers of polygamy because he assumed that in relying on the opinion of Professor Lieber he had done all that was required. In *Political Ethics* Lieber wrote, "The family cannot exist without marriage, nor can it develop its highest importance, it would seem, without monogamy.[35] Lieber detailed his conception of monogamy and its significance in an unsigned article published in *Putnam's Monthly* in 1855. Monogamy

> is one of the primordial elements out of which all law proceeds, or which the law steps in to recognize and protect. . . . Wedlock, or mono-gamic marriage, . . . is one of the frames of our thoughts, and moulds of our feelings; it is a psychological condition of our jural conscious-ness, of our liberty, of our literature, of our aspirations, of our religious convictions, and of our domestic being and family relation, the founda-tion of all that is called polity.[36]

The link to Christianity is explicit in later Mormon cases. Thus, the Supreme Court said in *Mormon Church v. United States* (1889) that polygamy was "contrary to the spirit of Christianity and of the civilization which Christianity has produced in the Western World," and again, that "[b]igamy and polygamy are crimes by the laws of all civilized and Christian countries." It may be noted that Justice Field was not even willing to call the advocacy of polygamy "a tenet of religion."

In fact, Lieber's provision on polygamy did not come into the federal Constitution. The Mormon Church was pressured by other means into giving up polygamy, and the later history of Utah as a state reveals not a commitment to the restoration of polygamy but rather a fairly intense commitment to a traditional version of monogamy. The church excommunicates those currently practicing polygamy.[37]

---

[34] See Aviam Soifer, "Contributions: Facts, Things, and the Orphans of Girard College: Francis Lieber, Protopragmatist," *Cardozo Law Review* 16 (1995): 2305.

[35] See Francis Lieber, *Manual of Political Ethics* (Philadelphia: J. B. Lippincott, 1876) (designed chiefly for the use of colleges and students of law.)

[36] Lieber, "The Mormons. Shall Utah Be Admitted into the Union?" *Putnam's Monthly,* May 1855, 225, 234.

[37] Kenneth D. Driggs, "After the Manifesto: Modern Polygamy and Fundamentalist Mormons," *Journal of Church and State* 32 (1990): 367, 388.

Utah is understood by historians to have a special role among the American states because of its intense and unique religious background. Utah, whose population is 70 percent Mormon,[38] is committed to family life, temperance, clean living, and the traditional work ethic: "[O]ne need only look, in the 1980s, at the size of the Mormon family, at the Mormons' health code, at their participation in a church wide welfare system, and at contemporary politics in Utah to see that Latter-day Saints continue to be a 'peculiar people.'"[39] The list of differences continues: "Despite their educational status and relative affluence, the Mormon birth rate is now twice the national average. The LDS death rate and the low incidence of a variety of diseases appear to be linked to their now strict adherence to the 'Word of Wisdom" which, among other things, proscribes tobacco and prescribes temperance." Additionally, "Regular assignments on welfare projects ranging from picking oranges to canning meats keep the communitarian spirit alive in a sea of individualism." Finally, it has been noted that majority opinion in Utah on a variety of issues, including right-to-work, feminism, liquor-by-the-drink, right to life, anti-Communism, and the equal rights amendment reflect "the still powerful influence of the Mormon Church when the leadership obliquely or directly defines a Mormon position."[40]

B. D. Williams, in discussing Mormon theories of separation of church and state, noted, "Whenever one church claims the membership (in fact or nominally) of 72% of the people of a state, as the Mormon Church does in Utah, its doctrines and practices are certain to have a pervasive influence on the folkways of the state." This will be true, he said, whatever the church does. "[E]ven if it never took a stand on a political question, the Mormon church would still significantly influence the metes and bounds of the political struggle in Utah." "Sale of liquor by the drink,

---

[38] Frank Jonas, "The Different State," in *Politics in the American West* (Salt Lake City: University of Utah Press, 1969), 327–29. The Mormon majority in Utah constitutes the major population of a state. Such a majority could, of course, also exist in a town. See description of Mormon town(s) in Alberta in Brigham Y. Card, Herbert C. Northcott, John E. Foster, Howard Palmer, and George K. Jarvis, eds., *The Mormon Presence in Canada* (Logan: Utah State University Press, 1990), 275. The influence of "Mormonism" can be based on church teaching, church influence or directive, or simply unofficial ideas of Mormon culture, perhaps to be considered folkways. Thus it may be that the support for capital punishment in Utah is linked to the idea of "blood atonement." See Brigham Young, quoted in Thomas O'Dea, *The Mormons* (Chicago: University of Chicago Press, 1957), 101.

It is often said that Mormons refer to non-Mormons as Gentiles (so that in Utah Jews are called Gentiles.) But see A. Mauss, "Mormon Semitism and Anti-Semitism," *Sociological Analysis* 29 (1968): 11–27.

[39] Grant Underwood, "Revisioning Mormon History," *Pacific Historical Review* 55 (1986): 413 (footnotes omitted)

[40] Richard Poll, quoted in ibid., 413. The Mormons opposed an MX missile base in Utah.

taxation of church welfare properties (farms, clothing mills, etc.), pari-mutuel betting and legalized gambling are all probably among the political questions that lie 'beyond the pale' in Utah because of the folkways of its predominant Mormon population."[41] Cheryl Preston identifies the differences in terms of Mormons' commitment to higher education and more traditional family patterns.[42]

In this instance, however, one can say that the family values with which the Mormon Church is associated in 1996 are for the most part the same family values articulated by the Christian nation in 1896: heterosexual monogamy, family stability, large families,[43] and traditional family structures.

Reynolds itself continues to be reaffirmed. As recently as 1985 the Tenth Circuit reaffirmed the case in *Potter v. Murray City* (10th Cir. 1985).[44] At another level, however, in the child custody case, *Sanderson v. Tryon* (Utah 1987) the Utah Supreme Court noted that "polygamous practices should only be considered as one among many other factors regarding the children's best interests."[45]

In the nineteenth century polygamy was associated both with the Mormons and with the literary versions of Islamic and Middle Eastern polygamy. Today we associate polygamy also with Muslim immigrants, excommunicated Mormon fundamentalists, and, sometimes with individual figures, as when Bertolt Brecht is described as a polygamist.[46] But public defenses of polygamy have begun to appear, and it may be nineteenth-century polygamy, at least, is not altogether condemned. Thus, a Utah judge wrote, "I cannot say, as the main opinion seems to imply, that polygamy is *morally* wrong. It is neither morally nor legally wrong in Turkey and elsewhere. It is questionable whether it was morally or legally wrong in Utah Territory in the 19th Century, and I like to think, at least, that my great-grandfather was not only a law-abiding citizen, but was not immoral according the mores of his time. Whether it is moral, or legal, depends in most part upon time, place and circumstance."[47] In 1991 the

[41] Williams, "Separation," 38.

[42] Cheryl B. Preston, "Joining Traditional Values and Feminist Legal Scholarship," *Journal of Legal Education* 43 (1993): 511, 514.

[43] Timothy Egan, "Utah's Claim to Fame: No. 1 in a Family Way," *New York Times,* April 23, 1995.

[44] *Potter v. Murray City,* 760 F.2d 1065 (10th Cir. 1985). See also *Barlow v. Blackburn,* 798 P.2d 1360 (Ariz. App. 1990).

[45] *Sanderson v. Tryon,* 739 P.2d 623 (Utah 1987). See also Matter of Adoption of Waiting, 157 Utah Adv. Rep. 26, 808 P.2d 1083 (Utah 1991).

[46] Martin Esselin, *Berthold Brecht: A Choice of Evils,* 4th ed. (London: Methuen, 1993), xii.

[47] Judge Henriod, in *In re State in Interest of Black,* 3 Utah 2d 315, 283 P.2d 887 (Utah 1955).

plural wife Elizabeth Joseph, wrote an op-ed piece in the *New York Times* defending contemporary polygamy as allowing a larger variety of choices for women. This can be taken as an indication of change in the current discussion.[48] Whereas defenses of polygamy had previously been available through, for example, the material of Joseph Musser,[49] one can now refer to a sympathetic discussion published in the *New York Times*. At the same time, one must also note that in 2001 there was a conviction of a polygamist living in Utah with several wives and many children.

In short, Utah's commitment to monogamy continues, reflected by two other legal events, the first a case upholding Utah's adultery statute,[50] the second the statute passed to block any attempt to ask Utah to recognize homosexual marriages performed elsewhere.[51] The statute provides that marriages between persons of the same sex are "prohibited and declared void."[52]

The possibility of looking at Mormon history in terms of two snapshots taken in different centuries, or to suggest a contrast between Mormons then and now, is not, of course, new. Indeed, it is fairly standard to stress a transformation of Mormon life after the turn of the century as the assimilation and Americanization of Mormonism.[53] But another kind of analysis may add something to an account focused either in separatism or assimilation (from the point of view of the group) or rejection leading to acceptance (from the point of view of the state).[54] Such an analysis focuses on two modes of interaction between church and state, distinguished by universalist or particularistic objectives.

The reconstitution of Mormonism and Utah after 1896 begins with a rejection of church control of state politics. The Utah Supreme Court recently noted that "[t]he Mormon majority at the 1895 convention acted

---

[48] Elizabeth Joseph, "My Husband's Nine Wives," *New York Times,* May 23, 1991.

[49] Joseph W. Musser, *Celestial or Plural Marriage* (Salt Lake City: Truth Publishing, 1944). Musser had five wives and twenty children (Driggs, "After the Manifesto," 382). See Martha Sonntag Bradley, "Joseph W. Musser: Dissenter or Fearless Crusader for Truth," in *Differing Visions: Dissenters in Mormon History,* ed. R. Launius and Linda Thatcher (Urbana: University of Illinois Press, 1994).

[50] *Oliverson v. West Valley City,* 875 F. Supp. 1465 (D. Utah 1995). The adultery statute litigation, a statement of a commitment to traditional monogamous forms, is perhaps somewhat complicated by the fact that Mormon doctrine assumes the potential for plural marriages in the next world.

[51] Following the Hawaii decision in *Baehr v. Lewin,* 74 Haw. 530, 852 P.2d 44 (Haw. 1993).

[52] Utah Code Ann., sec. 30–1-2(5) (1893).

[53] Generally, A. Mauss, *The Angel and the Beehive: The Mormon Struggle with Assimilation* (Urbana: University of Illinois Press, 1994).

[54] As Leo Pfeffer once noted, *marginal religion* is not a legal category in the United States. "The Legitimation of Marginal Religions in the United States," in *Religious Movements in Contemporary America,* ed. Irving Zaretsky (Princeton: Princeton University Press, 1974), 9.

deliberately to distance itself from any suggestion that the new government of Utah could justifiably be viewed as theocratic."[55] Utah had "struggled for statehood for nearly fifty years,"[56] and the church had been threatened with destruction and forced to abandon polygamy. The court concluded that "the Church, following the Manifesto of 1890, had worked to convince Congress of the sincerity of its renunciation of polygamy and of its intent to forswear control of civil affairs."[57] Thus, "statehood was obtained, but at a high cost."[58]

The narrative of the change from the nineteenth century to the twentieth century has been analyzed by historians and sociologists, sometimes in terms of early sectarianism followed by later assimilation. Recently Armand Mauss discussed the change in terms of assimilation followed by a current period of retrenchment.[59]

Much of this analysis draws on the familiar typology of Ernest Troeltsch, relating to churches and sects.

> The Church is that type of organization which is overwhelmingly conservative, which to a certain extent accepts the secular order, and dominates the masses; in principle, therefore, it is universal, i.e. it desires to cover the whole life of humanity. The sects, on the other hand, are comparatively small groups; they aspire after personal inward perfection, and they aim at a direct personal fellowship between the members of each group. From the very beginning, therefore, they are forced to organize themselves in small groups, and to renounce the idea of dominating the world. Their attitude towards the world, the State, and Society may be indifferent, tolerant, or hostile, since they have no desire to control and incorporate these forms of social life; on the contrary, they tend to avoid them; their aim is usually either to tolerate their presence alongside of their own body, or even to replace these social institutions, by their own society.[60]

One distinction in Troeltsch addresses attitudes toward a larger unit, the church seeking cooperation, the sect seeking separation. Mauss can thus observe that the Mormons are more churchlike in Utah and less churchlike in other parts of the country or, indeed, the world.

[55] *Society of Separatists v. Whitehead*, 870 P.2d 916 at 936 (Utah 1993) (upholding opening prayer in council meetings). Ibid., 935–36.

[56] Ibid., 936.

[57] Ibid.

[58] Ibid.

[59] Mauss, *Angel and Beehive*, 85. Mauss identified five areas in which the modern Mormon Church is concentrating on sectlike behavior, as an aspect of retrenchment. The church is particularly interested in continuing revelation, missions, temples and genealogical research, family renewal, and religious education.

[60] Ernst Troeltsch, *The Social Teaching of the Christian Churches*, trans. Olive Wyon (New York: Macmillan, 1931).

The scheme described here, that is, the distinction between mode 1 and mode 2, is similar to church/sect analysis in many ways, but it does not focus, as the latter often does, on transformation over time in a single institution or form of organization. Rather, it looks at the way in which that institution relates to a larger unit, even taking the religious institution itself as constant (counterfactually, of course). Mode 1 and mode 2 are labels given to two strategies of religious institutions in dealing with the state, the first involving a co-option of the state, the second an attempt to carve out space with the state for a religious life. Size and socioeconomic status have no defining relevance, and religious institutions may use both strategies at the same time.

Applying these distinctions to the history of the Mormons, before and after statehood, involves a different version of constitutionalism from the one conventionally used. Whereas some discussion focuses on the "words on parchment" definition of constitutionalism, the present section uses constitutionalism as a framework, a way of being, or a set of folkways, rather than emphasizing language or the interpretation of language.[61]

Modes 1 and 2 do not necessarily follow one another in historical succession, but may operate in combination. One can also see a different emphasis in the use of these modes depending on the nature of the larger group. A mode 1 picture of Mormon behavior would emphasize its attempts to influence state and federal governments so as to have governments adopt Mormon values as universal. A mode 2 picture would stress ways in which the LDS church sees to make room for its own values within a larger system. A mode 1 relationship focuses on engagement; a mode 2 relationship focuses, in the end, on disengagement.

Utah is a state in a federal union, dominantly populated by one religious group. It is natural, even inevitable, Mauss notes, that the Mormons should attempt to dominate the policies of the state.[62] Using the language of modes 1 and 2, one can say that the Mormon relation to Utah is a mode 1 relationship, parallel to that relationship evident in the nineteenth century (after formal disestablishment) between Christian denominations and the federal government. Thus, the *Reynolds* case reveals a mode 1 relationship in the Court's analysis of the Christian nature of marriage. The Mormons in *Reynolds* attempted a mode 2 objective with reference to the federal system—space for its own institution—but did not manage to establish it. Federal recognition of the free exercise right (sought by the Mormons) was in effect a mode 1 strategy in the interest of a mode 2 objective.

---

[61] On Llewellyn and Hamilton on folkways and constitutionalism, see Weisbrod, "Family, Church, and State."

[62] Mauss therefore turns his attention to the relations between the Mormons and the federal government (*Angel and Beehive,* 109).

Modern Utah also can reveal mode 2 relationships, as religions that are not part of the Mormon Church attempt to create space for themselves. Here an example is the excommunicated Mormon fundamentalists seeking recognition for polygamy (despite its illegality) through litigation over custody or adoption. This space is created not through an exemption like the one sought in *Reynolds,* but rather by a general—mode 1—rule broad enough to validate their activities. Thus: "Polygamous or nonpolygamous families may adopt."

In relation to the federal government, the Mormon Church in the twentieth century engaged in both mode 1 and mode 2 strategies. Examples of mode 1 are the efforts to defeat the ERA or the MX missile program. An example of mode 2 is a use of the special exemption for religious groups in the federal statutes against discrimination.[63] Modes 1 and 2 are, again, operating together.

The Supreme Court case *Bishop v. Amos*[64] can illustrate mode 1 and mode 2 in operation in the modern setting. In 1964 Congress passed an act forbidding employment discrimination and added a limited exemption for churches with reference to religiously connected work. In 1972, that exemption was broadened so that religious groups could discriminate, in effect, even where the work was secular by general standards. Senator Ervin explained that "the amendment would exempt religious corporations, associations, and societies from the application of this act insofar as the right to employ people of any religion they see fit is concerned. That is the only effect of this amendment."[65] This is mode 2 objective—autonomy for churches—achieved by a mode 1 recognition of the exemption by the state. The exemption was upheld against a challenge to a Mormon Church employer's use of the exemption to "discriminate" against an employee who could not get a "temple recommend."[66]

Whatever may have been true in the past, a church attempting today to create its own world as to family and education will necessarily involve itself in the structuring of the state environment. Its choice of mode 1 or mode 2 stances, in what sequence or combination, depends on circumstances, but even in Utah, even in a "sovereign state," a religious group cannot control its environment in the way that was possible in the nineteenth century. This is increasingly true also in sovereign national states.[67] The constitutionalism of federal-state relationships and the constitution-

---

[63] Through the Religious Freedom Restoration Act (1991).

[64] *Corporation of Presiding Bishop v. Amos et al.,* 483 U.S. 327 (1987).

[65] He continued, "In other words, this amendment is to take the political hands of Caesar off of the institutions of God, where they have no place to be."

[66] On temple recommend, see LDS brief in *Bishop v. Amos,* 4.

[67] See Mark W. Janis, Richard S. Kay, and Anthony Bradley, *European Human Rights Law* (Oxford: Oxford University Press, 1995).

alism of church-state relationships, frameworks including the ideas of the world constitutional documents, make that sort of isolation fundamentally impossible.

These observations are not about changes in the characteristics of institutions, for example churches becoming sects over time. That all churches are, in a manner of speaking, sects is a given of the American legal situation. The effort here is to describe the strategies that institutions adopt in working with and within larger units. The two larger units considered are the federated state and the federal government, both with reference to a church, the Latter-day Saints, which is in fact strong in many states and indeed many countries.

The attempt is to see the Mormon Church as representing, not simply the church standing against the state, but also the church overlapping and penetrating the state in the form of the religious consciousness of individual voters or religious affiliations of state officials, constrained by both their official roles and their religious consciences.

The interactive strategies described involve using political power to achieve particular state-issues as universal objectives, or using arguments based on religious status to achieve protection and recognition by the state for particularistic goals, often autonomy. This mode 2 objective is achieved often by a religious liberty argument that is in effect a mode 1 argument, since the church seeks to have the state recognize religious liberty as a universal value. The modern history of the Mormon Church reveals clear instances of these strategies, as well as one case, polygamy, where the mode 1 policy reflects both the official position of the church and certain ambivalence within the Mormon culture, so that as a matter of state law polygamy is both illegal and to some limited extent acknowledged.

Addressing the fame of Zane Grey's *Riders of the Purple Sage* (1912), Loren Grey writes, "Perhaps it is [popular] because the practice of polygamy which the Mormon church repudiated long ago, but which endures among rebel sects scattered over many parts of the world—still holds a somewhat morbid fascination for many people all over the Christian world."[68] Whatever the reason, Grey's story of the Mormons is still told.

In the film version of 1996, however, the Mormon aspect of the background is largely excised.[69] Some viewers will recognize the nineteenth-

---

[68] See Loren Grey, foreword to *Riders of the Purple Sage*, by Zane Grey (Lincoln: University of Nebraska Press, 1994). Grey suggests that "this may be the result of their frustration over the puritanical dogma which pervades most Christian religions even today, and which still stifles so powerfully in many what we view as freedom of personal choice and sexual expression" (viii).

[69] The plot concerns Jim Lassiter's attempt to find the Mormon abductors of his sister, Millie Erne.

century Mormons from the settings, the strict obedience to group discipline, and the suggestion of polygamous arrangements among the
group.[70] Others may think the sect a group out of time and place, believers
from another planet. The 1996 *Riders* is hard on the religious group and
hard on polygamy, but suppresses the identification with the Latter-day
Saints. It pursues a quite different approach from the 1940 Zanuck pro-
duction of *Brigham Young,* which was friendly toward the Mormons and
quiet on polygamy.[71] Both films raise the issue of the group and the larger
society and reveal the tensions between the two.

When Brigham Young announced the removal of the Latter-day Saints
to Utah, he said, "The exodus of the nation of the only true Israel from
these United States to a far distant region of the west, where bigotry,
intolerance and insatiable oppression lose their power over them—forms
a new epoch, not only in the history of the church, but of this nation."[72]
The effort of this chapter has been to consider the constitutional framework of that new epoch in which the nation-state becomes dominant, and
all internal groups exist within a federal constitutional frame.

But there is an aspect not yet raised, which is the status of individuals
in relation to churches in the constitutional system in which the state is
sovereign but concedes considerable autonomy to churches. For this, we
turn, in the next chapter, to a tragic piece of the history of the Amish in
America.

---

[70] One commentator referred to the group in the new film as the "not-Mormons." Jim
Molpus, "Press the Remote: Rider Remake Ruined by Mishmash Morality," *Nashville Ban-
ner,* January 19, 1996, C2.

[71] See James D. Arc, "Darryl F. Zanuck's *Brigham Young:* A Film in Context," *BYU
Studies* 29, no. 1 (1986): 5–33.

[72] Gaustad, *Documentary History,* 1:159–60.

CHAPTER 4

Another Yoder Case: The Separatist Community and the Dissenting Individual

> "It is for the Amish to decide what Amish traditions are, but it
> is for all of us to decide collectively what our American tradi-
> tions are, to decide what 'American' means on the other side of
> the hyphen in Italo-American or Asian-American."
>
> —E. D. HIRSCH JR., *Cultural Literacy*

✦ THE Amish Church, a separatist group historically rooted in the left wing of the Reformation, has survived in its traditional form only in the United States. In this country, it occupies a particular cultural space as a benign separatist community.[1] This is evidenced by (to take only two examples) the treatment of the group in the film *Witness* as well as the group's appearance in the science fiction television series *Earth: The Final Conflict*.[2]

In some of these appearances in the wider culture, the positive aspects of the Amish are balanced by an awareness of the group's internal disciplinary mechanism, the *meidung,* or shunning, which is seen as presenting a threat to individual members of the community.

In law, the well-known Supreme Court decision of 1972, *Wisconsin v. Yoder* (406 U.S. 205 (1972))(exempting Amish children from two years of high school) reinforced the image of the Amish as a self-supporting, independent, and highly valued religious community. There have also, however, been decisions dealing with the *meidung,* and one of these is the subject of this chapter.

Shunning provides an appropriate context for examining the difficulties involved in state-dominated theories of pluralism. Although shunning sometimes is seen simply as a bad practice, it widely is understood as the

---

[1] In general, see John Hostetler, *Amish Society,* rev. ed. (Baltimore: Johns Hopkins University Press, 1968); Donald B. Kraybill, ed., *The Amish and the State* (Baltimore: Johns Hopkins University Press, 1993).

[2] Another appearance is in a comic context, *The Frisco Kid. Holy Matrimony* shows a comparable use of the Hutterites.

sanction on which a highly valued religious community depends. This means, to begin with, that some group other than the state is trying to operate a legal system. Further, when the state attempts to provide a remedy, the limits in state power in fact may be all too evident.

John A. Hostetler and Gertrude E. Huntington describe Amish shunning as "the church-community's means of dealing with obdurate and erring members and of keeping the church pure. How shunning should be practiced was the central question in the controversy that led the Amish to secede from the Swiss Brethren. The doctrine was intrinsic in the Anabaptist movement from its very beginning."[3] They explain the New Testament background.

> The Anabaptist concept of the church was of a pure church consisting of believers only; persons who violate the discipline must first be excommunicated, then shunned. This method of dealing with offenders, the Amish say, is taught by Christ (Matthew 18:15–17), and explained by the Apostle Paul (I Corinthians 5:11) that members must not keep company with unrepentant members nor eat with them. The passage is interpreted to mean that a person who has broken his vow with God and who will not mend his ways must be expelled from the fellowship just as the human body casts off an infectious growth . . .[4]

Hostetler and Huntington go on to describe the variations that are possible in different groups. The Swiss Mennonites excluded the banned person from communion. "A more emphatic practice was advanced by Jacob Amman." Amman said that the excommunicated person would be shunned "not only at communion but also in social and economic life." Thus, the ban "means that members may receive no favors from an excommunicated person, that they may not buy from or sell to an excommunicated person, and that no member shall eat at the same table with an excommunicated person." This includes the family. "If the person under the ban is a husband or wife, the couple is to suspend their marital relations until the erring member is restored to the church fellowship."

Shunning is unlike many issues that create tensions between groups and the state, because the group practice is different from the state practice. Familiar examples of such issues are controversies over medical or education. By contrast, shunning, as a group practice, can be viewed as similar to the practices of other groups or, indeed, of the state itself. That is, we can construe expulsion and exclusions, outlawing, incarceration, and even capital punishment as forms of avoidance (or shunning). The point

[3] John A. Hostetler and Gertrude E. Huntington, *Children in Amish Society* (New York: Holt, Reinhart and Winston, 1971), 6.
[4] Ibid.

here is that shunning is a practice that in large part defines the group. It is a prime mechanism, in addition to group education and religious ritual, through which the *we* that constitutes the group is maintained.

In general we belong to many groups, so that the term *we* has a shifting reference. These groups—"intermediate groups"[5]—are often understood to play a significant role in life. Sometimes the role the intermediate groups play is attacked as a form of private government.[6] Sometimes the groups are seen as establishing normative codes to which individuals choose to be committed.[7]

Sometimes, however, the codes do not fit together. In such cases, a group may find that its norms have been violated, and the group will respond. Amish shunning cases may involve such tensions among codes for an individual, who may be an American, Amishman, father, husband, and farmer. At one moment these codes fit together, and then suddenly they do not.

A particularly difficult problem arises when the group disciplines an individual member for breaking its code in a manner that ordinarily would be a basis for civil liability in the state system. In such a case the individual first must decide whether or not to seek help from the state.[8] In response, the state then must decide whether to intervene, recognizing that not intervening also is taking a substantive position.

A typical shunning case that includes state intervention would involve an individual who is shunned by the community as a sanction after withdrawing or being expelled from it, and who then sues the community in tort.[9] Although recent cases of this type have involved an individual's

---

[5] The term *intermediate groups* refers to those various groups to which an individual may belong. These groups are conceptually intermediate between the individual and the state. Some groups extend over many nations.

[6] See generally Samuels and Miller, *Corporations and Society*, 241–312 (including essays on the issue of the corporation as a private government); see also Stewart Macaulay, "Private Government," in *Law and the Social Sciences*, ed. Leon Lipson and Stanton Wheeler (New York: Russell Sage Foundation, 1986), 445.

[7] This is discussed further in chapters 9 and 10.

[8] Some groups and some individuals will neither litigate nor defend in the state system.

[9] A well-known example of such a case is *Bear v. Reformed Mennonite Church,* in which Robert Bear brought suit against the Reformed Mennonites, following his excommunication from and shunning by the community. 341 A.2d 105, 106 (Pa. 1975). The Reformed Mennonites argued that they had a complete defense in the free exercise clause of the First Amendment (107). The lower court accepted this defense, but the Pennsylvania Supreme Court rejected it and remanded the case for trial (108). The conflict between Robert Bear and the Reformed Mennonites continued in various legal forums, including a federal case that was dismissed in 1986. "*Shunned*" *Mennonite Loses Another Court Battle*," UPI Feb. 28, 1986 (LEXIS, Nexis library, UPI file). For further discussion of *Bear*, see text accompanying notes 36–37.

For general discussions of shunning see John A. Hostetler, "The Amish and the Law: A

relations with groups that are primarily religious, individuals, in theory, also could raise tort claims in response to discipline by secular groups.[10] An individual might base such a claim for avoidance on a theory of conspiracy to boycott, alienation of affections, defamation, or tortuous interference with contract. The claim also might allege malice. The community's defense (if it is a religious community) typically would be that the shunning was a religious practice protected by federal and state constitutions. Any community also might raise a common-law tort defense arguing that the behavior, if tortuous, was privileged.

Religious groups provide a particularly useful context for addressing questions about pluralism because the issues raised by their interaction with the state are presented so clearly. I am less interested here in the legal categories in which these problems are discussed (that is, tort, contract, First Amendment) than in the issues that underlie those categories. Because shunning involves the conflict of two legal systems, it tests and defines our commitment to pluralism and diversity. Because these cases suggest that the state's power is limited by the group's ability simply to refuse to comply with any court order, the cases highlight the limits of law.

We begin with the assumption that a crime is not excused even when described as a group sanction. For example, the state forbids private executions, whether as a family sanction[11] or a group sanction. The state similarly forbids private incarceration.

Thus, we are as surprised as Charles Merriam when he describes the university jail at the University of Berlin, the "academic hoosegow" in which Bismarck and others were held. "This was a revelation to me," Merriam writes, "for in my day the school authorities could throw a man out but they could not throw him in."[12]

Merriam's image of a university jail evokes the world of legal pluralism, in which multiple authorities operate within parallel systems of rules and sanctions. In the age of the modern state, the world of legal pluralism is a difficult one to keep in focus. Our idea of law is monist: one authority,

Religious Minority and Its Legal Encounters," *Washington and Lee Law Review* 41 (1984): 33, 36–40; Justin K. Miller, "Damned If You Do, Damned If You Don't: Religious Shunning and the Free Exercise Clause," *University of Pennsylvania Law Review* 137 (1988): 271; John H. Yoder, "Caesar and the Meidung," *Mennonite Quarterly Review* 23 (1949): 76. For a discussion of problems arising out of contract cases involving former members of nineteenth-century utopian communities, see Weisbrod, *The Boundaries of Utopia*.

[10] Various sorts of exclusions from trade unions and professional associations might provide an example.

[11] See "Missouri Couple Sentenced to Die in Murder of Their Daughter," *New York Times*, December 20, 1991, A33 (reporting the conviction of fundamentalist Muslim parents for killing their rebellious teenage daughter).

[12] Charles E. Merriam, *Public and Private Government* (New Haven: Yale University Press, 1944), 2 n. 3

one set of rules. This is particularly true to the extent that our sense of law is dominated by criminal law. Criminal law in general is not a major impetus toward legal pluralism, whether in the form of claims of religious exemption, local or customary law, or the so-called cultural defense. Criminal law is associated with the unity of law—law indifferent to persons, law rooted in a sense of impersonal justice—ideas that go deeply to our sense of what the rule of law in the modern state is about. Similarly, we are largely committed to the preserving the state's monopoly on the *we* of violence.

At the same time, in some other significant contexts, most obviously contracts and commercial law, we acknowledge that pluralism is intrinsic to the subject. Contracts are exactly about the law of the individual parties; commercial law is filled with references to the custom of the trade. In recent times—though not historically—the field of domestic relations has moved from the criminal law model, in which the state had a single conception of the good family and the good life, to a contracts model, in which the law provides a fairly open framework for individual choices. These fields are inheritors of the tradition of decentralization and of a pluralist view of the social structure as a whole.

Other questions are raised in other dimensions of this problem, however, particularly in relation to pluralist theory. John Hostetler comments on the issue of the Amish and the larger society in these terms: "It is clear that the Amish will not tolerate the removal of their children from their homes to distant schools where they are placed in large groups with narrow age limits, taught skills useless to their way of life and exposed to values contradictory to their culture."[13] As he points out, "There have been no studies of acts of violence against the Amish. Amish are frequently helpless, as pacifists, to defend themselves or their property. Members typically do not report acts of violence or destruction of private property to law enforcement officials."[14]

Our images of traditional societies often involve monoliths. It is clear, however, that even in such societies there are internal differentiations, which sometimes rise to the level of splits and separations. Further, "Small groups may be far more oppressive to the individual than larger ones."[15]

Andrew Yoder had been a member of a conservative Amish group, the Old Order of the Amish Mennonite Church. Disagreeing with them over several matters (including his need of a car to get a sick child to medical

[13] Hostetler,"Amish and the Law," 44.

[14] Ibid., 46.

[15] Morris R. Cohen, quoted in Aviam Soifer,"Freedom of Association: Indian Tribes, Workers, and Communal Ghosts," *Maryland Law Review* 48 (1989): 350. For Morris Cohen's later view on groups and the state, see *The Meaning of Human History* (La Salle, Ill.: Open Court, 1947).

treatment), he left the group's church for that of a more liberal group.[16] He then was shunned by his first group.[17] He felt, he said, "like a whipped dog."[18] Yoder brought suit and alleged that the defendants "willfully, intentionally and maliciously entered into a secret combination and conspiracy" to boycott him in accordance with the rules of the Old Order of the Amish Mennonite Church.[19] *Yoder v. Helmuth,* decided in Ohio in 1947,[20] did not result in an elaborate judicial discussion, but the facts of the case are particularly useful for present purposes, first because the plaintiff said that he was no longer a member of the group that shunned him, and second because the case, which was not appealed, resulted in the award of damages and an injunction directed against the shunning.[21] William Schreiber gives an extensive account of the proceedings in *Our Amish Neighbors.*

In 1947 the *Meidung* (also termed *mite, avoidance, shunning, boycott*) had been in effect for about five years. At that point, Yoder sued, saying that the *Meidung* had been imposed to force him "to submit to church officials in the management of his trade, religious and business affairs." The ban "excluded him from all social and business relations with the members of said church by persuasion and intimidation." Yoder said that the ban had reached into his family, and that his "own brother had been requested to boycott and avoid him and to have no dealings with him and had been told that his refusal to do so would place him, the brother, under the ban and make him also an object of the boycott." The church authori-

---

[16] Plaintiff's Petition, 1–2. Yoder argued that he had not been expelled (ibid., 3). The church version of the events spoke of an expulsion (Defendant's Answer, 1).

[17] Plaintiff's Petition, 1–2.

[18] "Wins Ostracism Suit," *New York Times,* November 8, 1947, 2.

[19] Plaintiff's Petition, 2.

[20] *Yoder v. Helmuth,* No. 35747 (Ohio C.P. Wayne County Nov. 7, 1947). Material on *Yoder v. Helmuth* has been provided to me by the Mennonite Historical Library at Goshen College, Goshen, Indiana, and by the Wayne County Common Pleas Court, Wayne County, Ohio. I appreciate the courtesy of both of these institutions. The case is unreported but extensively described in William I. Schreiber, *Our Amish Neighbors* (Chicago: University of Chicago Press, 1962), 97–117 and in *Yoder.* See also Note, "The Right Not to Be Modern Men: The Amish and Compulsory Education," *Virginia Law Review* 63 (1967): 925, 936. See generally Hostetler, *Amish Society.* Note that issues of shunning or disfellowship can arise also in conventional custody cases. See, e.g., *Johnson v. Johnson,* 564 P.2d 71, 76 (Alaska 1977) (holding that liberal visitation rights would overcome the access problems of a noncustodial father who had been disfellowshipped by the Jehovah's Witnesses), cert. denied, 434 U.S. 1048 (1978). See generally Carl E. Schneider, "Religion and Child Custody," *University of Michigan Journal of Law Reform* 25 (1992): 879 (exploring the ways courts may consider a parent's religiously motivated behavior in making child-custody decisions).

[21] Plaintiff's Petition, 1; Journal Entry, 1; Court's Finding, 204–5.

ties, Yoder said, had also asked his father to "remove him, Andy, from the farm which he had been operating under lease."

Yoder listed ways in which he had been affected by the *Meidung*: on various occasions, he had been forced to eat separately under a tree. A farmhand had requested Andy eat at a separate table, in the cellar. "Worst of all, and here the boycott had showed its ugliest side, he had not been able to obtain help for his own harvesting operations, and the men he did get to help him were likewise banned from the church."

Yoder had offered a number of reasons for leaving the Old Order Amish church: some related to transportation, for his farm and for his daughter, who had to be driven to a town fifteen miles away for treatments for polio. He also was opposed to the rule of his church that prohibited male members from wearing rubber suspenders. And finally, he "had a natural and indefeasible right to worship God according to the dictates of his own conscience" and opposed the *Meidung*. He requested damages of $40,000 and asked for an injunction.[22]

Yoder's general claim was that the boycott violated his civil rights.[23] The judge's charge to the jury also framed the question in those terms:

> The law gives to each and every individual the right to believe and belong to any Church that he chooses, or to no Church, if he so chooses. And no church or its ruling body has the right, under the law, to deny any of its member these rights, including the right, if he so chooses, to withdraw from membership in the Church.[24]

The judge also referred to the action/belief dichotomy, familiar in discussions of religious exemptions from valid state laws: "When one puts his religious belief into practice and thereby interferes with the civil rights of another it is unlawful."[25]

The charge to the jury continued with an argument to the effect that there can be no acquiescence to evil acts, even when performed by religious groups. "Sincerity of religious belief . . . is no valid legal excuse to deny anyone his guaranteed human rights."[26] The judge concluded that

---

[22] Schreiber, *Our Amish Neighbors*, 98–99 (quoting Plaintiffs Petition, 3).

[23] See Plaintiff's Petition, 6–7; Charge to the Jury, 189–90; see also Charles E. Westervelt Jr., "Torts-Disciplinary Action by Religious Society as Infringement of Civil Liberty," *Ohio State Law Journal* 9 (1948): 370. Westervelt approved of the granting of the injunction in these terms: "Under no circumstances can a religious group be permitted to resort to concerted action in derogation of an individual's civil rights. It seems evident that the 'mite' was an intentional and coercive interference with the plaintiff's right to be unmolested in business and society, and was, therefore, properly enjoined" (371).

[24] Charge to the Jury, 196.

[25] Ibid.

[26] Ibid., 197.

under the right of freedom of religious worship, the Plaintiff had a legal right to withdraw from the Helmuth Congregation and to buy an automobile if he so chose, and not to be disciplined. . . . He also had the legal right to freely enjoy the relationship of his entire family and the freedom of business intercourse unrestricted by any unlawful restraints thereon.[27]

The jury awarded damages, but only a portion of those requested.[28] Schreiber writes that "[t]he verdict was not appealed, but neither were steps taken to comply with the court order."[29] As a result, some Amish property was sold, though some of the award was paid by an unknown third party.[30] The judge also issued an injunction against the defendants, ordering them to stop their boycott of Yoder.[31] One commentator notes,

The consequences of this inference with a religious practice were truly tragic. One of the ministers against whom the judgment was rendered lost his farm at a forced sale to provide money to satisfy the judgment. He subsequently died, his wife claims, of a broken heart. Andy Yoder's daughter died shortly after the trial, and Andy Yoder hung himself.[32]

As noted above, this case and others like it raise a general question whether such state interventions into relations between individuals and groups serve the function of state dispute settlement or whether they are examples of what Charles Merriam referred to as the "poverty of power."[33] The controversy in *Yoder* clearly continued after the law had spoken, and those watching the case knew that the court order was not the end of the story. An article in *Time* magazine noted that Yoder "would be permitted to worship in an Amish Church but he would have no voice in the church or be admitted to communion."[34] The article concluded that "[t]o the stubborn Amishmen, who frown upon court actions, God's law came before that of men. Andrew would still be under a mite of a mite."[35] A *Newsweek*

---

[27] Ibid., 198–99. The charge to the jury did not reach such issues as admission to communion.

[28] Journal Entry, 1 (jury's verdict on damages); see also Schreiber, *Our Amish Neighbors*, 113.

[29] Schreiber, *Our Amish Neighbors*, 113.

[30] Ibid., 113–14. Schreiber reports that the third party was a prominent businessman who had extensive business dealings with the Amish (115).

[31] Court's Findings, 204–5.

[32] "Right Not to Be Modern," 936 n. 62.

[33] Charles E. Merriam, "Political Power," in *A Study of Power* (Glencoe, Ill.: Free Press, 1934), 156–83.

[34] "The Mited Man," *Time*, November 17, 1947, 26.

[35] Ibid.

article commented that while the judgment would not be appealed, "The Amish have their own ways of meeting such ausländer edicts."[36]

Few court cases arise out of shunning, but *Yoder* demonstrates that the state-centered system seems inclined to react for a victimized member of a group and against the particular intermediate community. A non-Amish jury found for the victim in the 1947 *Yoder* case, and the judge gave priority to the individual's right against the group, noting that he believed that religious freedom was an individual matter.[37] The shunning improperly burdened the individual's right to leave the group.

A ruling in favor of the shunned member, or former member—a distinction to which I will return—is not, however, inevitable. In this area of law many rules exist, and a great deal of legal language is available. But as is true in any complex case, the rules and the language do not dictate a single answer.

One approach might be to say that the larger state should defer to the community on this issue, either through a free exercise defense or because according to common-law tort approaches, the behavior was privileged. This was the position of the lower court in *Bear v. Reformed Mennonite Church*,[38] another shunning case that reached into the family. Bear claimed tortious interference with his business and alienation of his family's affections.

> The short answer to plaintiff's averments of injury to his business and marital interest would be, in light of the foregoing, a summary a fortiori dismissal. More considered analysis reveals that the fatal defect of Plaintiff's allegations is the fact of privilege, the presence of which will bar a cause of action for *[inter alia]* interference with business relations.
>
> With respect to Plaintiff's allegation of interference with business relations, it is determinative that Defendants' "shunning," as a religious practice, has for its partial purpose maintenance of Defendant Church's spiritual integrity. . . . Likewise, it is dispositive of Plaintiff's allegation of alienation of affections that the practice of "shunning" is within the constitutional immunity afforded by the First Amendment.[39]

We could reinforce this conclusion by referring to contract law concepts. We could say that the member, in exercising his freedom of religion, knowingly joined a church that used shunning as a sanction and was now subject to that sanction. John Howard Yoder put the argument this way:

[36] "The Amish 'Mite,'" *Newsweek,* November 17, 1947, 30; see also "Wins Ostracism Suit," 2.

[37] Schreiber, *Our Amish Neighbors,* 112–13.

[38] *Cumberland Law Journal* 24 (June 1973): 168, rev'd, 341 A.2d 105 (Pa. 1975).

[39] "Bear," *Cumberland Law Journal,* 172.

"[I]n contractual terms, Andrew Yoder was suing the church for consistently applying a forfeiture clause in a contract which he had freely made (in awareness of the existence of a forfeiture clause) and had intentionally broken."[40]

We thus can consider the individual who is subjected to discipline as a member of the smaller community without the right to appeal to the larger authority. We might decide to do this because we believe it effectuates individual's choices, because it strengthens intermediate communities' power against the state, or because we believe that the state's intervention here would not be effective.

Alternatively, we could advocate legal relief for the individual on the theory that she had rights as a member of the larger community, that these rights had been infringed by a group claiming greater power than it was entitled to, and that the interests of the larger community require protection of the individual. This concern for state interests is revealed in the position of the Pennsylvania Supreme Court in *Bear:*

> In our opinion, the complaint, in Counts I and II, raises issues that the "shunning" practice of appellee church and the conduct of the individuals may be an excessive interference within areas of "paramount state concern," i.e. the maintenance of marriage and family relationship, alienation of affection, and the tortuous interference with a business relationship, which the courts of this Commonwealth *may* have authority to regulate, even in light of the "Establishment" and "Free Exercise" clauses of the First Amendment.[41]

We may take this position because we believe that the tyranny of small groups is more intense and dangerous than the tyranny of large ones, or because we are not sympathetic to the particular group and assume that a person victimized by it must be protected. This could be true whether or not we are sympathetic to the individual victim.

Of course there is no reason to assume that the victim in a shunning case is fighting for democratic principles or for a more open society. Although he may be doing precisely that, it is equally possible that the per-

---

[40] Yoder,"Caesar and the Meidung," 88.

[41] *Bear,* 107. John T. Noonan Jr. labeled the issue in *Bear* as"Preserving the Purity of the Membership." See *The Believer and the Powers That Are* (New York: Macmillan, 1987), 288. In sociological terms, this issue relates to questions of deviance and community self-definition. See generally Kai T. Erickson, *Wayward Puritans: A Study in the Sociology of Deviance* (New York: Wiley, 1966), 3–25 (discussing the proposition that deviant behavior may be a necessary element in the definition of society as well as an important element in the long-term development of society); Robert Ian Moore, *The Formation of a Persecuting Society* (Oxford: Blackwell, 1987), 106–12 (examining the history of persecution in Western Europe in relation to general deviance theory).

son shunned is denouncing the group for deviating from the true faith, which may be narrow and oppressive by the standard of the outside society. In contrast to the positive image of the Amish presented by the court in *Wisconsin v. Yoder,* the well-known education case referred to above, an Ohio Court treating an Amish shunning problem wrote in 1919 of the "strange and peculiar sect composed of Low Germans [which] 397 years ago construed portions of the Bible as shown by Art. 16 of the Amish Confession of Faith."[42] The Ohio court was not impressed with the group's history:

> Some things become more precious by age, but the crude and unnatural conceptions as disclosed are in sharp conflict with modern legal civil rights. [They] tend to infringe upon inherent family and business life, and [harmonize] better with the views of his Satanic Majesty and his satellites or representatives on earth. Of course courts have nothing to do with men's religious views howsoever antiquated, except when such acts infringe civil right; all we need to state is that no religious views can be the means of infringing civil rights.[43]

On the basis of this negative view of a particular intermediate group, the larger culture may be unsympathetic to many religious groups that use strong forms of shunning because of the groups' commitment to unusual religious beliefs and social forms, and because of the groups' willingness to engage in social ostracism to the extent of even rejecting family members.

But even if the outside world is sympathetic to the victim rather than the group, does this mean that the state should intervene? What other possibilities are there? Are there cases in which we expect a certain amount of self-help from the victim? This position is illustrated by a contemporary comment on the 1947 *Yoder* case in the journal *United Evangelical Action,* in which the writer stressed that Andrew Yoder had a remedy:

> Yoder could, with ease, move a bare mile away and then have dealings to his heart's content with other farmers. Likewise, he could easily have all business dealings with non-Amish if he so chose. Instead, Yoder insists on living within a communal body which he himself does not advocate. Horace Greeley would say, "Go West; young man, go West."[44]

---

[42] *Ginerich v. Swartzentruber,* 22 Ohio N.P. (n.s.) 2, 16 (1913).

[43] Ibid. See also Zechariah Chafee Jr. and Edward D. Re, *Cases and Materials on Equity* (Brooklyn: Foundation Press, 1958), 1221–22 (using *Ginerich* among illustrative cases dealing with equitable intervention).

[44] Ford Berg, "The Other Side of the Yoder Suit," *United Evangelical Action,* December 1, 1947, 7. For a discussion of what effectively amounts to "exit," see Frederick M. Gedicks,- "Toward a Constitutional Jurisprudence of Religious Group Rights," *Wisconsin Law Re-*

Historically, excommunication from a small community could be described in terms of prison and fetters,[45] rather than as a merely psychological restraint, perhaps because one could not leave the physical environment for another community easily, or at least not without a letter of identification and a good character. But what if one could leave? The notions of decentralized pluralism and voluntary association assume that people can pass freely into and out of communities.[46] One notes the importance of what one exits *into*. That is, does the largest group require membership in some internal subgroup, or is it possible to be, in effect, a citizen of the world? What happens when no other group will accept an individual who must be a member of some group and who has been excluded from his original group? This is part of the meaning of outlawry. We generally assume that the state is available as a membership for all individuals and that the "exit" option from, in general, internal groups cannot be eliminated altogether,[47] but we question how heavily it can be burdened. The practice of shunning or excommunication is, after all, designed in part to keep people in or to restore them to communion.

Sometimes leaving the group or the jurisdiction is not an effective remedy. For example, what if a church not only shuns—typically described as passive behavior—but actively denounces and defames? A church might do this either on the theory that it was disciplining a present member for the (ultimate) good of the member or for the good of the others, who observe and are fortified by the example.

If a church takes the position that one cannot renounce membership and that, therefore, jurisdiction over members is perpetual, what position should the state take? From a contract perspective, much might depend on whether the individual, in joining the church, knew of the group's posi-

---

view (1989): 99, 155 n. 252 (comparing the burden on individuals of securing another job with the burden on the church of state intervention). On "exit" generally, see Albert O. Hirschman, *Exit, Voice, and Loyalty* (Cambridge: Harvard University Press, 1970).

[45] See Yosef Kaplan, "The Social Functions of the *Herem* in the Portuguese Jewish Community of Amsterdam in the Seventeenth Century," in *Dutch Jewish History,* ed. Joseph Michman (Jerusalem: Tel Aviv University, 1984), 111, 115 (describing excommunication as "[a] prison without bars" or "iron fetters which the eye cannot see but which the body feels very strongly" (citations omitted).

[46] Whether they can enter all communities is a separate issue, complicated by our expanding conceptions of impermissible discriminations.

[47] This reaches the issue of voluntary slavery. See James Crawford, "The Rights of Peoples: Some Conclusions," in *The Rights of Peoples,* ed. James Crawford (Oxford: Clarendon Press, 1988), 159 (raising the question "Should individual rights, including the right to opt out of groups or communities, prevail over the interests of those groups or communities?"). Crawford also notes that "[t]he crucial issue is that of 'minorities of minorities': if minority rights are genuinely collective, then it presumably follows that dissenting members of minority groups can be compelled to comply with the wishes of the majority" (60).

tion on the issue or of how severe the sanctions were. Clearly, whether the church declares eternal membership is not the end of the debate. It may be that religious groups see themselves as units that one can join but not leave. But one can in fact join different groups. From the original group's point of view, that is apostasy; from the new group's point of view, it is conversion. And from the state's point of view? The answer to that question will require examination of the context in which it is asked, not an automatic conclusion that one identification or another must control.

In one case, for example, a court might say that the group can shun the former member because (1) in the group's view one is always a member, and (2) shunning is required by the internal discipline of the group and the example that must be set for present members. In another case a court might say that the individual who left his money ambiguously to "my church at the time of my death" must be taken to mean the church he was most recently attending rather than the church that was boycotting him though still claiming him as a member.

On this point it was said of Andrew Yoder, "Yoder lives in a free country and if he does not want to obey the Amish law he can quit the Amish church. Despite this, Yoder has insisted on remaining an Amishman, continues to wear a beard and wants to be a unit of the Amish body."[48] But perhaps the "Amish body" has many parts. But even if it does, we have the question of whether some parts, or would-be parts, cannot really be called Amish at all. And that question raises another, which is who is to decide the substantive issue. The *Yoder* case indicates that Yoder's position was that he was no longer a member of the more conservative group.

In another case, the court allowed a tort action by a former member against a church that believed that members could join the church but could not withdraw from it.[49] In *Guinn,* the court distinguished between the church's behavior toward members while still members and its behavior toward former members.[50]

In addition to whether an individual's exit is possible, financially or psychologically,[51] or whether we see the membership issue in the way that a church sees it, serious questions remain as to what types of interventions would resolve the disputes.[52] If damage awards are ordered, the individu-

[48] Berg, "Other Side," 7.

[49] See *Guinn v. Church of Christ,* 775 P.2d 766, 786 (Okla. 1989).

[50] Ibid., 769–75, 777–85. See generally Lynn R. Buzzard and Thomas S. Brandon Jr., *Church Discipline and the Courts* (Wheaton, Ill.: Tyndale House, 1987) (discussing remedies for churches in dealing with church discipline issues).

[51] John Hostetler has discussed the issue of freedom of movement and relocation as a way of avoiding the strict *meidung* among the Amish (*Amish Society,* 311).

[52] Although we can view the law as involving the application of rules, it is generally thought that law also focuses on resolving disputes. Discussions of the use of law as a tool

als held liable may or may not pay them. Others may come forward to pay, or the state may take more stringent measures to enforce the awards, possibly creating a new victim class. Injunctive relief—orders directed against the behavior itself—are likely to be futile, both because the courts cannot mandate intimate relations and because avoidance tactics would make it difficult to know whether an order had been respected. It is not difficult to imagine the shift from collective ostracism under the command of a religious authority to individual ostracism (which the court order would not prohibit) once the religious directive had been withdrawn through state coercion. Indeed, it is tempting to think that the state legal system, faced with this problem, might turn to the defense of privilege as one way of avoiding the issue.

The lower court in *Bear* was extremely sensitive to the issue of remedies:

> Weighing heavily in this court's adjudication of the instant dispute is the fact that if any injunction were granted, its enforcement would be impossible, its effect nugatory. It is a suggestion both idle and vain that the elusive nuances of a marital relationship, or the varied complexities of economic and social intercourse could be coercively reinstated by injunctive relief.[53]

All of this would be true without reaching the specific issue of religious freedom. But, as the court pointed out, "Compounding the problem of enforcement is the collateral problem of the injury—denial of religious freedoms—an injunction would work upon Defendants. Neither precedent, nor conscience, nor logic can support injunctive relief in such circumstances."[54]

We might want to say that we are not looking for a framework within which to approach these issues because we already have one in the Constitution. But what do we mean by the Constitution?[55] And, what understanding of the relations between groups and the state does our Constitution assume at any point in time? A position on the question of group autonomy would seem to be part of the social-political reality that under-

---

for dispute resolution assume that the law's power is sufficient to terminate the dispute. A different view of the relation between law and society might cast judicial intervention as just one step in the total picture of power adjustment.

[53] "Bear," *Cumberland Law Journal,* 173. See generally Roscoe Pound, "The Limits of Effective Legal Action," *American Bar Association Journal* 3 (1917): 55.

[54] "Bear," *Cumberland Law Journal,* 173.

[55] For a discussion of different approaches to this question, see Richard S. Kay, "Comparative Constitutional Fundamentals," *Connecticut Journal of International Law* 6 (1991): 445. On the issue of underlying assumptions, see Richard S. Kay, "Pre-constitutional Rules," *Ohio State Law Journal* 42 (1981): 187.

lies a constitution. This is the level of "inclination" that Chafee invoked when he analyzed internal disputes and associations as raising a classical conflict between the state and groups:

> Our reaction toward any particular dispute in a club or trade union or church or college is almost sure to be influenced by our inclination toward one side or the other in this undying controversy. We shall be a bit more favorable to judicial intervention if we believe that the state is the sole ruler of all that goes on within its borders, and is the necessary safeguard of the individual against the closely pressed tyranny of associations. We shall be more doubtful of the probable wisdom of state participation in the affairs of such a group if we are accustomed to think of the state itself as just one more kind of association, which, like the others, should keep to its own functions, and which must be judged according to the value and efficiency of the services it renders us in return for rather high annual dues.[56]

But what does the political world look like if the state is understood as just another association, and an expensive one at that? It may be that we do not seek the ideal state because, as Robert Dahl suggested, we find the costs too great.[57] Some, however, have tried to outline relations in a framework that, if not "ideal," is at least closer to a pluralist empirical reality than the models of the uniquely sovereign state. A number of these efforts are the subject of part 2 of this book. Before reaching those models, we must review some situations in which the group presence has been acknowledged by states, sometimes to the detriment of the groups, and where the group, rather than the individual, has been taken as the political unit. The idea of corporatism in chapter 5 is necessary background for the discussion of part 2.

---

[56] Chafee, "Associations Not for Profit," 1029 (citations omitted). Chafee's list of groups is instructive. I think that we read Chafee's observations as if they were directed either to churches (to which deference is owed under the First Amendment) or to social clubs (the same, except, arguably, when implicated in business or professional life). Chafee, however, did not restrict his concerns in this way. His distinctions were between business (profit-making) and nonbusiness groups. The question that Chafee raised is still vital for us.

[57] See Robert A. Dahl, *After the Revolution?* rev. ed. (New Haven: Yale University Press, 1990), 36–37.

CHAPTER 5

Melting Pots and Pariah Peoples

Surely there is here a mine for Silver and a Place for Gold where it can be refined.

—JOB 28:1

For the thing which I greatly feared is come upon me, and that which I was afraid of is come unto me.

—JOB 3:25

✦ A PHOTOGRAPH from 1947 credited to the Associated Press and published in *Time* magazine shows Andrew Yoder in an Ohio courtroom.[1] Four of the defendant Amish men sit around a table in an identical posture, each resting his head on his hand, all looking at each other. In the background, a number of spectators talk to each other and watch the proceedings. A photograph of Yoder himself has been superimposed on the center bottom of the picture, placed by the photographer in such a way as to reinforce the alienation of the individual from the group. The caption reads, "Andrew Yoder (center) & Fellow-Amish men: The plain people called it pride."[2]

The discussion of the Amish in chapter 4 stressed that despite the insularity and separateness of the Amish community, it was in fact located within a larger jurisdiction, whose tolerances and rules framed the life of the community to some degree. Initially the church's history is that of a Mennonite splinter, so that it has roots in a European experience. We add to that a particularly American dimension that even played back on the Mennonites who stayed in Europe.[3] We can see that framing in the Yoder courtroom, walls that represent the outside state.

One major frame[4] is the context provided by state law. We organize our experience as citizens of a state. We distinguish between our identity

[1] "The Mited Man," 26. On the Amish rejection of photographs, see Donald B. Kraybill, *The Riddle of Amish Culture* (Baltimore: John Hopkins University Press, 1989), 34.

[2] "The Mited Man," 26. *Yoder* is a common Amish name.

[3] Not the only influence, of course.

[4] See generally, on the concept of framing, Erving Goffman, *Frame Analysis* (Cambridge: Harvard University Press, 1974). Goffman's book addresses the organization of experience, not the organization of society.

groups and our casual or ad hoc associations,[5] between groups that are official creatures of the state and groups that are not, a distinction that may for some correspond to major and minor affiliations.

But the framing provided by the state and state law can take quite different forms.

Chapters 3 and 4 offered detailed histories of two religious groups in the United States. The present chapter attempts a wide-angle presentation of various ways in which group-state encounters can be structured. We start with a discussion of corporatism, a mode or strategy of political organization in which the group receives a status as a group within the larger society, and individuals are conceived primarily in terms of group affiliation.

There are many kinds of corporatism. One of particular interest here involves the treatment of religious groups in Europe. A strikingly clear version of traditional corporatist structure is the history of the Mennonites. A brief account is offered by the Mennonite historian H. S. Bender, who stresses the essential feature of the corporatist idea: "To understand the system of privileges [in pre-unification Germany] it must be pointed out that in this period people did not live under equal rights for all, but that rights were differentiated according to the political, social, ecclesiastical, and economic position of the person in question."[6]

Bender outlines different privileges sought by the Mennonite churches. One is of particular illustrative interest, an exemption from military service granted in deference to the Mennonite creed of nonresistance. This privilege vanishes in the course of the widespread adoption of the goals of the French Revolution. "For the history of the Mennonites in Germany a turning point came when the French Revolution did away with local independence and local privileges, in 1789 proclaiming 'Liberty, Equality, Fraternity' as the rights of all men, and in 1793 introducing universal compulsory service."[7] Bender notes that Napoleon moderated this law in 1800 by allowing substitutes under special conditions, but enforced it anew in 1806.

Nonresistance became less and less insisted on as an aspect of Mennonite practice in Germany. Even when nonresistance was accepted as an article of the creed, there was no insistence on a particular method of proving it. How "each congregation and each young man will indeed prove our old-Mennonite nonresistance, in order to satisfy his own con-

[5] See generally Meir Dan-Cohen, "Beyond the Public/Private Distinction: Between Selves and Collectivities: Towards a Jurisprudence of Identity," *University of Chicago Law Review* 61 (1994): 1213–43.

[6] Harold Stauffer Bender, "Germany," *Mennonite Encyclopedia* (Hillsboro, Kans.: Mennonite Brethren Publishing House, 1955).

[7] Ibid., 495.

science and the demands of the authorities, we leave to the judgment of each of them." This was the formula, Bender tells us, "later often repeated to save the principle and at the same time abandon it."[8]

The issue of nonresistance was dealt with in various ways over a long time. Some of the Mennonites emigrated to Russia, and some went to America. Those remaining were divided between the nonresistant and those who were willing to serve with arms.[9]

As the story continues into the twentieth century, we reach the events of the Third Reich: "The German martyrs of nonresistance in World War II included only one Lutheran and many Jehovah's Witnesses, but no Mennonites." But after the war, American and Dutch Mennonite influences, as well as the impressions of the war, resulted in a new nonresistant trend. The "new German constitution of 1950 makes provision for alternative service for conscientious objectors."[10]

The tendency to assimilation among the German Mennonites was, in Bender's account, very evident. "As to nonconformity nobody wanted to be very conspicuous, different, or shocking." By the end of the nineteenth century even the Amish in Germany had dropped nonconformity. "Technical progress often did away with traditional fashions. Thus the world overcame nonconformity."[11]

The Mennonite story is one of corporatism in which the removal of a privilege threatens the practice of the group, but we see that the group itself survived and in fact returned to its original stance when the state environment was less restrictive. There is little in Bender's account to suggest direct limitation or discrimination against the Amish-Mennonites.

Other groups experience corporatism in a more intensely oppressive form. We may use the Jews in czarist Russia as an illustrative case.

Here, the internal life of the pariah group is relatively familiar though the images of *Fiddler on the Roof*. That same community after a massive immigration to America is shown, for example, in the film *Hester Street* and is also chronicled in a well-known literary tradition.[12] It is a community in which Law is religious law, Torah. The point is made in the index of *Life Is with People*, a well-known book on the sthetl.[13]

---

[8] Ibid., 496.

[9] Even the American Mennonites, however, had a surprising regard for Bismarck. James C. Juhnke, *Vision, Doctrine, War* (Scottdale, Pa.: Herald Press, 1989), 90–94.

[10] Bender, "Germany," 497.

[11] Ibid., 497–98, 498.

[12] E.g., Henry Roth, *Call It Sleep* (New York: Robert O. Ballou, 1935).

[13] Mark Zborowski and Elizabeth Herzog, *Life Is with People: The Jewish Little-Town of Eastern Europe* (New York: International Universities Press, 1952) (Law is Torah, not czarist law).

Still, the outside world was there, and its law was there. Even in the most heartwarming depictions of shtetl life—*Fiddler on the Roof,* for example—we can see the outside world as well as the tradition of the group. Sholem Aleichem's original Tevye stories, on which *Fiddler* is based, are clear on the point. As has been noted, Tevye's daughters respond to the outside environment in various ways, by marrying a gentile, or by joining the revolution, and finally the Jews are told to leave.[14] Still, the overwhelming theme is one of isolation and relative autonomy.[15]

The situation of the Jews in Russia has been described many times, by those who experienced it, those who observed it, and by historians looking back. Christian Wilhelm Dohm (1751–1820), a friend of Frederick the Great, described the status of Jews in the second half of eighteenth-century Europe generally: "In almost all parts of Europe," he wrote, "the laws of the state aim to prevent as much as possible the influx of these unfortunate Asiatic refugees—the Jews. . . . Everywhere the Jew is denied the privilege of service to the state. He is not allowed to engage in agriculture, nor is he permitted to acquire property. The only branch of economic activity left for him in which to eke out a livelihood is petty trade. When a Jew has several sons, he has the privilege of having with him only one, since the oldest alone is allowed to marry and raise a family. The others he must send away. His daughters remain with him only if they are lucky enough to marry Jews of his own city who have the right to stay there."

"Very rarely," Dohm noted, "is a Jewish father fortunate enough to live among his children and grandchildren, and to establish the welfare of his family on a permanent foundation."[16]

The pariah status of the Jews also resulted in outbreaks of violence. In some of these, officials were the instigators.[17]

---

[14] Sholem Aleichem, *Tevye* (New York: Pocketbooks, 1965).

[15] A less well remembered Sholem Aleichem story ("Dreyfus in Kasrilevka"), which ends with Job-like attack on God, begins with a problem of information. "How did Kasrilevka get wind of the Dreyfus case? Well, how did it find out about the war between the English and the Boers, or what went on in China? . . . So how did Kasrilevka learn about the Dreyfus case? From Zeidel. Zeidel, Reb Shaye's son, was the only person in town who subscribed to a newspaper, and all the news of the world they learned from him, or rather through him. He read and they interpreted." "The Old Country," in *Collected Stories of Sholem Aleichem,* trans. Julius Butwin and Frances Butwin (New York: Crown, 1946). On Dreyfus and later, see Paula Hyman, *From Dreyfus to Vichy* (New York: Columbus, 1979) and Pierre Birnbaum, *Jewish Destinies: Citizen, State, and Community in Modern France,* trans. Arthur Goldhammer (New York, Hill and Wang, 2000).

[16] Quoted in Louis Greenberg, *The Jews of Russia* (New Haven: Yale University Press, 1944), 13.

[17] Vladimir Nabokov, father of the novelist, condemned the Kishinev pogrom of 1903, and particularly the role of officials in that violence. See Vladimir Nabokov, *Speak, Memory* (New York: Vintage, 1989), 174 ff.

In 1910 Albert Venn Dicey wrote that the "worst evil of Russian despotism is that it threatens the Jewish subjects of the Tsar with moral degradation." Dicey thought that "[t]he existence of the Pale of Settlement, the denial to Russian Jews of the ordinary rights conceded by every civilized government to all its subjects; above all, the absolute dependence of the Russian Jews on the varying caprice of every person, degrades, and must degrade, the victims of tyranny." He concluded, "The heroic endurance of persecutions and ill-usage lasting for centuries is the highest glory of Judaism. . . . But no race and no body of men ever as a whole lives up the level of heroism and martyrdom. . . . Despotic power first degrades its victims and then defends its own existence by the plea that its victims and unworthy of freedom and justice."[18]

But even here, in connection with the Russian Jews, the idea of corporatist status as privilege can surface. An English barrister who became an American lawyer described the special legal status of the Jews as it related to marriage and divorce in terms of tolerance and benefit. "The law of marriage and divorce which governs the Jews of Russia differs in many particulars from the rules applicable to adherents of other sects." Hyacinthe Ringrose noted, "This special set of regulations comes from the people of Israel themselves and is an outgrowth of the ancient Mosaic code of jurisprudence." He concluded that in permitting this system of regulation, "we find at least one attitude of wise tolerance for which the Russian Empire is entitled to credit."[19]

But of course tolerance was not the hallmark of the regime. At least one case became an international issue. It was described this way in the *Great Soviet Encyclopedia.*

> Beilis Case, legal proceedings organized in Kiev in September and October 1913 by the tsarist government and the Black Hundreds against the Jew Mendel Beilis, a shop assistant in a brick plant, who was slanderously accused of the ritual murder of a Russian boy, A. Iushinskii. The actual murderers were protected from the court with the aid of I. G. Shcheglovitove, the minister of justice.
>
> The investigation of the Beilis case lasted from 1911 to 1913. At a time when there was a revolutionary upsurge in Russia, the Black Hundreds, having launched an anti-Semitic campaign, tried to use the

---

[18] Albert Venn Dicey, introduction to *The Legal Sufferings of the Jews in Russia,* ed. Lucien Wolf (London: T. F. Unwin, 1912).

[19] Hyacinthe Ringrose, *Marriage and Divorce Laws of the World* (London: Musson-Draper, 1911). See also Ringrose, introduction to the William Shakespeare, *Merchant of Venice* (New York: Heath, 1916), viii–ix. Ringrose was describing a version of the millet system, used in the Ottoman Empire (and in the Middle East today, for example) under which religious minorities are, at least to some extent, governed by their own religious law.

Beilis case to attack democratic forces and to bring about a coup d'état. Representatives of the progressive Russian Intelligentsia, public figures abroad (the Frenchman Anatole France and others) spoke out in defense of Beilis. Despite the pressure of the government and the Black Hundreds, the jury acquitted Beilis.[20]

The encyclopedia saw no need to define ritual murder.[21]

After his acquittal Beilis went first to Israel (then under the Turkish rule) and finally, in 1922, to America. While living in New York he published "The Story of My Sufferings" (1926).

The introduction to that work makes clear the meaning that this trial in Russia had to the Jews on the Lower East Side of New York. "The publishers of Mendel Beilis' memoirs were confronted with a double opportunity," we are told.

> The first was of national concern for the Jewish people. It was not only Mendel Beilis who was indicted but the Jewish people; it was not Beilis alone who was acquitted of the terrible charge of ritual murder but his entire race. It is thus important to preserve this notorious incident in the history of Jewish life in the Diaspora in the form of a book to record the fate which almost befell every Russian jew, as also the sufferings which fell to the share of Mendel Beilis, scapegoat for a people.
>
> It was also true the publishers said, that Beilis needed the community's support.[22]

In Israel, under the British mandate, Beilis would have found a church-state system with which he was familiar, in which religious denominations had authority over certain areas of life and in which everyone was as-

---

[20] *Great Soviet Encyclopedia*, 3d ed. (New York: Macmillan, 1970). Some observers demurred on the point of whether there could ever have been a ritual murder. This is rather like the approach Dostoyevsky has Alyosha take: When asked if the Jews engaged in the practice of ritual murder, Alyosha says that he does not know. See Maurice Samuels, *Blood Accusation* (New York: Knopf, 1966). See also on the Beilis trial Albert S. Lindemann, *The Jew Accused* (Cambridge: Cambridge University Press, 1991), also Ezekiel Leikin, *The Beilis Transcript* (Northvale, N.J.: Jason Aronson, 1993).

[21] The idea of blood libel has been generalized in language like *ritual murder. Demonic murder* extends to groups other than Jews.

[22] "The second purpose of this publication is to ensure in some slight measure the continued existence for the martyr. Mendel Beilis could very easily have benefited financially from the tale of his own experiences and that of his people. He refused, however. He regarded those experiences too holy for commercialization." This book would, the publishers believed, "give the Jewish people the opportunity to repay in slight measure the onerous duties which Beilis undertook for the Jewish people, to show him a portion of the honor befitting a martyr for his people." Mendel Bellis, *The Story of My Sufferings* (New York: Mendel Beilis Publishing, 1926), 7.

sumed to be affiliated with one religion or another.[23] The situation in America was different. The United States in 1922 had had a century's experience with working out the applications of the First Amendment to the United State Constitution. While the nineteenth century knew the Christian nation as a vital living association, secular and humanistic ideas had, by the 1920s became ever more acceptable. Civil disability for Jews and Catholics had long since been eliminated.[24]

While America might have been unique and exceptional, America was a place in which the Jewish community was not unique and exceptional. Rather, America was a place in which the situation of the Jews was in a sense normal.[25]

The American Jewish immigrants found themselves in legal circumstances to some quite new, a legal equality marked by ideas of separation of church and state. The religious community, still the dominant legal order of some of the old countries, was no longer, for example, empowered to handle marriage and divorce. Jews were full citizens, who voted, stood for office, had aspirations for their children in public life.[26]

At the same time, they had come to a country that knew anti-Semitism in various forms, ranging from the blood libel[27] to discrimination in housing and employment[28] and social clubs to the expulsion of Jews from a town in Georgia.[29]

One issue in the United States was a conversation, in a rather new setting, regarding the problem of individuals and groups in the political order. For the Mennonites, as noted by Bender, that issue is conventionally dated from the time of the French Revolution. This is also true for the Western Jews. The French Revolution's rejection of status and privilege was one version of citizenship in the modern state. French emancipation meant the end of pariah status for the Jews. It also meant the end of communal privilege. It reflected the liberal view of individuals and the

---

[23] Ibid. An unusual statutory example of the millet in America is a Rhode Island statute exempting Jews from the incest statute as it relates to marriages between an uncle and niece, permitted by Jewish law.

[24] See Morton Borden, *Jews, Turks, and Infidels* (Chapel Hill: University of North Carolina Press, 1984).

[25] Zionist theory had reinforced the idea that a Jewish state was needed to normalize the situation of the Jews in modern nation-states.

[26] On Jewish civil rights, see Borden, *Jews, Turks, and Infidels*.

[27] On definitions of anti-Semitism, see below. Generally, see Jonathan Sarna, ed., *The American Jewish Experience* (New York: Holmes and Meier, 1997).

[28] On anti-Semitism in law, see Jerold Auerbach, *Unequal Justice* (Indianapolis: Bobbs-Merrill, 1969).

[29] Leonard Dinnerstein, *Anti-Semitism in America* (Oxford: Oxford University Press, 1984).

state, which left little room for group life. But group life had its own history, even in liberal settings.

The group pattern was clear in the earliest history of New York City, when the English resumed control of the city. "The intensity of Dutch resistance to assimilation was also demonstrated by their loyalty to Holland's Roman-Dutch legal tradition. With the resumption of proprietary authority in 1674, the use of Dutch was no longer permitted in New York courts. But Dutch New Yorkers showed little inclination to accept the English notion of a common law or to yield to the unfamiliar procedures of English court (Dutch courts relied on arbitrators and referees rather than juries)."[30] The Dutch, like many groups after them, effectively "boycotted the English judicial system for the resolution of commercial as well as private disagreements, often appealing instead to the consistory of the Reformed Church. Dutch residents of New York City rarely sue one another after 1674."

In America, everyone but the original Native American was an immigrant. Because there was no majority religion, in theory there could be no minority religion. Nathan Isaac's army experience is telling. He notes that "the Germans taunted our prisoners of war by telling them that they had yet to find an American in the American army. They did not consider the Levies, DuBois, O'Briens, Knutsons, and Pappandrikopolouses Americans."[31] But America was not a tribal state. Everyone was involved in insider/outsider, we/they issues. Ringrose's account of the experience of Catholics in a jury pool demonstrates that certain group issues were unresolved.

During the last year of the late Mayor Gaynor's service as a justice of the New York supreme court, it was my privilege to appear before him in Brooklyn at trial term, as counsel for a husband who was suing his wife for an absolute divorce. The issues of fact were framed under our practice for a jury trial and I felt it necessary to be most careful in the selection of the jury. I realized the likelihood that many talesmen, being Roman Catholics, might be constitutionally reluctant to decide the questions of fact in such a manner as to permit my client obtaining a decree of absolute divorce founded upon their verdict.

While great latitude is given to counsel in our state in the examination of talesmen, it is an exceedingly delicate and dangerous thing to inquire into a proposed juryman's religious faith. So, with hesitation

---

[30] Edwin Burrows and Mike Wallace, *Gotham* (Oxford: Oxford University Press, 1999), 89.
[31] Nathan Isaacs, "In Hope of the New Diaspora," *Menorah Journal*, 1919, 190. On the *Menorah Journal*, see Robert Alter, "Epitaph for a Jewish Magazine: Notes on the *Menorah Journal*," *Commentary*, May 1965, 51–55.

not unmixed with apprehension of a rebuke from the bench, I asked the talesmen this question: "Have any of you gentlemen such a conscientious objection to the granting of an absolute divorce that your taking a part in the trial of this case would embarrass you?" Before anyone had a chance to answer this question, Judge Gaynor turned quickly around in his chair and asked in positive tones: "Are any of you members of the Roman Catholic Church?" Four of the talesmen answered, "Yes." "Then you can leave the jury box," said the judge. "This is a court of law, and not a church. We are deciding cases in this courthouse according to the laws of the state of New York, and the doctrines or rules of any religious faith concerning the marriage relation must not be allowed to interfere with the orderly course of transacting the state's business."

Ringrose notes that Judge Gaynor's remarks to the jury in this case were "severely criticized at the time by a number of prominent members of the bar." Still, Ringrose thought "what he said was true and wise, even if it was expressed in a brusque fashion." Ringrose insisted that "[m]odern divorce laws are not founded on theological dogmas or theories, but upon practical social science and humanity." He included that "[t]here is no such thing as Catholic justice or Protestant justice in our courts of law. Our judicial system, without claiming perfection or infallibility, is the finest expression of the wisdom and experience of the ages."[32]

The Ringrose of the courtroom, however, took a more subtle position than the Ringrose of the article in *Case and Comment*. Justice Gaynor was imposing a disqualification for jury service based on religious affiliation or membership alone. Ringrose the lawyer saw the question in terms of individual conscience and allowed the possibility that a Catholic could participate in granting a civil divorce.[33]

In 1922, at about the time that Beilis arrived in New York, English writer Hilaire Belloc published a book in London, reviewed in England and America, that opened again the issue of legal distinctions between groups.[34] Belloc's argument was that the Jews were alien, and unassimila-

---

[32] Hyacinthe Ringrose, "Conflict between Church and Divorce Court," *Case and Comment* (1914): 16. Ringrose (d. 1986) was the author of a work on the Inns of Court and the editor of an anthology of Catholic literature. Mayor Gaynor had given up the Catholicism of his childhood and become an Episcopalian.

[33] The discussion of Catholicism and political issues continues. See Peter Seinfields, "Thinking Catholics," *New York Times,* March 4, 2000.

[34] Hilaire Belloc, among the outstanding English Catholic apologists of his time, wrote a large number of books and engaged with G. K. Chesterton in a variety of political discussions. His work included an attack on the modern state, *The Servile State* (Indianapolis: Liberty Classics, 1977). He was also interested in the restoration of a medieval value structure often called today *distributivism*. This vision related to groups and decentralization

ble, and that the solution to the Jewish problem was segregation and "privilege." He was thinking of the model discussed above in connection with the Mennonites.

He had once urged,

> The Jewish nation ought to be recognized as a nation in some way or another, with all the advantages and disadvantages that follow from the recognition of any truth. I express that policy in the word *privilege*. Where there is conscription the obvious bargain would be not to submit Jews to military service. In England, where there is no conscription, I would have registration and charters, Jewish Courts and so on. But all that is mere Utopia.[35]

Some thought that Belloc's argument proved too much, in that the very claims raised by him in relation to Jews could as easily be made in relation to Catholics.

> Now the Jews do not claim sovereign rights; indeed, the vast majority of Jews do not desire them. And, consequently, on this point breaks down the contention of Mr. Belloc that the Jews are undesirable citizens in any country because they have a dual nationality. Roman Catholics, for instance, have, so to speak, a dual nationality, because they are bound on the one hand by the decrees of the Pope and on the other by the laws of the country in which they reside—yet no one has ever suggested that, because of this, they should be segregated, either hostilely or amicably, within the precincts of a larger Vatican.[36]

Writing in the *New Republic*, Carlton Hayes noted that in the United States, one saw anti-Catholicism that was almost as strong as anti-Semitism, and that it was said of Catholics, as well as Jews that " 'they are

---

based on harmony in social relations within a Christian order. The example of the medieval world in which Jews, a small internal community understood to be outside of that order rather than an internal constituent part, may well have provided Belloc with his conception of the proper relations between Christians and Jews in the world he described at various points, most particularly in *The Jews*, 3d ed. (Boston: Houghton Mifflin, 1937). For biographical material, see Andrew Norman Wilson, *Hilaire Belloc* (London: Hamish Hamilton, 1984); Robert Speaight, *Life of Hilaire Belloc* (New York: Farrar, Straus and Cudahy, 1957). See generally, Colin Holmes, *Anti-Semitism in British Society, 1876–1939* (London: E. Arnold, 1979). See Moore, *Formation of Persecuting Society;* Gavin Langmuir, *History, Religion, and Anti-Semitism* (Berkeley and Los Angeles: University of California Press, 1990) for medieval material. It has been suggested that French nationalism was a source: John Patrick McCarthy, *Hilaire Belloc, Edwardian Radical* (Indianapolis: Liberty Press, 1978), 42.

[35] Letter of January 1, 1916, to Maurice Baring, quoted in Speaight, *Life of Hilaire Belloc,* 453.

[36] Lewis Benjamin, "The Jewish Problem in England," *Fortnightly Review* 3 (1922): 971.

different,' that they are clannish, that they are un-American, that they below to an 'international organization,' that they are under foreign domination."[37]

The issue of groups was, at the time of these discussions, very much marked by discussions of nationality—which had surfaced as part of the aftermath of the First World War. Group affiliation as it related to religion was considered a matter of private choice and cognizance.

By the middle of the twentieth century, corporatism had become associated with fascist forms as much as with medieval forms. As to fascism, the suppression of individuals altogether was obvious. Fascism could not conceive of any sphere of human activity remaining immune from intervention by the state. "We are, in other words, a state which controls all forces acting in nature. We control political forces, we control moral forces, we control economic forces . . . everything in the State, nothing against the State, nothing outside the State."[38] These were Mussolini's ideas.

For Mussolini, Sternhell writes, the fascist state was not only a living being, an organism, but a spiritual and moral entity: "The fascist state is wide awake and has a will of its own. For this reason, it can be described as 'ethical.'" Sternhell continues, "Not only does the existence of the State imply the denial of the individual's rights—'the individual exists only insofar as he is within the State and subjected to the requirements of the State'—but the State asserts the right to be 'a State which necessarily transforms the people even in their physical aspect.' Outside the State, 'no human or spiritual values can exist, much less have value': 'no individuals or groups (political parties, cultural associations, economic unions, social classes) outside the State.'"[39]

Liberal theory rejected all of this. Emancipation and liberal political theory also meant, however, lack of interest in what group issues looked like, how they could be defined, even discussed. The issue for liberal democracies was whether there was a way to think of groups as formed by individuals—so that individuals retained their primary place—while still possessing a group identity.

The problems for us, as heirs of the Enlightenment, are more complex perhaps than for those who considered these matters earlier. The experience of the Holocaust provided an example of race hatred in which recantation or conversion were not among the options for the hated group.

[37] Carlton J. H. Hayes, review of "The Jews," *New Republic*, July 12, 1922, 193. See also Speaight, *Hilaire Belloc*, 454, regarding similarities between Jews and Catholics: Belloc "did not see how easily his arguments could be turned against the Catholics."

[38] Mussolini, quoted in Zeev Sternhell, "Fascist Ideology," in *Fascism: A Reader's Guide*, ed. Walter Laqueur (Berkeley and Los Angeles: University of California Press, 1976), 356.

[39] Ibid.

Nazi Germany (or South Africa) also provided an example of separation that was precisely intended to denigrate and stigmatize.[40] As we entered the twenty-first century, the bloody story of group identification was still being told in many places.

We assume the desirability of a world in which such denigration and stigmatization is unacceptable. We see that memberships are multiple, overlapping, transitory.[41] We are more conflicted, perhaps, than earlier generations about the problem of identifying groups, about seeing individuals as members of groups, and about raising issues of group characteristics. We have trouble relating our expectations of a state that, if we are political liberals, we see as properly activist and more than minimal with our commitment to the ideals of group autonomy and flourishing diversity in a pluralist order. We are surprised to find that some of our images of this order take us back to the Middle Ages and various centers of authority. Some of those images invoke independence and sovereignty.

The history of Hawaii and the American treatment of a sovereign indigenous people was argued before a People Tribunal in 1993.[42] The tribunal was sponsored by one hundred Hawaiian groups dedicated in one way or another to the sovereignty of the island's indigenous people.[43] The tribunal intended to try the United States for its violation of Hawaiian sovereignty. As Milner Ball notes, the proceeding was in the line of trials that had their origins at Nuremberg, and went on to trials not backed by state force. In the case of Hawaii, the complainants were, however, invoking the idea of sovereignty.

In an action unrelated to this trial the United States government apologized to the Native people of Hawaii, but this apology had no legal consequences. The apology is referred to by the U.S. Supreme Court's *Rice v. Cayetano*,[44] which held unconstitutional a Hawaiian statute restricting the right to vote for certain state offices to those of Hawaiian ancestry.[45]

[40] See Aviam Soifer ("Involuntary Groups") and Carol Weisbrod comment ("Groups in Perspectives") *Washington and Lee Law Review* 48 (1991): 437.

[41] See recently Franklin Snyder on Robert Cover, "Nomos, Narrative, and Adjudication: Toward a Jurisgenetic Theory of Law," *William and Mary Law Review* 40 (1999): 1623.

[42] Milner S. Ball, *Called by Stories: Biblical Sagas and Their Challenge for Law* (Durham, N.C.: Duke University Press, 2000).

[43] Ibid., 93.

[44] *Rice v. Cayetano,* 528 U.S. 485 (2000) at 503.

[45] See also, Sally Engle Merry, Tenth Anniversary Symposium's New Direction, Law, Culture and Cultural Appropriation, *Yale Journal of Law and the Humanities* (10 1988): 575. Merry has also written on the 1993 tribunal in "Legal Pluralism and Transnational Culture," in *Human Rights, Culture, and Context: Anthropological Perspectives,* ed. Richard Wilson (London, Pluto Press, 1997). For a comment on *Rice v. Cayetano,* see Aviam Soifer, "A Very Troubling Supreme Court Precedent: Race, Hawaii, and History," http://www.tompaine.com/history/2000/04/20/1.html.

A central difficulty is that this sovereignty may not be recognized. Here is the theme of nonrecognition in an Australian short story: a white man shoots a black man. The following is, in effect, a statement in the white man's defense: "[H]e did not know that black was a messenger. Who had the right to pass through all territories without harm. How could he know that? And even if he had, he mightn't have cared anyway that it was a consideration in their world. It wasn't one in ours. That they should even have considerations—that there might be rules and laws hidden away in what was just makeshift savagery, hand-to-mouth getting from one day to the next and one place to another a little further on over the horizon— that would have seemed ridiculous to him."[46]

The desperation that hostile political and social environments can create for groups is well documented. Sometimes the hostility is expressed mildly, and we call it discrimination; sometimes more intensely—and we call it genocide. But hostility once experienced is unlikely to be forgotten by individuals or groups. And of course we might conclude that it is the group itself taken as a whole that is good or bad. Group practices may, from the point of view of the outside society, be bad, or incomprehensible, or simply unenlightened. Particular groups can be presented in a highly sympathetic manner—as in Anne Fadiman's account of the tragic encounter of Hmong and Western medicine in *The Spirit Catches You and You Fall Down*[47]—or as perpetuators of barbaric customs, as in the discussions of the Hmong use of a cultural defense. Is "marriage by capture" (seen as rape in the state system) in any way excused by a cultural context?[48]

And the pogroms are never far from one's mind. Even when the groups is fully accepted, the historical experience is part of its narrative. Thus, the Mormons (above, chap. 3) continue to stress nineteenth-century persecution in explaining their present political stance.

The cultural lives of law exist not only in time but over time, and thus the blood libel trial of Mendel Beilis in Kiev 1913 has a life in its own time and place, a later life in the minds of the Jewish immigrants of New York among whom Beilis lived after 1920, and a later life in the general

---

[46] David Malouf, *Dream Stuff* (New York, Pantheon, 2000). "Sovereignty" and "recognition" are, of course, much-discussed subjects. See Mark W. Janis and John Noyes, *International Law*, 2d ed. (St. Paul: West, 2001), 400 ff.

[47] Anne Fadiman, *The Spirit Catches You and You Fall Down: A Hmong Child, Her American Doctors, and the Collision of Two Cultures* (New York: Farrar, Straus and Giroux, 1997).

[48] On the cultural defense in an anthropological perspective, see Deirdre Evans-Pritchard and Alison Dundes Renteln, "The Interpretation and Distortion of Culture: A Hmong 'Marriage by Capture' Case in Fresno, California," *Southern California Interdisciplinary Law Journal* 4 (1994).

society when Malamud's *The Fixer* was published in the 1960s. It remains a cultural reference for the idea State-and-Groups, particularly on the question of what the medieval corporatist tradition can mean.

In the 1960s, in Malamud's novel *The Fixer* and Maurice Samuel's account, *Blood Accusation,* the Beilis trial was inevitably read against the European Holocaust. "The wave of international indignation and protest which was aroused when the Beilis case was launched forms a striking contrast to the comparative equanimity with which Hitler's preparations for the extermination of the Jews were received outside Germany," Leonard Shapiro wrote.[49]

Where one stood in 1913 for the Russian Jews in New York, who had escaped the anti-Semitism of czarist Russia, in the 1960s one stood for six million who had not escaped Hitler.

"To begin with, before I had read the book, I wondered why Malamud should expect his readers to be concerned about what had happened to this one Jew half a century ago, in view of what had happened to six million Jews during the Second World War" wrote a reviewer of *The Fixer.* "It did not take me long to realize that Malamud had deliberately set himself this problem. Six million was a figure, but a man was a man. If he could tell this story well enough, he must have decided, this one unprepossessing man, this Yakov Bok, could represent not only the martyrs of Belsen and Auschwitz but all victims of man's inhumanity. We the readers could be made to feel for this one man what we could not possibly feel for the six million."[50]

Moreover, in mind of Malamud, one stood for many who were not necessarily Jews in a variety of different contexts: civil rights workers, Sacco and Vanzetti, Dreyfus. Malamud wrote, "After my last novel I was sniffing for an idea in the direction of injustice on the American scene, partly for obvious reasons—this was a time of revolutionary advances in Negro rights—and partly because I became involved with this theme in a way that sets off my imagination in terms of art." He thought of civil

---

[49] Leonard Shapiro, review of *Blood Accusation, New York Review of Books,* June 1, 1967, 32.

[50] Granville Hicks, "One Stood for Six Million," *Saturday Review,* September 10, 1966. Explaining his intentions in *The Melting Pot* in the second edition of the play, Zangwill noted that the "Jewish immigrant" selected as the "typical immigrant" is the "toughest of all the white elements that have been poured into the American crucible." The Jews, had by their "unique experience of several thousand years of exposure to alien majorities, developed a salamandrine power of survival." This may or may not be true, as one observes that the issues of group survival and ethnicity characterize many ethnic and religious groups. But it seems to be true, as Zangwill also believed, that the "conditions offered to the Jew in America are without parallel throughout the world," partly related to separation of church and state, partly to the sense of experimentation and development in American institutions generally. And it was true not only for Jews but for many groups.

rights workers in the South, of Sacco and Vanzetti, of Dreyfus, of Caryl Chessman, and then he remembered Mendel Beilis, about whom his father had told him, and something happened. "In *The Fixer,*" he explained, "I use some of his [Beilis's] experiences, though not, basically, the man, partly because his life came to less than he had paid for by his suffering and endurance, and because I had to have room to invent. To his trials in prison I added something of Dreyfus's and Vanzetti's, shaping the whole to suggest the quality of the afflictions of the Jews under Hitler."[51]

One version of a solution to state-group problems is the melting pot. But that image of assimilation has, from the start, been contested. Thus, Rabbi Judah Magnes argued in 1909 against the image of the melting pot that Israel Zangwill had offered in his play.[52]

> The Melting Pot is not the highest ideal of America. America is rather the refining pot. Here, indeed, men have the opportunity of losing their old-world hatreds, their petty spites and jealousies. . . . In the refining process the dross will be lost. But "surely there is here a mine for silver and a place for gold where it may be refined." Each man as he strikes root here is no more obliged to yield his individuality, his race, his speech, his culture, his ideals, than he is obliged to yield his religion.[53]

Magnes's argument was echoed by his brother-in-law, Louis Marshall, in a brief he presented to the Supreme Court in *Pierce v. Society of Sisters.*[54] The language evokes entities placed between the individual and the state,[55] or in some cases, sees the state as an association.[56]

---

[51] Quoted in Hicks, "One Stood for Six Million."

[52] Israel Zangwill, *The Melting Pot* (New York: Macmillan, 1909, 1914) (first produced in Washington in 1908, and dedicated with permission to Theodore Roosevelt). Magnes's sermon was given at Temple Emanuel in New York on October 9, 1909.

[53] Judah Leon Magnes, in *Dissenter in Zion,* ed. Arthur Goren (Cambridge: Harvard University Press, 1982).

[54] See below. Conceivably in fact, Magnes echoed Marshall, or both some other speaker. The chronology here is to cited printed sources. When he addressed this issue in the amicus curiae brief submitted on behalf of the American Jewish Committee to the Supreme Court of the United States in *Pierce v. Society of Sisters,* Louis Marshall said, "There is no such thing as a melting pot, anthropologically speaking. If there were, it would be a misfortune. However much iron and copper and lead and zinc and gold and silver may be mixed, the net result is a product which possesses none of the virtues of the original metals and is utterly useless. Far better would it be to purify and refine the original metals, for then their individual values would be enhanced."

[55] The term used by Sally Falk Moore, the anthropologist, in *Law as Process* is *semi-autonomous groups.* Related terms might be *groups, associations,* and *mediating institutions.*

[56] The reification of the "state" see John Griffiths, "Legal Pluralism and the Theory of Legislation—with Special Reference to the Regulation of Euthanasia," in *Legal Polycentricity,* ed. Hanne Petersen and Henrik Zahle (Aldershot, U.K.: Dartmouth, 1995), 201, 228 n.

The image of group life goes back to ideas of Maitland. "There seems to be a genus of which state and corporation are species. They seem to be permanently organized groups of men; they seem to be group-units; we seem to attribute acts and intents, rights and wrongs to these groups, to these units." Even if the state is a special sort of group, Maitland said, we should ask questions about the species itself.[57]

Pierre Birnbaum has noted that many discussions of these questions take place at a fairly theoretical level, in which particular national histories are not taken into account. Our debates over liberalism/communitarianism and citizenship, he notes, are engaged "on the plane of normative philosophy."[58] He urges that "historical sociology" be taken into account. It is not clear, he argues, that "the debate takes the same form in countries with 'strong' states as in countries with 'weak' ones. Or in countries where universal values dominate, as opposed to countries in which citizenship is easily compatible with membership in various types of community."[59]

Of course the American story is not the only story. The discussions are domestic in many countries and are also international. The efforts to think again about these issues through the twentieth century (and into the twenty-first) are the subject of part 2.

---

18. See generally Griffiths, "What Is Legal Pluralism?" *Journal of Legal Pluralism and Unofficial Law* 24 (1986): 1–55.

[57] See Frederick William Maitland, introduction to Otto Friedrich von Gierke, *Political Theories of the Middle Age* (Boston: Beacon Press, 1960), ix. See also Carol Weisbrod, *Butterfly, the Bride* (Ann Arbor: University of Michigan Press, 1999), and particularly the discussion of the psychological theory of law advanced by Leon Petrazycki.

[58] Birnbaum, *Jewish Destinies*, 114–15.

[59] Ibid.

The Peaceable Kingdom

Part 2 of this book examines another vision of federalism. It is horizontal, pluralist, and includes public and private groups in various relations to each other. We could speak of an "essential federalism" of America, Alexander Pekelis wrote, "and we would not, of course, have in mind just forty-eight or forty-nine American jurisdictions. We think of a wider and deeper network composed of a plurality of legal systems enjoying an extremely great amount of autonomy."[1]

Essential federalism, while still drawing in the idea of the state, sees groups without reference to a public-private line. It also evokes autonomy in the situation of stability and harmony that we also sometimes associate with the peaceable kingdom.

"Perhaps the best-known icon of The Peaceable Kingdom is one of Edward Hicks' many paintings of it." Milner Ball writes: "To one side of the canvas we see William Penn under an elm covenanting with Indians. To the other side are stylized figures from Isaiah 11: leopards, lions, fatlings, forest, and children together—all staring out at us, their eyes wide and a little startled."[2] The Hicks painting is, Ball continues, "logically, historically, and zoologically incongruous, but it works. All of the elements are there: politics, the natural world, law in the form of a treaty relating disparate peoples. The harmony of beasts with each other and with humans is esthetically linked to the politics of the treaty, not as cause and effect but as companion parts of the whole."

Will Kymlicka also has discussed Hicks's painting, featured on the cover his book on pluralism:[3] "[T]he jacket illustration is a painting called 'The Peaceable Kingdom' by Edward Hicks, painted around 1834. It illustrates the signing of a treaty in 1682 between a group of Quakers and three local Indian tribes, the Leni Lenape, Susquehannock, and Shawnee, allowing for the establishment of a Quaker community in Pennsylvania. (The Quakers were one of the few groups to honor their treaty commitments.) Hicks, a devout Quaker, viewed this treaty as the beginning of the 'peaceable kingdom' prophesied in Isaiah, in which love will

---

[1] Alexander Pekelis, "Legal Techniques and Political Ideologies: A Comparative Study," in *Law and Social Action*, 67–68. Some of Pekelis's work is directed to limitations on the power of "private governments." See below.

[2] Milner Ball, *Lying Down Together: Law, Metaphor, and Theology* (Madison: University of Wisconsin Press, 1985), 173. On Hicks, see Carolyn Weekley, *The Kingdoms of Edward Hicks* (Williamsburg, Va.: Rockefeller Art Center, 1999).

[3] Will Kymlicka, *Multicultural Citizenship: A Liberal Theory of Minority Rights* (Oxford: Oxford University Press, 1995), vii.

replace hostility and competition both amongst humans and in the natural world (e.g. 'the lion will lie down with the lamb')." Kymlicka explains that he "chose this painting because it portrays and celebrates a form of multiculturalism that we often ignore. Most discussions of 'multiculturalism,' at least in North America, focus on the case of immigrants, and the accommodation of their ethnic and racial differences within the larger society. Less attention has been paid to the situation of indigenous peoples and other non-immigrant 'national minorities' whose homeland has been incorporated into the boundaries of a larger state, through conquest, colonization, or federation."[4]

But there is no human ruler in the Hicks's painting. Kymlicka's issues arise in the world and history and politics, a world instantly closer to that of Erastus Field's monumental federalism.

Using the *Peaceable Kingdom* as an emblem and contrasting it with the *Historical Monument of the American Republic,* we can identify at least four differences:

First, we are no longer describing the nation-state.

Second, we are in a world in which difference, perhaps the difference of the animals, the difference of the Indians, the difference of gender, will feature prominently. The single figures in this sense can represent groups.

Third, each of the figures may taken as a representative of a group, but each is also an individual, individual animal, individual human being. What is that individual like? What is its self?

Fourth, we can say that the Hicks painting, of which he painted many versions, raises explicitly the issue of the lion: How big is it?

Part 2 of this book considers these questions, in discussions that move away from American law to draw widely on the experiences of different countries and different groups. The last chapters, on education and on the self as negotiator, continue the stress on the individual as the basic unit.

Some explorations of groups assume static (natural, involuntary) memberships that are relatively few in number (one is black or white, male or female, etc.). Others see a spectrum in which some afflictions are based on birth and others on choice.[5] The present inquiry assumes that the affiliations of individuals are multiple and changing. Moreover, as chapter 10 suggests, the issue of individual choice of affiliations and attitude toward affiliation has a weight of its own.

The issue can be caught in the difference between *I, the subject* and *me, the object,* that is, the object in effect of labels used by others, including oneself.[6] Some aspects of the self, the subject, will be considered in the last chapters. Chapters 6 and 7 will consider the groups more than individuals.

[4] Ibid., 102.

[5] Donald Horowitz, *Ethnic Groups in Conflict* (Berkeley and Los Angeles: University of California Press, 1985), noting that both elements are often present.

[6] See William James, "The Consciousness of Self," in *Principles of Psychology,* vol. 1 (New York: Dover, 1950), using "the words Me and I for the empirical person and the judging Thought" (371).

Daniel Bell addresses possible group labels this way: "At particular times—but usually in relation to an adversary, which gives it its political character—one specific identification becomes primary and overriding and prompts one to join a particular group; or, one is forced into a group by the action of others."[7] He points out, however, that "there is no general rule to state which identification it might be."[8] Bell adds a discussion on the "range of diverse identities available."[9] His category *socially deviant* raises serious issues for pluralism, since some identities may be antisocial or criminal. One problem is that of creating political forms large enough to hold not only different ethnicities but groups—and new groups—that compete ideologically, groups whose differences cannot be described as "merely" physical or cultural, but must be treated as significant and even possibly disturbing. This issue is litigated often in the United States in terms of the protection of the First Amendment's guarantee of religious liberty. But it raises problems that go beyond religious differences to competing visions of the world, whether these are religious or secular.

It is also possible to distinguish between good and bad kinds of pluralism. Thus historian David Hollinger argues for a postethnic America, in which "affiliation on the basis of shared descent would be voluntary rather than prescribed."[10] He distinguishes between pluralism and cosmopolitanism, noting, "Cosmopolitanism is willing to put the future of every culture at risk through the critical, sympathetic scrutiny of other cultures . . . [while] pluralism is more concerned to protect and perpetuate particular, existing cultures."[11] "Cosmopolitanism is more oriented to the individual, whom it is likely to understand as a member of a number of different communities simultaneously, while pluralism is more oriented to the group, and is

[7] Daniel Bell, "Ethnicity and Social Change," in *Ethnicity: Theory and Experience,* ed. Nathan Glazer and Daniel P. Moynihan (Cambridge: Harvard University Press, 1975), 141, 159.

[8] Ibid.

[9] Ibid., 159 n. 9. Bell lists the following as *intermediate social units:*
1. Political parties
2. Functional groups
   a. Major economic interests: business, farm labor
   b. Segmented economic interest: for example, professional associations
   c. Economic communal groups: for example, the poor, the aged, the disabled
3. Armies
4. Voluntary associations (for example, consumer, civic)
5. Age-graded groups (for example, youth, students)
6. Ethos communal groups (for example, the "community" of science)
7. Symbolic and expressive identification
   a. Regional (for example, Texans)
   b. Socially "deviant" (for example, drug cultures, homosexual)

For a list of groups not limited to traditional ethnic or religious groups that might in some contexts produce public disorder, see W. M. Reisman, "Responses to Crimes of Discrimination and Genocide: An Appraisal of the Convention on the Elimination of Racial Discrimination," *Journal of International Law and Policy* 1 (1971): 29, 45. For a list of groups not limited to traditional groups that need protection, see Leon Lipson, "Piety and Revision: How Will the Mandarins Survive under the Rule of Law?" *Cornell International Law Journal* 23 (1990): 191, 197.

[10] David A. Hollinger, "Postethnic America," *Contention* 2 (1992): 79.

[11] Ibid., 83.

likely to identify each individual with reference to a single, primary community."[12] The idea of "cosmopolitan" self used by Jeremy Waldron is used in the concluding chapter to consider this question of multiple memberships.

The international community provides another substantive level for consideration of the same questions. In that case, the nation-state becomes an intermediate level.[13] If we view "living law pluralism"[14] as good or inevitable, the question is what form of global or state political organization can sustain difference without disintegration.

Part 2 of this book explores these questions through consideration of theories and practices, particularly as to education, that have either placed a higher value on pluralist understandings of the human situation or have been built, however reluctantly, on what could be seen as the unavoidable pluralism of that situation.

It is possible that the division of the book into part 1 and part 2 suggests a false dichotomy in this presentation and that the two pictorial emblems are not alternatives but simply different emphases, each of which is prominent at some particular time. Certain highly accommodating readings of the free exercise clause look a great deal like a fairly strong version of pluralism. Certain descriptions of the organizing and sanctioning role of the framework state look a good deal like hierarchy. The book could, in short, have been organized with the two emblems placed side by side as a beginning, with all the textual rhetoric offered as commentary on both. As I have suggested elsewhere, Rex, the king, and Pontifex, the bridge-builder, may be the same official in different moods.[15]

---

[12] Ibid.

[13] This assumes a politically active and effective international community.

[14] F. S. C. Northrop, "Contemporary Jurisprudence and International Law," *Yale Law Journal* 61 (1952): 623, 648.

[15] See Carol Weisbrod, "Women and International Human Rights: Some Issues under the Bridge," in *Religion and the Law: Obligations of Citizenship and Demands of Faith,* ed. Nancy Rosenblum (Princeton: Princeton University Press, 2000).

CHAPTER 6

Theoreticians: Questions Left Open

> [T]here has been no generation and no country which could
> not count among its best legal minds one or more opponents to
> [the] monistic theory. Rousseau and Bentham, Savigny and
> Gierke, Durkheim and Duguit, William James and John
> Dewey, Calhoun and Horace Kallen, Croce and Figgis, Morris
> R. Cohen and Harold Laski—all approached the problem from
> different angles: the legal character of rules made by the so-
> called private groups, the multiplicity of legal orders, the plural-
> istic structure of the state, guild socialism, vocational represen-
> tation, concurrent majorities.
>
> —ALEXANDER PEKELIS, "Private Governments and the
> Federal Constitution"

◆ THE DISCUSSIONS reviewed in this chapter, ordinarily called pluralist, address issues of sovereignty. Pluralist theories often reject one view of sovereignty and invoke another. Before examining pluralist theories themselves, it may be useful to set out as background some of the general theoretical material on sovereignty.

In twentieth-century Germany, Carl Schmitt offered what has been called a modernized version of Hobbes and Bodin[1] that sees the sovereign as the source not of the rule but of the exception. It is a version of absolutism. This European sovereignty is visible in Foucault, who contrasts it with "new type of power." This nonsovereign power, which lies outside the form of sovereignty, is called, in Foucault, disciplinary power.[2]

"Schmitt's jurisprudence puts sovereignty—in the exception rather than the norm—at the center. The sovereign as uncommanded commander."[3] Carl Schmitt's discussion of pluralism (in *The Concept of the Political* and also in an essay called "Ethic of State and Pluralistic State')[4] examines the theories of English pluralism particularly. It finds them inadequate because they fail to locate a specific sense of the political. Schmitt's

---

[1] See Paul Hirst, "Carl Schmitt's Decisionism," in *The Challenge of Carl Schmitt,* ed. Chantal Mouffe (London: Verso, 1999).

[2] Foucault, *Power and Knowledge,* ed. Colin Gordon (New York: Pantheon, 1980).

[3] Ibid., 12.

[4] Essay in Mouffe, *Challenge of Carl Schmitt.*

critique of Laski and Cole accepts many of their descriptions of the social universe. It finally rejects their vision, however.[5] Schmitt's sentence is that the sovereign decides on the exception. Agamben, quoting Schmitt, adds Walter Benjamin: The modern world is one of permanent exception.[6]

When Giorgio Agamben talks about sovereignty, he quotes Carl Schmitt and Walter Benjamin. Agamben notes that "the paradox of sovereignty consists in the fact that sovereign is, at the same time, outside and inside the juridical order. If the sovereign is truly the one to whom the juridical order grants the power of proclaiming a state of exception and, therefore, of suspending the order's own validity," then—and here he quotes Carl Schmitt—" '[T]he sovereign stands outside the juridical order and, nevertheless, belongs to it, since it is up to him to decide if the constitution is to be suspended *in toto*' (Schmitt, Politische Theologie, p. 13)." Agamben continues: "The specification that the sovereign is *'at the same time* outside and inside the juridical order' (emphasis added) is not insignificant: the sovereign, having the legal power to suspend the validity of the law, legally places himself outside the law." "This means," Agamben concludes, that the paradox can also be formulated this way: 'the law is outside itself,' or: 'I, the sovereign, who am outside the law, declare that there is nothing outside the law.' "[7]

One hundred years ago, C. E. Merriam published his doctoral thesis, a history of the theories of sovereignty since Rousseau. In his review of the many competing theories in various countries over several centuries, he attempted not to defend a correct theory, but to describe the variety of theories and to summarize them broadly in categories, so that one could deal with the sense in which a writer understood sovereignty. Thus, the conclusion of Merriam's thesis noted that those who might admit that there was half, double, limited, or relative sovereignty, might actually mean that something is sovereign in one sense but not another. He stressed the importance of knowing the sense in which the speaker referred to sovereignty.[8]

Merriam's point is still important. The word sovereignty is used in a wide variety of senses, and, to the extent that the conversations about sovereignty are disciplinary, the senses conventional within disciplines

---

[5] See Carl Schmitt, *The Concept of the Political,* trans. George Schwab (Chicago: University of Chicago Press, 1996), 41ff. See discussion by David Dyzenhaus, "Putting the State Back in Credit," in Mouffe, *Challenge of Carl Schmitt.*

[6] Schmitt, quoted in G. Agamben, *Homo Sacer,* trans. Daniel Heller Roazan (Stanford: Stanford University Press, 1998), 15.

[7] Agamben, *Homer Sacer,* 15.

[8] Charles E. Merriam Jr., *History of the Theory of Sovereignty since Rousseau,* Columbia University Studies in the Social Sciences (New York, 1900; repr. New York: AMS Press, 1968), 226–27.

provide a boundary that may or may not be noted. In short, we are often in a disciplinary conversation, and we would not require or expect material on the "sovereignty of justice" or the "sovereignty of self" in a book that deals with sovereignty in international law.

Sovereignty in the American discussion from the start moved away from the qualities of the absolute sovereign. In *Democracy in America,* Tocqueville described a dual or divided sovereignty.[9] But there were attacks on sovereignty in general, and one writer, Philemon Bliss, suggested that the idea be abandoned, arguing, "Justice is the only true sovereign."[10]

The separate states retained sovereignty while also ceding some to the federal government. National sovereignty was used as part of the international discussion to determine (or describe) those admitted to the community of "nations," while Indian sovereignty was a term used in the domestic discussion to treat the status of an internal group that was understood to have a claim to autonomous status. The autonomy of the individual described in terms of sovereignty is a step beyond this. Perhaps the link to the point made by Jack Rakove, that in the United States, the argument on sovereignty was associated not with the assertion of a claim to power but rather with the effort to resist power.

> Sovereignty had thus acquired a new meaning in American usage. To acknowledge state sovereignty was to accord the states a final say, not in exercising the power to command obedience, but in nullifying the commands of an authority perceived, in particular cases, to be external and illegitimate. The effect was to invert the original formulation. Sovereignty now lay much closer to a theory of resistance than of command—closer to Locke, in a sense, than to Hobbes. The states, in the final analysis, would act as an unchecked checker, the court of last resort in determining when an exercise of national supremacy had gone a measure or two too far.[11]

Further, Rakove stress that the "American concept of sovereignty, that is, has always had a profoundly negative, defensive, reactive character." The concept "ironically expresses the dominant anti-statist currents that have swirled through our political culture since the eighteenth century."[12]

Today, we tend to speak more of legitimacy than of sovereignty, but, as Ernest Gellner noted in a clever paraphrase, "Roughly speaking, legiti-

[9] Tocqueville, *Democracy in America,* 1:114, 364.
[10] Bliss quoted in Merriam, *Theory of Sovereignty,* 167.
[11] Jack N. Rakove, "Making a Hash of Sovereignty II," *Green Bag* 3 (1999): 51, 55.
[12] Ibid., 54.

macy is sovereignty recollected in tranquillity."[13] There is an argument that small communities (assuming that they pass the Austinian test of numbers—"considerable" or "not extremely minute") might be sovereign in Austinian terms, even though located within another state. This argument can be made by an analogy to the feeble but sovereign state that obeys the rare commands of the more powerful state.[14] This would work best for the nineteenth century, on the theory that the larger state made few demands.[15] Today, we may want to say that groups have a role in shaping official law (i.e. pressure groups that file amicus briefs) and also in translating, enforcing, and re-creating law.[16]

But, in general, state law remains paramount in thinking about law.

In law, we may take Willard Hurst's summary as a statement of the conventional wisdom on the questions of the state's relation to other groups: "Possession of the legitimate monopoly of violence within a territory was the most distinctive attribute of our law."[17] Of course, law shared rule making and the imposition of penalties with other institutions. Thus, "[p]rivate clubs, trade associations, labor unions, and religious congregations fixed terms of admission, made regulations for the behavior of members, and fined violators or withdraw their privileges, or suspended or expelled them. [So, too,] [i]ndividuals governed much of their everyday relations by social customs which they enforced by recognized signs of social disapproval or by ostracism. But to take life, inflict physical pain, or confine the body were ways of enforcing rules which this legal order recognized as properly held only at the command of law."[18]

The state is sovereign and, despite federalist theory, is conceived as unified.[19] Frug notes that "the need for a single unified sovereign has become a fundamental premise of Western political thought." Federalism has not replaced the notion of unified sovereignty because the American version of federalism retains sovereignty and places it in the people. In the twentieth century, "For all practical purposes, the unified sovereign has become the federal government (absent a constitutional convention), exercising

[13] Ernest Gellner, *Legitimation of Belief* (Cambridge: Cambridge University Press, 1974), 24.

[14] See Austin, "Lecture VI," 1:223.

[15] Cf. Robert Cover, "The Supreme Court, 1982 Term—Foreword: Nomos and Narrative," *Harvard Law Review* 97 (1983): 4 (on law creation by internal groups); Weisbrod, "Family, Church, and State" (for a discussion of pluralism in this sense and for the material on legal and political pluralism cited there).

[16] See, e.g., Daniel Givelber, William Bowers, and Carolyn Blitch, "Tarasoff, Myth, and Reality: An Empirical Study of Private Law in Action," *Wisconsin Law Review* 1984:443.

[17] James W. Hurst, *Law and Social Process in United States History* (Ann Arbor: University of Michigan Law School, 1960), 267.

[18] Ibid., 267–68.

[19] Frug, "City as Legal Concept," 1057, 1126, 1127 n. 301.

power by virtue of the commerce clause, § 5 of the 14th amendment, the spending power, or, if necessary, another source."

For lawyers at least, the state coincides with the legal system. As already indicated, D'Entreves says that if we look for the state we find officials.[20] As Joseph Tussman observed, "Taking law as central we develop theories of the state as a legal order or as the 'rule of law.'"[21]

We translate the question "What is to be done?" into the question "What should the state, acting through its judges, do?" "The legal foray into republicanism," Kathryn Abrams notes, "has been sidetracked by its intellectual premises. Straitened by the distinctive problems and perspectives of liberal legalism, it has produced a muted hybrid, oddly focused on the role of the courts."[22] It is a major effort for law teachers to focus on other parts of government or even on the influence of lower courts.

There are, however, other views.

For those accustomed to a postmodern discussion, the idea that the center is not all powerful and that power is dispersed throughout the society may well be associated with the work of Michel Foucault. For those coming to similar questions from the orientation of law or political theory, Foucault's insights on this point may seem familiar and even undeveloped. Although Foucault can be viewed as a pluralist, his work does not analyze either responses to power or particular ways in which groups and individuals with power respond to each other.[23] Moreover, as has been noted (by, for example, Duncan Kennedy), Foucault's view of law is prerealist. Some of what Foucault describes as nonlaw or some change in the legal regime may well be, to those raised on realist approaches, simply law operating in one of its several modes.[24]

Perhaps more to the point is that Foucault was not using the insights of European sociology of law as we find it, for example, in Eugen Ehrlich's *Fundamental Principles of the Sociology of Law*.[25] The argument, then, is that the centrist focus on state law was an exaggeration, and that one had to study the inner law of associations.

These distinctions were foundational not only for legal realists but for a good deal of empirical research, some of it carried out under the heading

---

[20] D'Entreves, *Notion of the State*, 5.

[21] Joseph Tussman, *Obligation and the Body Politic* (Oxford: Oxford University Press, 1960), 73.

[22] Kathryn Abrams, "Law's Republicanism," *Yale Law Journal* 97 (1988): 1591.

[23] See Michael Walzer, "The Politics of Michel Foucault," in *Foucault: A Critical Reader,* ed. David Couzens Hoy (Oxford: Blackwell, 1996).

[24] Duncan Kennedy, "The Stakes of Law: Hale and Foucault," *Legal Studies Forum* 15 (1991): 327.

[25] Eugen Ehrlich, *Fundamental Principles of the Sociology of Law,* trans. Walter L. Moll (Cambridge: Harvard University Press, 1962).

sociology of law (studies through the University of Wisconsin), and some under the heading law and anthropology.

These ideas are found also in other places.

Our traditional focus on English political theories of eighteenth-century writers has tended to keep us from other political ideas that might have been important in fact, to a population that included substantial elements that were not English. Peter Kropotkin, the Russian anarchist prince, and Abraham Kuyper, then leader of the Dutch Anti-Revolutionary Party and later the country's prime minister, both visited America in the late nineteenth century.[26] Their writings help to illustrate two versions of nonstate federalism that could have been familiar to a hypothetical late-nineteenth-century American. These authors spoke from different, if not opposed, traditions; one is associated with the Left and anarchism,[27] the other with the religious Right and conservatism.[28] But their ideas could easily have been available to Americans thinking about political structures.

---

[26] See Paul Avrich, *Anarchist Portraits* (Princeton: Princeton University Press, 1988), 79–106 (discussing Kropotkin's tour of America); "Ex-Dutch Premier, Dr. A. Kuyper, Dead," *New York Times,* November 9, 1920, 15 (mentioning Kuyper's lecture tour of the United States).

[27] E.g., Kropotkin.

[28] Dirk Jellema makes it clear that it is difficult to categorize Abraham Kuyper: "[I]n the same year that an English historian dubbed him as a clerical reactionary, the leader of the Dutch anarchists saluted him as a kindred spirit." Jellema concludes his article on Kuyper by saying that he was the most notable figure produced by the Netherlands' Christian political movement. Dirk Jellema, "Abraham Kuyper's Attack on Liberalism," *Review of Politics* 19 (1957): 472, 485. Kuyper, who lived from 1837 to 1920, developed his ideas in the context of Dutch society, notably pluralistic and structured on the basis of religious and ideological "pillars." See generally David O. Moberg, "Religion and Society in the Netherlands and in America," *American Quarterly* 13 (1961): 172. Moberg suggests that this concept could be followed in the United States. It may be, in fact, that a study of Dutch society and its approach to problems of pluralism is important for any student of federalism, diversity, or tolerance. Harold R. Isaacs, *Idols of the Tribe: Group Identity and Political Change* (New York: Harper and Row, 1975; repr. Cambridge: Harvard University Press, 1989), 156–57. It may be that the high point of Dutch pluralism has passed. See Arend Lijphart, *Democracy in Plural Societies: A Comparative Exploration* (New Haven: Yale University Press, 1977), 52 (referring to the structure as consociationalism, or "segmented pluralism").

Kuyper's publications are largely available only in Dutch, though a few of his works have been translated into English. The commentary on his work often is written from within the Reformed Church and is published in religiously focused journals. Useful articles discussing Kuyper in one such journal include James D. Bratt, "Abraham Kuyper's Public Career," *Reformed Journal,* September 1987, 9, and George Marsden, "Where Have All the Theologians Gone?" *Reformed Journal,* April 1986, 2. The debate over Kuyper's theology is detailed in James Bratt, *Dutch Calvinism in Modern America: A History of a Conservative Subculture* (Grand Rapids, Mich.: W. B. Eerdmans, 1984), 14–33. See generally James W. Skillen, introduction to Abraham Kuyper, *The Problem of Poverty,* ed. Skillen (Washington, D.C.: Center for Public Justice, 1991), 9–22 (discussing Kuyper and his ideas); see also

Kuyper was in the United States in 1898 in part to receive an honorary degree at Princeton. The lectures that he gave at that time were published under the title *Calvinism*. His ideas are of interest here primarily because of their focus on antistate sovereignty arguments in a theological context. Kuyper's emphasis on what he called *sphere sovereignty* is strikingly parallel to that presented by other nontheological schools of political thought. Dirk Jellema provides a useful introduction to Kuyper's theoretical approach:

> Society is made up of social groups, related organically, rather than of individuals related impersonally. These groups, or spheres, received their sovereignty from God, not from the state. They are prior to the state. The state is necessary because of sin, and is due to God's *gratia universalis*. The state's function is to serve society; that is, to serve the social spheres which make up society. This means that the state's role is to uphold and strengthen the sovereignty of the social spheres. It has been the partial destruction of the sovereignty of these social spheres intermediate between individual and state which has brought about the present social crisis.
>
> These spheres include, in the narrow sense, such things as family, town, province, church, school, occupational groups; and, in the wider

---

James W. Skillen and Rockne M. McCarthy, eds., *Political Order and the Plural Structure of Society* (Atlanta: Scholars Press, 1991), 397 ("At the basis of Kuyper's entire social philosophy is his faith in the Trinitarian God who establishes or casts down, blesses or curses, all human formative efforts in culture and society"). The tradition of pillarization in the Netherlands undoubtedly provided a basis for at least one discussion of decentralization in education. See Rockne M. McCarthy, Donald Oppewal, Walfred Peterson, and Gordon Spykman, *Society, State, and Schools: A Case for Structural and Confessional Pluralism* (Grand Rapids, Mich.: W. B. Eerdmans, 1981), 141–43 (describing the system of educational pluralism in the Netherlands).

Ideas of decentralization and pluralist frameworks can take people to different places when they respond to specific political questions. Those influenced by Kuyper, for example, went in different directions on the New Deal. For some, Roosevelt's administration was understood as an extension of state power into fields better left alone. Bratt characterizes this as "reactionary Kuyperianism (*Dutch Calvinism*, 148–49). A "more moderate brand" of Dutch Calvinism tended to see the New Deal more positively, "approving of its Social Security, collective bargaining, and regulatory measures" (149). Still, Bratt concludes, "instinctive wariness of the state balanced every positive note with a precaution" (150).

Kuyper was described in the *Independent* as "the most prominent of Dutch theologians and . . . Professor of Hebrew and Dogmatic Theology in the Free University of Amsterdam. He is also a member of the Dutch Parliament and a leader of the Anti-Revolutionary Party, as well as editor of its organ, *The Daily Standard*." Abraham Kuyper, "False Theories of Sovereignty," *Independent* 50 (1898): 1918. See also John Witte Jr., "The Biography and Biology of Liberty: Abraham Kuyper and the American Experiment," in *Religion, Pluralism, and Public Life: Abraham Kuyper's Legacy for the Twenty-First Century*, ed. Luis E. Lugo (Grand Rapids, Mich.: W. B. Eerdmans, 2000), 243–62.

sense, such things as science, literature, art, ideology. The state may not interfere with the sovereignty of these spheres. Thus it may not interfere with municipal autonomy, or artistic freedom, or freedom of conscience, or freedom of speech, or freedom of education. A sound theoretical notion of freedom, said Kuyper, is possible only with a correct view of society, one which recognizes sphere sovereignty; otherwise there is no theoretical check on the power of the majority.

"Kuyper's social thought thus tends more towards syndicalism or Guild Socialism," Jellema writes, "than it does towards a hierarchically organized corporative state." But clearly, "Society is not arranged vertically but horizontally. The state's task is to protect the social spheres." Jellema notes, "This may, of course, mean extensive state intervention in certain cases, notably when a social sphere is too weak to exercise its true sovereignty; then the state must help it become strong. Each sphere has its own specific sovereignty which it must not go beyond; if it attempts to, the state must intervene."[29]

In addressing the problem of conflict between the spheres and the issue of government regulation of the spheres, Kuyper would have authorized state intervention in only three cases:

> 1. if different spheres should clash, the State government may compel mutual regard for the boundary lines of each; 2. it may also intervene to defend individuals in those spheres against abuse of power by others (e.g. in the case of excessive unemployment, cruelty to a child); 3. it may coerce all spheres to contribute financially and with whatever means are necessary to maintain the natural unity of the State.[30]

Kuyper saw some of the problems of conflict between spheres, but he also seemed to assume solutions in particular intellectual contexts. If, for example, we believed in the "natural unity" of states, we probably would not be so concerned about creating institutions to define and preserve that unity.[31] Moreover, James Bratt raises a "troubling question that Kuyper never resolved."[32] The question is, "What place would the secular have in the reformed nation? How could Kuyper simultaneously assert, as he

[29] Jellema, "Kuyper's Attack on Liberalism," 482–83 (citations omitted).

[30] Anthony H. Nichols, "The Educational Doctrines of Abraham Kuyper: An Evaluation," *Journal of Christian Education*, August 1975, 26, 35.

[31] See generally Ivo Schöffer, "Abraham Kuyper and the Jews," in Michman, *Dutch Jewish History*, 237; "The Jews in the Netherlands: The Position of a Minority through Three Centuries," *Studia Rosenthakiana* 15 (1981): 85, 97–98. Schöffer refers to Kuyper as "the founder of the Calvinist 'pillar'" and notes that Kuyper "would have preferred the Jews to retire within their close community also, sacrificing so to speak what he considered their wrong-headed emancipation" (97).

[32] Bratt, *Dutch Calvinism*, 26.

did, pluralistic tolerance and spiritualized politics?"[33] Bratt also suggests that Kuyper's assumption that "a high degree of harmony and equity naturally existed among [the spheres]" is problematic.[34] It also has been noted that "Kuyper's political philosophy does not grow and deepen to the point where he is able to elaborate the notion of public justice as the norm of state life."[35]

The pluralist vision and the detailed questions it raises are visible again when we look at the ideas of Peter Kropotkin.[36] Kropotkin outlined one version of his view of federalism in his autobiography, *Memoirs of a Revolutionist*:

> We saw that a new form of society is germinating in the civilized nations, and must take the place of the old one. . . . This society will be composed of a multitude of associations, federated for all the purposes which require federation: trade federations for production of all sorts,—agricultural, industrial, intellectual, artistic; communes for consumption, making provision for dwellings, gas works, supplies of food, sanitary arrangements, etc.; federations of communes among themselves, and federations of communes with trade organizations; and finally, wider groups covering all the country, or several countries, composed of men who collaborate for the satisfaction of such economic, intellectual, artistic, and moral needs as are not limited to a given territory. All these will combine directly, by means of free agreements between them.[37]

[33] Ibid.

[34] Ibid.

[35] Skillen and McCarthy, *Political Order*, 402 (noting that while Kuyper sees that the "government's task is to protect confessional and societal pluralism," the meaning of public justice is loose and ambiguous).

[36] Prince Peter Kropotkin was born in Moscow in 1842 to a Russian aristocratic family. He worked as a geologist and zoologist, developing in the course of his investigations a critical perspective on Darwinian theory that is reflected in his book *Mutual Aid*. See Ashley Montagu, foreword to Peter Kropotkin, *Mutual Aid* (Boston: Extending Horizon Books, 1955). In that book Kropotkin wrote that "neither the crushing powers of the centralized State nor the teachings of mutual hatred and pitiless struggle which came, adorned with the attributes of science, from obliging philosophers and sociologists, could weed out the feeling of human solidarity, deeply lodged in men's understanding and heart, because it has been nurtured by all our preceding evolution" (292). In the course of his career as a philosophical anarchist, Kropotkin was arrested and imprisoned several times. He spent many years living in Europe and England and made two visits to the United States. After the 1917 revolution, the Kropotkin family returned to Russia, where he died in 1921.

[37] Peter Kropotkin, *Memoirs of a Revolutionist* (New York: Horizon Press, 1968). Kropotkin's "Memoirs" originally were published in the *Atlantic Monthly*. See Peter Kropotkin, "The Autobiography of a Revolutionist," *Atlantic Monthly*, September 1898, 346, through September 1899, 410. The forum suggests a general audience.

He noted that

> there will be full freedom for the development of new forms of produc-
> tion, invention, and organization; individual initiative will be encour-
> aged, and the tendency toward uniformity and centralization will be
> discouraged. Moreover, this society will not be crystallized into certain
> unchangeable forms, but will continually modify its aspect, because it
> will be a living, evolving organism; no need of government will be felt,
> because free agreement and federation take its place in all those func-
> tions which governments consider as theirs at the present time, and
> because, the causes of conflict being reduced in number, those conflicts
> which may still arise can be submitted to arbitration.[38]

Kropotkin's ideas, and those of anarchism generally, always have been
associated with a no-government position. But Kropotkin was led quite
naturally to emphasize not only no-government, but also limited government[39] and on decentralization and communitarianism. In this respect,
Kropotkin can be associated with movements ranging from guild socialism to syndicalism, which saw the state's role as providing a framework
within which group life would be possible.[40]

Kropotkin summarized his general position in a speech he gave in the
United States, in which he declared that mankind's progress "points in
the direction of less government of man by man, of more liberty for the
individual, of freer scope for the development of all individual faculties,
for the greatest development of the initiative of the individual, for home
rule for every separate unit, and for decentralization of power.[41] Kropotkin also said,

> I am a strong federalist ... and I think that even under the present
> conditions the functions of government could be with great advantage
> decentralized territorially. Your theory of home rule in America I con-
> sider a distinct step in advance of the European centralized state, and
> it ought to continue in all directions.[42]

---

[38] Kropotkin, *Memoirs of a Revolutionist*, 398–99.

[39] These issues arise in Pierre Proudhon's work as well. See Richard Vernon, introduction
to Pierre Joseph Proudhon, *The Principle of Federation,* trans. Richard Vernon (Toronto:
University of Toronto Press, 1979), xi, xiv– xvi (noting the conflict between Proudhon's
ideas of anarchism and federalism). See generally Alan Ritter, *The Political Thought of
Pierre-Joseph Proudhon* (Princeton: Princeton University Press, 1969), 155–60 (discussing
Proudhon's theory of federalism as a view of minimal government).

[40] For an account of Kropotkin, see Avrich, *Anarchist Portraits,* 53–106.

[41] Ibid., 87–88.

[42] Ibid., 85.

English pluralism was also seen as a direct attack on the conventional theory of the state. Laski wrote,

> The medieval worship of unity in fact is inherited by the modern state; and what changes in the four centuries of its modern history is simply the place in which the controlling factor of unity is to be found. To the Papacy it seemed clear that in medieval times that the power to bind and loose had given it an authority without limit or question. The modern state inherits the papal prerogative. It must, then, govern all; and to govern all there must be no limit to the power of those instruments by which it acts.[43]

Although in America there was no "immediately sovereign body,"[44] as in England or France, the idea of the sovereignty of the people, operating through the device of representation, came to roughly the same point. But, said Laski, echoing Maitland, once it becomes clear that "the state is only a species of a larger genus,"[45] other issues emerge. Churches deny the state absolute sovereignty, "by which they mean that the canons of [the church's] life are not subject to the control of [the state's] instruments."[46] Because of this, Laski said, "there will be instances in which the state may find it wise to forego its claim to supremacy. Acts of authority are thus limited by the consciences that purposes different from that of the state can command."[47]

An easy adjunct to English political pluralism was the rejection of the definition of law as commands emanating from the state, in favor of a definition seeing Austinianism only as a form of prejudice or convention. The idea was that each group could issue its own law and provide authority for that law.[48] Along with the insistence on the importance and independence of group life came a view of the social order as one based not on law-as-command but on some principle of association. Thus, G. D. H. Cole, writing in 1920, criticized classical political theory for treating the

---

[43] Harold Laski, *Authority in the Modern State* (New Haven: Yale University Press, 1919), 23. American political federalism, as early Laski saw it, did little to change this picture. "The multiplicity of governmental powers demanded by the federal system makes no difference; it is merely a question of administrative convenience" (25–26).

The work of the English pluralists is still invoked in American discussion of these issues, though, as Nancy Rosenblum has noted, Americans tend not to follow the English pluralist approach on issues of "autonomy and priority." Nancy Rosenblum, *Membership and Morals* (Princeton: Princeton University Press, 1998), 42–43.

[44] Ibid., 25.

[45] Ibid., 27.

[46] Ibid.

[47] Ibid., 45.

[48] For a general discussion of legal pluralism, see Griffiths, "What Is Legal Pluralism?"

state as the "embodiment and representative of the social consciousness," so that "over against the State and its actions and activities, this form of theory has set indiscriminately the whole complex of individuals and other associations and institutions, and has treated all their manifestations as individual actions."[49] Cole argued that this was a false view, arising "mainly from the conception of human society in terms of force and Law."[50] This view, said Cole, "begins at the wrong end, with the coercion which is applied to men in Society, and not with the motives which hold men together in association."[51] Cole saw three sources of live social theory for his time: the church, industry (including Marxist and guild socialist thought), and history (where he included Gierke and Maitland with their stress on association).[52] A later discussion by G. D. H. and Margaret Cole offered this description of groups and the state: "Every modern society is a network of associations. Very often, these particular associations are spoken of as if they existed, in some sense 'within the State, and even as if they owed their being to the State's willingness to grant them recognition.'"[53] It is true, the Coles wrote, that the state's attitude toward an association can be immensely important to it.[54] And while group consciousness is ordinarily not a problem, it sometimes produces conflict between the group's members and the state; "it may at any time affect them, calling up a loyalty which will influence their behaviour and perhaps bring them into group conflict with other groups or associations or with the state itself."[55]

English pluralism of the early part of the twentieth century thus differed substantially from American interest group pluralism. The English idea was that group life was real, independent of, and often competing with, the state. English pluralism saw state behavior as bounded by the behavior of other groups, with law emanating from several sources. American interest group pluralism, on the other hand, saw the various interest groups as competing for the largess of the central state. This approach did not diminish the state in theory, as English pluralism tended to, but rather saw the state as the monitor of competition for the allocation of limited re-

---

[49] G. D. H. Cole, *Social Theory* (New York: Frederick A. Stokes, 1920), 6.

[50] Ibid., 7.

[51] Ibid.

[52] Ibid. If one looks for the sources of guild socialism, one finds, in addition to political pluralism, the tradition of English utopianism and "distributivism," the program of Belloc and Chesterton. See Gilbert Chesterton, *The Napoleon of Notting Hill* (New York: John Lane, 1904); see generally S. T. Glass, *The Responsible Society* (London: Longmans, 1966).

[53] G. D. H. Cole and Margaret Cole, *A Guide to Modern Politics* (New York: A. Knopf, 1934), 370–71.

[54] Ibid., 372.

[55] Ibid., 372–73.

sources.[56] Although the English pluralists did not all believe the same thing, they had strong points in common. It has been said that "[t]he chief political interest of Cole's scheme, or of other contemporary schemes in the English pluralist mold, lies of course in the proposed dissolution of the state, understood here as a set of central institutions invested with final authority and wielding coercive power."[57] Pluralism was "a movement which set out above all to devolve responsibilities, to reinforce horizontal relationships, and to dispense with or at least divide up vertical ones."[58]

Several critiques of English pluralist thought have been made. Hocking wrote that pluralists stop short of the only thing that would matter—an attack on the issue of force. Pluralism "proposes no return to the former distribution of armed forces among the various social powers. It does not advocate the abolition of force against recalcitrant citizens and groups."[59] Hocking thus concluded that "so long as the locus of force remains untouched, political pluralism is hardly more than an assertion of the importance of group authority and of its migrations and an appeal for modest deference to these and other authorities on the part of governments."[60] It is possible that this modest deference is all that is asked for by present advocates of group life. At the same time, a deeper appreciation of group life is sometimes suggested, and if some deeper sense of pluralism is invoked, serious questions about the meaning of pluralist theory must be confronted.

The questions have often been suggested. Nicholls, for example, criticizes Figgis by suggesting that he was not sufficiently explicit either on the "extent to which the state might interfere with groups"[61] or the cir-

---

[56] On American interest group pluralism, as contrasted with English political pluralism, see Anthony H. Nicholls, *Three Varieties of Pluralism* (London: Macmillan, 1974) (discussing Bentley, Truman, Dewey, Lippmann, Latham, and Dahl). Cultural pluralism is yet another idea that may not discuss the theory of the state at all, but simply refers to the fact or desirability of various different communities within the state. See David Myers and Nomi Stolzenberg, "Community, Constitution, and Culture: The Case of the New York Kehillah," *Michigan Journal of Law Reform* 25 (1992): 633.

[57] Richard Vernon, foreword to G. D. H. Cole, *Guild Socialism Restated* (New Brunswick, N.J.: Transaction Books, 1920), xxxv.

[58] Ibid. Guild socialism, in Cole's version at least, tried to be rid of the state. See G. D. H. Cole and Walter Lippmann, *Public Opinion* (New York: Harcourt, Brace, 1922), 296 (noting that, functionally, the coordinator seemed to have all the power of the state). Other guild socialists saw the state as an arbiter. See generally A. Wright, *G. D. H. Cole and Socialist Democracy* (Oxford: Clarendon Press, 1979); Wright, "Guild Socialism Revisited," *Journal of Contemporary History* 9 (1974): 165–80.

[59] William E. Hocking, *Man and the State* (New Haven: Yale University Press; London: H. Milford, Oxford University Press, 1926), 88.

[60] Ibid. See also Francis W. Coker, *Recent Political Thought* (New York: D. Appleton-Century, 1934), 497–517 (examining pluralistic attack on state sovereignty).

[61] Nicholls, *Three Varieties of Pluralism*, 13.

cumstances in which the state might interfere. "The formal freedom of the individual to leave the group may be nullified in practice by powerful economic and social pressures. Also, may there not be groups whose way of life cripples the character of their members?"[62] Other difficulties with pluralism were suggested by the American Mary Parker Follett in 1918:

> Society . . . does not consist merely of the union of all these various groups. There is a more subtle process going on—the interlocking of groups. And in these interlocking groups we have not only the same people taking up different activities, but actually representing different interests. In some groups I may be an employer, in others an employee. . . . The state cannot be composed of groups because no group nor any number of groups can contain the whole of me, and the ideal state demands the whole of me.[63]

Yet another problem is suggested by the possibility that underneath the English pluralist approach is a commitment to a society based on fundamental value consensus.[64] If this is true, how useful can the English pluralism of the first half of the twentieth century be to us, when it is exactly the existence of that consensus on important questions that is in doubt?

At the same time, it would also seem impossible to be committed to pluralist group life without seriously examining historical pluralist thought. Cole wrote that "the demand for functional devolution"[65] meant

---

[62] Ibid.

[63] Mary Parker Follett, *The New State: Group Organization, the Solution of Popular Government* (New York: Longmans, Green, 1918), 289–90. Cf. Harold Laski, *Grammar of Politics* (New Haven: Yale University Press, 1925), 67 ("To exhaust the associations to which a man belongs is not to exhaust the man himself").

On Follett's sense of the importance of the state, see Coker, *Recent Political Thought*: "Miss Follett criticizes the pluralists' conception of the state as 'competing' for the citizen's loyalty; and she explains so fully the state's unifying functions, and its direct contact with individuals, that she is hardly to be classed properly among the pluralists" (513). See also Henry S. Kariel, *The Decline of American Pluralism* (Stanford: Stanford University Press, 1961), 157–63 (critiquing Follett's views on natural harmony and the creative role of conflict); Kariel, "The New Order of Mary Parker Follett," *Western Political Quarterly* 8 (1955): 425.

[64] See Vincent, *Theories of the State*, 182, 216.

[65] Guild socialism stressed functional units rather than geographic units. Morgan notes that while, in the eighteenth and nineteenth centuries, "the fiction of representation was sometimes explained and defended as a means by which all the different economic or social interests in a country had a voice in government," in fact, representation in England and America has always been geographic. Edmund Morgan, *Inventing the People* (New York: Norton, 1988), 41.

For a critique of guild socialism's idea of representation, see Robert Dahl, *Democracy and Its Critics* (1989), and for a discussion of guild socialism/syndicalism and fascist corpora-

"not a demand for the recognition of associations by the State, but a demand that the state itself should be regarded only as an association."[66] The state, he thought, might be the elder brother, "but certainly in no sense father of the rest."[67]

The last theoretician to be considered here is Alexander Pekelis.

"[O]ur devotion to the ideals of individual human dignity should not prevent us from realizing the limitations of individualism and emancipation or from recognizing the lasting value of the fundamental pluralistic traits of American society," Pekelis wrote. "Only to the extent, indeed, to which the United States is not a monolithic block, or a mere aggregate of individuals and not even a 'melting pot,' does it offer to the Jewish community, as such, a chance for survival in a modern setting."[68]

The approaches initiated by Marshall, and others in the 1920s were in effect expanded and conceptualized by Alexander Pekelis (1902–1946) in his tragically short career in America.

Pekelis, an Odessa-born Jew who studied in Europe, taught in Italy until 1938, when official anti-Semitism forced him to settle in Paris. In 1940, he emigrated to the United States. He studied at Columbia Law School, becoming editor in chief of the law review.[69] He died in a plane crash in 1946 while returning from a Zionist Congress.

Where Marshall is little remembered outside of the American Jewish community, Pekelis—like Nathan Isaacs—is recalled in mainstream scholarship.[70] His was a highly unusual voice in American legal scholarship, and his work could easily be considered with the work of others in the emigré generation (e.g., Kessler and Rheinstein) that brought civil law categories and experience to the United States. But where others left their mark within the academy, Pekelis worked in the world of the nonprofit agencies as what has been called a "Jewish civil servant." The work that

---

tism, see Cole and Cole, *Guide to Modern Politics,* 405. See also Soifer, "Freedom of Association," 364 (discussing American version of these ideas).

[66] G. D. H. Cole, "Conflicting Social Obligations," *Proceedings of the Aristotelian Society* (1915): 140; cf. Chafee, "Associations Not for Profit" (raising the possibility that the state is only another kind of association).

[67] Cole, "Conflicting Social Obligations," 159.

[68] Pekelis, "Full Equality in a Free Society," in *Law and Social Action,* 223.

[69] Pekelis taught at the New School and, in 1945, became chief consultant to the Commission on Law and Social Action of the American Jewish Congress. (The present author worked for the commission for some years after graduating from law school in 1961. The commission was then headed by Leo Pfeffer.)

[70] E.g., citation in Ellen Peters, *Commercial Law* (Indianapolis: Bobbs-Merrill, 1971), 64, of Alexander Pekelis, "Comparative Legal Techniques and Ideologies," *University of Michigan Law Review* (1943); also Mirjan R. Damaska, *The Faces of Justice and State Authority: A Comparative Approach to the Legal Process* (New Haven: Yale University Press, 1986), 118 n. 36f.

is left includes a number of law review articles, and the posthumous collection *Law and Social Action* (1950) edited by Milton Konvitz.

In *Law and Social Action,* Pekelis laid the framework for a political theory of *essential federalism,* based on crossing the public-private line in thinking about groups and governments.

On the one side, Pekelis worked on the problem of private government, stressing the impact that private governments have on the lives on individuals and urging the necessity of extending constitutional protections to those injured by the acts of private governments. On the other side, while on the staff of the American Jewish Congress, Pekelis worked out a scheme of group social action and self-government, within the context of Jewish issues and organizations, that worked toward the extension of group autonomy.

Pekelis understood the impact that community would have on political power: "When we see the individual challenging the power of the central authority he does not, as a rule, act as an individual. . . . He leans upon the power that even the smallest community has."[71]

Pekelis was, like Louis Marshall before him, concerned with the institutional forms of the semiautonomous community. In 1945, he wrote on the Jewish community and his program for the American Jewish Congress. "To state our basic belief at first negatively, we do not intend to define our task as that of a Jewish 'defense agency' or to confine it to the attempt of painless integration of individuals of Jewish faith or descent into the society in which they live."[72] He believed that many Jews "would be content if every single Jew—or at least those in the United States—were permitted to enjoy full and genuine political, economic, and social equality." And some would not reject assimilation to achieve this. Pekelis did not agree.[73]

He respected medievalism without concluding that it provided models for the contemporary situation. "The structure of modern societies makes the resurrection of Jewish autonomy in its traditional, *kahalistic* form as utterly impossible as it is undesirable."[74] While "we may recognize certain values inherent in the pluralistic structure of medieval societies," still, Pekelis insisted, "our stake and our share in the great struggles for individual freedom, the Renaissance and the Revolution, guarantee our immunity from the romantic virus of neomedievalism."[75] The problem then was to institutionalize cultural pluralism.

[71] Pekelis, "Legal Techniques," 68.
[72] Pekelis, "Full Equality," 279.
[73] Ibid.
[74] Ibid., 223.
[75] Ibid.

The philosophy and practice of cultural pluralism offer the opportunity for a new form of Jewish autonomy. Not as an "official" institution but as a private group, the Jewish community has a legitimate place in an essentially federalistic country, and can perform a wide variety of vital functions which in rigidly regimented societies are reserved either to governmental or at least to officially recognized agencies. To the extent to which the belief is preserved that American unity is achieved through a wide cultural and national diversity; to the extent that the United States guarantees to its minorities their first and basic right, that of fully preserving their minority characteristics; to the extent to which it is thus, in some sense, a multinational state; to the extent to which its centripetal forces do not destroy the autonomy of the social units comprising it—to the extent to which all this is true, America is immune to the totalitarian danger of rigid uniformity and American Jewry has a fighting chance for survival.[76]

Pekelis was concerned, however, with the failure of the pluralists to deal with problems of private government.

He noted that "*de facto,* private governments could escape constitutional controls, either because by the doctrines of monistic sovereignty they are not governments, or because by the doctrines of pluralism they are as sovereign as the nation, which has nothing to say about them."[77] Since, however, pluralists are, in general, "less logical than are monists, and since absolute pluralism is in itself as grave a contradiction as absolute relativism, the pluralistic theories can be considered as the forerunners of those which today advocate the limitation on the powers of *de facto* governments."[78]

Broadly speaking, Pekelis rejected the idea that the Constitution controlled government only: "I maintain that *the protection of individual rights is the primary, direct, and basic content of constitutional guarantees rather than a derivative and indirect result of restraints on governmental power.*"[79]

Pekelis believed that the United States was peculiarly well suited to the sort of pluralist world he envisioned. "The Jewish cause in the United States thus depends on the traditional American aversion to a leveling centralized government and to the compulsory uniformity of all members of a society. It partakes of all the difficulties and complexities inherent in a pluralistic conception of society and—which may be but another way

[76] Ibid.
[77] Pekelis, "Private Governments and the Federal Constitution," in *Law and Social Action,* 104.
[78] Ibid.
[79] Ibid., 105.

of putting it—a pluralistic conception of human personality." The philosophy he put forward "claims our right to be, at the same time, loyal, devoted, and selfless members of a great variety of overlapping groups—American citizens and citizens of the world; American Jews and members of a world Jewish community; citizens of a state and citizens of a village; members of a political party and members of a religious association." Pekelis would speak from the experience of the Soviet Union and Italy in saying that "[t]his is a right unthinkable in a simplified, monolithic society, a right dreaded by all kinds of totalitarian tyrants but truly inestimable to free men."[80]

Pekelis elaborated his positions carefully. His arguments for government involvement in a number of areas assume the modern welfare state, including an expansive role for judges, while at the same time he insisted on the right of minority groups to self-determination at critical points. He too rejected the image of the melting pot in favor of Horace Kallen's "cultural pluralism." He meant by that more than cultural diversity, however, as is clear from his ideas on the self-regulation of internal communities, which would be parallel to the regulation of the outside community.

One structure that had been attempted to protect minority rights was the treaty system that had been undertaken by the League of Nations. Because that experiment forms a part of the experience of twentieth-century pluralist theoreticians, it is useful to discuss it here. The League experience is used to open the issue of groups as self-evident, as they are often taken to be, as against the idea of groups as defined in many different ways in different contexts.

---

[80] Pekelis, "Full Equality," 224.

CHAPTER 7

The Minority Treaties of the League of Nations

> The co-existence of several nations under the same State is a
> test, as well as the best security of its freedom. It is also one of
> the chief instruments of civilization; and, as such, it is in the
> natural and providential order, and indicates a state of greater
> advancement than the national unity which is the ideal of mod-
> ern liberalism.
>
> —LORD ACTON, "Nationality"

✦ AN experiment under the League of Nations was established under the
treaties imposed on a number of nations after the First World War whose
purpose, at least in part, was the protection of certain minorities, particularly ethnic, linguistic, and religious. These treaties were between governments, in the conventional sense.[1] They preserved the general structure of
the nation-state while attempting to give rights to certain minorities.
These treaties, broadly speaking, assured the rights of internal minorities
in countries whose majority populations were understood to be different
ethnically, nationally, or religiously. The treaties were signed between
1919 and 1920 by the Allies with five states: Poland, Czechoslovakia,
Romania, Yugoslavia, and Greece.[2]

---

[1] Thus the idea that the groups themselves might be sovereign and party to treaties is not
invoked here.

An initial caveat is in order. To say that rights are guaranteed by treaties or constitutions
is not to say that they will be honored in fact, or even that they will be ultimately vindicated
by a judicial system theoretically committed to the rule of law when they are violated by
governments that reject the rule of law. There are examples of constitutional statements too
unreal even to be considered in the category of legal propositions expressive of values even
when they are not the instrumental values of the society. And a rule of law that is honored
in fact may, as in the case of group libel legislation in Nazi Germany, not operate to the
benefit of groups that are in theory the beneficiaries of such legislation.

[2] Romania, Yugoslavia (Serb, Croat, Slovene State), and Greece were on the Allied side
during the war. Poland and Czechoslovakia were new states. The nations bound by the
treaties might be also minorities in other states. Thus, Theodore S. Woolsey wrote in support
of the provisions on minorities, "We recall the repeated efforts of Prussia to stamp out
language and spirit of nationality in her Polish subjects and still more those of Russia." "The

Some states (e.g., Albania) made declarations to the League on the question of minority rights. Minorities clauses were incorporated in treaties with four defeated states: Turkey, Austria, Bulgaria, and Hungary.

It was stressed in 1945 that the objective of the treaties, though involving protection of minorities, had not been primarily humanitarian, but rather political. Reviewing various forms of international protection, the former director of the Minorities Questions Section of the League of Nations, Pablo Azcárate, wrote, "The essential aim of [one kind of] protection might be to shield the minorities from the danger of oppression by the majorities and from the pain and suffering, both moral and material, which such oppression necessarily causes."[3]

A system like that could be called humanitarian. But the League system was not like that. "The object of the protection of minorities which those treaties committed to the League of Nations was to avoid the many interstate frictions and conflicts which had occurred in the past, as a result of the frequent ill-treatment or oppression of national minorities."[4]

The model for all the treaties was the Polish Minority Treaty, signed at Versailles in 1919. The treaty called for what were later termed negative and positive rights. The negative rights were what Americans would probably refer to as rights relating to equal treatment, or based on nondiscrimination.[5] The positive rights called for the state to act to promote group interests.

Rights of Minorities under the Treaty with Poland," *American Journal of International Law* 14 (1920): 392, 392.

[3] Pablo de Azcárate Y. Flórez, *League of Nations and National Minorities: An Experiment,* trans. Eileen E. Brooke (Washington, D.C.: Carnegie Endowment for International Peace, 1945), 14.

[4] Ibid. Writing in 1934, Macartney agreed that the treaties were not primarily humanitarian, seeing the goals as peace (first), through stability of the treaty countries (second), which had been often jeopardized by mistreatment of minorities (third). C. H. Macartney, *National States and National Minorities* (1934; New York: Russell and Russell 1968), 279. He also thought, as against the group or collective rights reading of the treaties (held then and now by various writers), that the treaties were essentially built on the modern idea of the nation-state, without intermediate sovereign or quasi-sovereign groups (283). Patrick Thornberry also writes that the treaties were not group centered. *International Law and the Rights of Minorities* (Oxford: Oxford University Press, 1991), 48.

More recently, Robert Cover read the treaties as premised on the idea "that the nation-state, ordinarily dominated by a single racial, religious, or ethnic group, might fail to afford the benefits of its political processes to the racial, religious, or ethnic minorities within the state." "The Origins of Judicial Activism in the Protection of Minorities," *Yale Law Journal* 91 (1982): 1287, 1298 (reading the treaties in relation to footnote 4 of *United States v. Carolene Products,* 304 U.S. 144, 152 n. 4 (1938)).

The treaties are also discussed in Hannah Arendt, *The Origins of Totalitarianism,* 2d ed. (New York: Meridian Books, 1958). The current discussion by political scientists and others has also revived interest in the treaties.

[5] See generally Paul Brest, "Foreword: In Defense of the Antidiscrimination Principle," *Harvard Law Review* 90 (1976): 1.

Articles 2, 7, 8, and 9 indicate the spirit and tone of all of the treaties. Article 2 provided that "[a]ll inhabitants of Poland shall be entitled to the free exercise, whether public or private, of any creed, religion or belief, whose practices are not inconsistent with public order or public morals."[6]

Article 7 provided for equality before the law and equal civil and political rights for all Polish nationals without distinction "as to race, language or religion."[7]

Article 8 provided:

Polish nationals who belong to racial, religious or linguistic minorities shall enjoy the same treatment and security in law and in fact as the other Polish nationals. In particular, they shall have an equal right to establish, manage and control at their own expense charitable, religious and social institutions, schools and other educational establishments, with the right to use their own language and to exercise their religion freely therein.[8]

Article 9 provided:

Poland [must] provide in the public educational system in towns and districts in which a considerable proportion of Polish nationals of other than Polish speech are residents adequate facilities for ensuring that in the primary schools the instruction shall be given to the children of such Polish nationals through the medium of their own language.[9]

The Polish government could, however, make the teaching of the Polish language obligatory. State funding of minority schools was also authorized where there "is a considerable proportion of . . . minorities."[10]

The Polish Minority Treaty contains two clauses directly referring to the rights of Jews (particularly Sabbatarian rights), a reference explained

[6] The Treaty with Poland, June 28, 1919, chap. 1, art. 2, 225 Consol, T.S. 412 (entered into force Jan., 10, 1920), reprinted in Thornberry, *Rights of Minorities,* 399, 400.

[7] Ibid., art. 7, in Thornberry, *Rights of Minorities,* 401.

[8] Ibid., art. 8, in Thornberry, *Rights of Minorities,* 401.

[9] Ibid., art. 9, in Thornberry, *Rights of Minorities,* 401.

[10] Thornberry, *Rights of Minorities,* 402. As historian Salo W. Baron notes, there is a range of claims associated with the idea of group autonomy rights. One idea relates to control of schools, cultural institutions and the goal of a plural society. But in addition, he writes, wherever possible, "the minorities also sought to secure the right to collect a proportionate part of the governmental expenditures for schools, hospitals, and other cultural and charitable institutions." *Ethnic Minority Rights: Some Older and Newer Trends* (Oxford: Oxford Centre for Postgraduate Hebrew Studies, 1985), 4. And, he adds, in some cases "national minorities demanded, and occasionally obtained, quotas in political elections, for the most part in the form of electoral *curias* with each minority being allotted a percentage of officials to be elected equal to its percentage in the population" (4). On this issue at the peace conference, see David Hunter Miller, *My Diary: At the Conference of Paris* (New York: Appeal Printing Company, 1924), May 16, 1919, 13:56.

by Georges Clemenceau, president of the peace conference, as necessitated by the history of the Jews in Poland.[11] In his letter transmitting the Polish treaty, Clemenceau wrote as to the special provisions for Jews:

> The information at the disposal of the Principal Allied and Associated Powers as to the existing relations between the Jews and the other Polish citizens has led them to the conclusion that, in view of the historical development of the Jewish question and the great animosity aroused by it, special protection is necessary for the Jews of Poland. These clauses have been limited to the minimum which seems necessary under the circumstances of the present day, viz. the maintenance of Jewish schools and the protection of the Jews in the religious observance of their Sabbath. It is believed that these stipulations will not create any obstacle to the political unity of Poland. They do not constitute any recognition of the Jews as a separate political community within the Polish State.[12]

The treaties generally are viewed as a failure.[13] They did not prevent the Second World War and they did not ultimately protect vulnerable minorities. And of course they were politically suspect insofar as they

---

[11] Letter from Clemenceau to M. Paderewski, June 24, 1919, in *A History of the Peace Conference of Paris,* ed. H. W. V. Temperley (London: H. Frowde and Hodder and Stoughton, 1921), 5:432 (transmitting the treaty to M. Paderewski, one of the signers for Poland). For Paderewski's view on the treaties generally, see his comments in Miller, *My Diary,* 171–79 (Report of Committee on New States, Memorandum by M. Paderewski, dated June 15, 1919).

See generally on the Jews in Poland in the period of the First World War, Arthur L. Goodhart, *Poland and the Minority Races* (New York: Brentano's, 1920). Goodhart was counsel to a fact-finding mission appointed by President Wilson to investigate reports of the murder of Jews in Poland.

Other treaties mentioned other minorities specifically. See e.g., Thornberry, *Rights of Minorities,* 43 (referring to the Szeklers and Saxons of Transylvania, the Vlachs of Greece, and the Ruthenes of the Carpathians).

In addition, some treaties made provisions for the application of personal (Muslim) law. E.g., the Serb-Croat-Slovene Treaty, art. 10, reprinted in Temperley, *Peace Conference of Paris,* 451.

See also the treaty with Czechoslovakia, providing in article 10 that Czechoslovakia undertakes to constitute the Ruthene territory as "an autonomous unit within the Czecho-Slovak State, and to accord to it the fullest degree of self-government compatible with the unity of the Czecho-Slovak state." Treaty between the Principal Allied and Associate Powers and Czecho-Slovakia, September 10, 1919, art. 10, no. 20, cmd. 479, quoted in Temperley, *Peace Conference of Paris,* 465. In general, the treaties did not speak of autonomous units.

For a description of minorities covered by the treaties, see Macartney, *National States,* 518–42 (appendix 3).

[12] Letter from Clemenceau to M. Paderewski, June 24, 1919, in Temperley, *Peace Conference of Paris,* 436.

[13] See generally Jacob Robinson et al., *Were the Minorities Treaties a Failure?* (New York: Institute of Jewish Affairs of the American Jewish Congress and the World Jewish Congress,

were imposed by the victors on others, but not on themselves, despite the fact that the victors also had significant minorities to deal with.[14] But the failures of the treaties are not the only effects recalled by those who have evaluated the treaties. Jacob Robinson and his coauthors, for example, saw the strengths of the system, and more recently, Natan Lerner has said:

> Among the merits of the system, the following should be stressed: Minority schools were established in several countries; neglected groups were rehabilitated; forced assimilation was resisted; and representatives of democratic minority groups could play a role in the political affairs of countries such as Czechoslovakia and Latvia. Moreover, the methods of mediation and conciliation produced some results, and the Permanent Court of International Justice contributed to the protection of minorities with important decisions, of great value even today.[15]

David Weissbrodt, one of a number of contemporary authorities in the field of human rights to include a discussion of the Minorities Treaties as a background to a current discussion, sees the system as "the first extensive multilateral system for the protection of minorities."[16]

A failure or not, the treaties were superseded by the current United Nations materials on international human rights.[17] It is often noted, however, that the current material does not focus explicitly on issues of minorities, or indeed of collectivities, but largely addresses issues in terms of the rights of individuals. This is sometimes viewed as a weakness in the present human rights effort. But it is also possible to see the question differ-

---

1943). For recent discussions on the rights of groups and indigenous populations, see generally Crawford, *The Rights of Peoples* (collecting essays on the subject of peoples or group rights in the international context); symposium, "The Rights of Ethnic Minorities," *Notre Dame Law Review* 66 (1991): 1195 (collecting essays on national, ethnic, and minority rights); Natan Lerner, *Group Rights and Discrimination in International Law* (Boston: M. Nijhoff, 1991). Articles on human rights often include at least a brief description of the Minorities Treaties as background to current issues. See, e.g., András B. Baka, "The European Convention on Human Rights and the Protection of Minorities under International Law," *Connecticut Journal of International Law* 8 (1993): 227.

The League in 1922 also adopted a provision referring to the obligation of loyalty to the state that was imposed on the minorities. See Asbjorn Eide, "Minority Situation: In Search of Peaceful and Constructive Solutions," *Notre Dame Law Review* 66 (1991): 1311, 1319.

For a detailed examination of the treaty provisions, see also Robinson et. al., *Minorities Treaties a Failure,* 36ff.

[14] Robinson et al. in *Minorities Treaties a Failure* offer an elaborate statement of the problems. In 1934, Poland in effect renounced its duties under the Minorities Treaties. (Robinson et al., *Minorities Treaties a Failure,* 178–79). By 1939, Thornberry concluded, the system had stopped functioning (*Rights of Minorities,* 46).

[15] Quoted in Lerner, *Group Rights,* 11.

[16] David Weissbrodt, "Human Rights: An Historical Perspective," in *Human Rights,* ed. Peter Davies (Guernsey: Guernsey Press, 1991), 1, 3.

[17] See Thornberry, *Rights of Minorities,* 52 ff.

ently. Arcot Krishnaswami, rapporteur of the United Nations Sub-Commission on Prevention of Discrimination and Protection of Minorities, writing in 1960, understood that the limitation to specified groups in the Minorities Treaties was a weakness. The guarantees "applied only in respect of members of racial, religious or linguistic minorities."[18]

The Minorities Treaties are the products of an intellectual world in which several different issues are treated as self-evident. The first relates to political units. The second is membership, that is, who is actually a member of a linguistic or religious or ethnic group. A third issue is the question of categories, and the distinct issue of which memberships are important, or which community memberships are relevant for what purposes.

Emancipation operates to free individuals from the restraints of groups. In modern conceptions of religious liberty, religious group membership is voluntary, at least as understood by the state. Exit from a group is a serious possibility, because, in effect, emancipation simultaneously opens both the doors of the larger society and the doors of the community. A situation in which everyone has to be a member of some community and exit from one either involves membership in another (conversion) or outlaw status is quite different from a situation in which state citizenship is a residual category for everyone and group membership is a private associative option. Emancipation and assimilation produce exits from communities, as well as changes in those communities. It may be noted on this point that groups themselves often adopt different definitions of affiliation. For some groups exit is impossible, at least from the point of view of the group. The state's answer to that question, where it becomes relevant, is often different depending on the legal system of the country in which the question is raised. In some legal systems (e.g., the United States), the issue turns almost entirely on a right to voluntary association or personal affiliation and commitment. In others, the matter is decided on the basis of formal religious or racial definitions. Group sanctions continue to exist, but some, such as expulsion and excommunication, operate most effectively on those most strongly identified with traditional structures. Thus the claim of the group to a permanent and irrevocable affilia-

---

[18] Krishnaswami, "Study of Discrimination," 12. Arcot Krishnaswami (M.A., Cambridge, and Ph.D., London), an Indian barrister, published *The Indian Union and the States,* a book on Indian federalism, in 1964. In the Universal Declaration of Human Rights, "Everyone has the right to freedom of thoughts, conscience and religion" (Krishnaswami, "Study of Discrimination," 12). See also the International Covenant on Civil and Political Rights: "In those States in which ethnic, religious or linguistic minorities exist, persons belonging to such minorities shall not be denied the right, in community with the other members of their group, to enjoy their own culture, to profess and practice their own religion, or to use their own language" ("International Covenant on Civil and Political Rights," December 19, 1966, art. 27, *United Nations Treaty Service* 999, 171).

tion is one that in the modern situation can be simply denied by an individual who chooses to reject the group and, in effect, move away into the larger society. The more open the social and practical situation, the more real the possibility of exit.

Self-evidence in this area seems to be created by history and experience. It might be said that those memberships for which people kill or die—now, in this place—are the relevant ones. Frankfurter wrote as a member of the most "vilified and persecuted minority in history."[19] His minority status had been relevant all too often.

Yet even here, one might wonder if this has not to do as much with cultural perceptions as universal truth. Those memberships for which people kill or die may be more complex than we are accustomed to think. We can attach the label *class* or *economic* to issues for which people have killed and died in the name of labels relating to race or ethnicity. Those persecuted for religious heresy may "really" (that is, through another lens) have been persecuted for intelligence or deviance. Physical differences and whether or not they are considered significant or disabling, differences or age or sex and whether they are judged positively or negatively in particular contexts, are similarly complex.[20] Individual group and national histories all bear the marks of construction and imagination.

Central to the question of minorities is the problem of identities and identification. It is not merely the question who or what is a minority, a highly contested issue in itself. It is also the general question, "Who, as individual, is a member of a minority group?" This relates essentially to another: "Who wants to know and for what purpose?" Some of the complications of this question are familiar. They may be illustrated here by a figure in Rebecca West's *Black Lamb and Grey Falcon*. In this book, Constantine is a poet and a Serb, "that is to say a Slav member of the Orthodox Church, from Serbia."[21] We are also told that his mother was a Polish Jew. His father was a Russian Jew. Constantine is "by adoption only, yet quite completely, a Serb."[22] Constantine would seem to have various possible identifications. And his is, perhaps, an entirely common case.

---

[19] *West Virginia State Bd. of Educ. v. Barnette,* 319 U.S. 624, 646 (1943) (Frankfurter, J., dissenting).

[20] Consider, for example, left-handedness or unusual weight. See Clyde H. Farnsworth, "Anti-woman Bias Basis for Asylum," *New York Times,* February 2, 1993, A8 (discussing sex-based persecution as a basis for asylum in Canada). It is common for gays and lesbians to be referred to as minorities denied rights. On whether a physical characteristic is an asset or a liability, see H. G. Wells, *The Country of the Blind and Other Stories* (New York: T. Nelson and Sons, 1911), 536–68.

[21] Rebecca West, *Black Lamb and Grey Falcon: A Journey through Yugoslavia* (1941; New York: Penguin, 1982), 41.

[22] Ibid.

There are cases in which one particular form of identification trumps all others, either in mind of the individuals or the practice an outside group. Constantine would have been a Jew under some definitions and usages.[23] People are in fact defined often by one measure, often a group into which they have been born.[24] But in the American setting at least we have focused more and more on self-definition and on limiting the impact of those identifications that are not voluntary and on permitting freer choices of identities over a lifetime.[25] Some of the contexts in which we deal with these issues are difficult and even technical.[26] The basic point, however, is that as a culture we are concerned about ascribed statuses.

It is clear that the central issue of those pluralist structures with which we are familiar, the millet system of the Ottoman Empire[27] perhaps, or the pillars of Dutch pluralism,[28] is that from the point of view of problems of individual identity, the structure itself imposes an answer to the question, "Which identity matters most?" (It may also impose an answer to the question, "How do we determine that identity?") But it may be that the millet system and the pillars of the Dutch—petrified versions of what we commonly invoke as a "rainbow"[29]—are not the answer for a perma-

---

[23] On what it means (in terms of religion or nationality) to be a Jew in different nation-state systems, see Salo W. Baron, *History and Jewish Historians: Essays and Addresses* (Philadelphia: Jewish Publication Society of America, 1964), 19.

[24] Aviam Soifer, "On Being Overly Discrete and Insular: Involuntary Groups and the Anglo-American Judicial Tradition," *Washington and Lee Law Review* 48 (1991): 381.

[25] See generally Lawrence M. Friedman, *Total Justice* (New York: Russell Sage Foundation, 1985).

[26] For a difficult context, see Schneider, "Religion and Child Custody." For a technical context, see Carolyn C. Jones, "Split Income and Separate Spheres: Tax Law and Gender Roles in the 1940s," *Law and History Review* 6 (fall 1988): 259.

[27] *Millet* is a term "for the organized recognized religion-political communities enjoying certain rights of autonomy under their own chiefs." Bernard Lewis, *The Political Language of Islam* (Chicago: University of Chicago Press, 1988), 39. See also Leon Ostrorog, *The Angora Reform* (London: University of London Press, 1927): "[I]n its spirit of extreme liberalism towards non-Moslem creeds, Mohammedan Law prescribes not only tolerance of, but strict non-interference with anything which, in the Mohammedan conception, is considered as being within the province of the special religious beliefs of Jews and Christians" (79).

[28] Pillarization refers to a system of differentiation in which the major social, political, and cultural institutions are segmented along religious-ideological lines. Lijphart, *Democracy in Plural Societies*, 5, calls it *consociationalism*.

[29] See Kathleen M. Sullivan, "Rainbow Republicanism," *Yale Law Journal* 97 (1988): 1713; Tony Hiss, "The End of the Rainbow," *New Yorker*, April 12, 1993, 43–44 (discussing the Rainbow Curriculum in New York City). On a "rainbow coalition," see Iris Marion Young, "Polity and Group Differences: A Critique of the Ideal of Universal Citizenship," *Ethics* 99 (January 1989): 250, 264. Note that the rainbow is limited to primary colors on a spectrum that we can see. It is used as an image of diversity, but in fact may not be the image we need.

nent or semipermanent structure. These work for a period of time when a number of groups are known, established, and of conceded importance within a particular society. Thus, Arend Lijphart suggested some time ago that the high point of Dutch pluralism—in the sense of pillarization—might already have been reached, and that now the society was not so segmented.[30] (Perhaps this is so because ethnic or religious affiliation is no longer as important as it once was, though class differences might remain significant.)[31] Or it might be that in the Dutch case even a society once segmented, then integrated, is now simply to be segmented again, but along different lines, as by the entry of new immigrants.[32] In which case there might be a role for pillars again.

Horace Kallen's "cultural pluralism," while the term sticks, may not be the answer either. To begin with, cultural pluralism is a description finally of an attitude toward difference and, at least as currently used, suggests no particular structures. Further, to the extent that Kallen himself thought in terms of "perfection of men according to their kind," his terms raised problems. What is "my kind" is exactly the point at issue.[33] Kallen thought that certain identifications were permanent and natural: "[A]n Irishman is always an Irishman, a Jew is always a Jew. Irishman or a Jew is born; citizen, lawyer or church-member is made. Irishman and Jew are facts in nature; citizen and church member are artifacts in civilization."[34] It is a stance that omits a fair number of questions—they are, in fact, involved in the limitations of the Minorities Treaties.

[30] Lijphart thinks that its high point is past because the society is no longer so fragmented (*Democracy in Plural Societies*, 1–2, 52). But doesn't the introduction of the new immigrants into Dutch society raise similar questions again?

[31] For a review of the American class structure, see generally Paul Fussell, *Class* (New York: Summit, 1984). See also *Memoirs of Michael Karolyi: Faith without Illusion*, trans. Catherine Karolyi (London: J. Cape, 1956), 15 (noting Karolyi's cousin's identification of himself, always, as an aristocrat).

See generally Jay A. Sigler, *Minority Rights: A Comparative Analysis* (Westport, Conn.: Greenwood Press, 1983).

[32] For writing on problems relating to new immigrants, see chapters 8 and 9 of Jeremy Boissevain and Jojada Verrips, eds., *Dutch Dilemmas: Anthropologists Look at the Netherlands* (Assen, the Netherlands: Van Gorcum, 1989). See also Janwillem Van de Wetering, *Outsider in Amsterdam* (New York: Pocket Books, 1978).

[33] Horace Meyer Kallen, *The Structure of Lasting Peace: An Inquiry into the Motives of War and Peace* (1918; New York: Haskell House, 1974). See also David A. Hollinger, *In the American Province: Studies in the History and Historiography of Ideas* (Bloomington: Indiana University Press: 1985); Milton M. Gordon, *Assimilation in American Life: The Role of Race, Religion, and National Origin* (Oxford: Oxford University Press, 1964), 141–45; Philip Gleason, "American Identity and Americanization," in *Harvard Encyclopedia of American Ethnic Groups*, ed. Stephen Thernstrom et al. (Cambridge: Belknap Press of Harvard University Press, 1981), 31. Kallen suggested some structures, including an internationalization of education (174).

[34] Kallen, *Structure of Lasting Peace*, 31.

The strength of the Minorities Treaties is the positive approach to the issue of minorities and group life. The limitation of the approach taken in those treaties is that in effect they perpetuate the understanding of group life that characterized the millet system or Dutch pillarization. That is, the treaties defined which particular group affiliations were important--as in fact they were--tending to make those affiliations important into the future.

If *groups* is shorthand for "created in fact or in meaning by individuals," saying that groups have rights is simply another way of saying that individuals have rights. Indeed, much of the American discussion is not about whether groups have rights but rather whether the group affiliations of individuals should be given more weight than has been traditional in the American legal system. Thus, when Aviam Soifer argues for the importance of group life or the historical group experience, he is not suggesting a shift to a group rights approach from an individual rights approach. Rather, he is adding depth to an individual right of association by adding a group dimension to our understanding of what is at stake in a controversy.

This observation may also be true of other academic explorations of these issues. When Yoram Dinstein says that the right to education must be thought of as a group right rather than an individual right because no individual can run a school, he seems to be saying simply that individuals can act collectively. He does not seem to be focused on a group right if by that we mean, for example, that the group right displaces any individual right of individuals (as it might under fascism, for example).[35] Indeed, Dinstein notes that "collective human rights retain their character as direct human rights" and are collective only in the sense, apparently, that "they shall be exercised jointly rather than severally."[36] Or perhaps they are collective because we believe that the individual has waived all rights by contract and given them to the group.[37]

---

[35] "Against individualism, the Fascist conception is for the State; and it is for the individual in so far as he coincides with the State." Benito Mussolini, "The Doctrine of Fascism," in *The Social and Political Doctrines of Contemporary Europe,* ed. Michael Oakeshott, 2d ed. (Cambridge: Cambridge University Press, 1941), 166.

And no groups, political, economic, or cultural, are outside the state. See generally Zeev Sternhell, "Fascist Ideology," in Laqueur, *Fascism,* 315.

Aviam Soifer has noted that at the time of the New Deal, "Odious comparisons to Mussolini's fascist brand of syndicalism helped to underscore a pervasive American distaste for government recognition of groups. Judicial opinions and lawyers' arguments are full of references to the contrast between good old American individualism and the treatment of people in old world group terms." "Freedom of Association: Indian Tribes, Workers, and Communal Ghosts," *Maryland Law Review* 48 (1989): 350, 366.

[36] Yoram Dinstein, "Collective Human Rights of Peoples and Minorities," *International Comparative Law Quarterly* 25 (1976): 102, 103.

[37] Does inalienable right mean only a right that others cannot take away? Does it include the idea that individuals or groups cannot alienate it? There was an attempt in at least one

A strong illustration of a group rights issue is a group's control over children lost through (illustratively) war, genocide, or even conventional adoptions. To the extent that the group has a claim independent of the claim or wishes of parents, one might say that this is a group right. But even here, the group can be understood as affiliated individuals, even though many of them are dead.[38]

From a certain point of view, the most powerful group claim is that of the state itself, for example, in enforcing compulsory education over the objection of parents. But even this circles back to the question of whether the state is or is not an association of individuals through real or fictional consent.

The debate over group rights is based fundamentally on the idea that individuals who have been persecuted as a group should be acknowledged as a group in any public remedies. This, more than logical necessity, would seem to justify reference to particular religious groups, for example, to Jews in the Polish Minority Treaty, where presumably a reference to Sabbatarians would have done as well.

Acknowledgment of the past as well as solutions in the present require a discussion of the group, but not because legal recognition of a group right is necessary for group life. Group rights can usually be easily understood in terms of individual rights. Individuals can associate in many forms, corporate and noncorporate, for various purposes. For example, land can be held collectively through corporations or a system of individual trustees. And, as Boris Bittker points out in his discussion of group rights, the German reparations paid to Israel or to the conference on Jewish material claims against Germany were primarily payments made to the state, which assisted refugee resettlement, and to the group, which, in effect, represented residuary legatees.[39]

---

case to renounce rights provided by the League, when minorities in Turkey said that they did not want to be protected by the Minorities Treaties. This was described by Julius Stone as a legal nullity (because the minorities were not parties to the treaties). Julius Stone, *International Guarantees of Minority Rights: Procedure of the Council of the League of Nations in Theory and Practice* (London: H. Milford, Oxford University Press, 1932), 22–23. Louis Marshall described it as an outrage, in "The Renunciation of Minority Rights by Turkish Jews," in *Louis Marshall, Champion of Liberty: Selected Papers and Addresses*, ed. Charles Reznikoff (Philadelphia: Jewish Publication Society of America, 1957), 2:575–76 (statement to the press on August 10, 1926, on the action of Turkish Jews renouncing all national minority rights guaranteed by the Treaty of Lausanne, July 24, 1923). See Robinson et al., *Minorities Treaties a Failure*, 81, 288.

[38] The Amish, for example, honor the past, and the views of members who died as Amishmen. Franklin H. Littell, "Sectarian Protestantism and the Pursuit of Wisdom: Must Technological Objectives Prevail?" in *Public Controls for Nonpublic Schools*, ed. Donald A. Erickson (Chicago: University of Chicago Press, 1969), 72.

[39] Boris I. Bittker, *The Case for Black Reparations* (New York: Random House, 1973), 78.

Perhaps we can ask what turns on the question. We can differentiate the kinds of demands made by individual members of groups on the larger system. Sometimes they simply request not to be targets of discrimination. In the strongest version of this idea, once the discrimination disappears, the group disappears also, since the group had no identification other than that caused by the injury imposed by the outside system. In the different contexts of group autonomy, the members seek cultural recognition, sometimes, as already noted, with claims for support or direct representation.

Often the demand for recognition is associated with education. The litigation over the minority schools in Albania was precipitated by an Albanian attempt to exercise exclusive control not only over the content of education but over the associational aspects of education, by closing the minority schools. The case on minority schools in Albania challenged a provision of the Albanian constitution of 1933 that gave the state entire authority over education: "The instruction and education of Albanian subjects are reserved to the State and will be given in State schools."[40] The Greek minority submitted petitions to the Council of the League of Nations under the procedures authorized.[41]

The issue was brought to the Permanent Court of International Justice[42] for an advisory opinion related to the status of minority schools in Albania, and the interpretation of article 5 of the Albanian Declaration of 1921, which states: "Albanian nationals who belong to racial, religious or linguistics minorities will enjoy the same treatment and security in law and in fact as other Albanian nationals. In particular they shall have an equal right to maintain, manage and control at their own expense or to establish in the future, charitable, religious and social institutions, schools and other educational establishments, with the right to use their own language and to exercise their religion freely therein."[43]

The background to the case is recalled by the historian Joseph Rothschild. He writes that Ahmed Zogu, upon becoming "Zog I King of the Albanians"[44] in 1928, attempted as part of a general political and cultural reform to deal with the schools: "The school system of the Roman Catho-

---

[40] Advisory Opinion No. 49, Minority Schools in Albania, 1938 Permanent Court of International Justice (ser. A/B), 485.

[41] See Stone, *International Guarantees,* for the necessary procedures.

[42] On the Permanent Court of International Justice, see Mark W. Janis, "The International Court," in *International Courts for the Twenty-first Century,* ed. Mark W. Janis (Boston: Martinus Nijhoff, 1992), 13.

[43] Advisory Opinion No. 49, 485.

[44] A formula, Rothschild remarks, which alarmed Yugoslavia, that had a substantial Albanian minority. Joseph Rothschild, *East Central Europe between the Two World Wars* (Seattle: University of Washington Press, 1990), 362.

lic church was closed in 1933, when Zog nationalized all education, but then reopened in 1936, upon the Franciscan Order's reluctant acceptance of state control and inspection."[45] Rothschild notes:

[The nationalization] was an assertion of Albanian national pride specifically vis à vis Italian and Greek "paternalism," as the supervisory and pedagogical staffs of most religious and private schools were citizens of these two states and the ideological thrust of their teaching programs was felt to be the inculcation of their own national values into Albanian children.[46]

In January 1935, the Council of the League of Nations requested the court give an advisory opinion on the interpretation of article 5 of the declaration of 1921. Albania and Greece were both represented before the court, as states best able to provide information to the court.

The Albanian government argued that any "interpretation which would compel Albania to respect the private minority schools would create a privilege,"[47] and further, that the "minority régime is an extraordinary régime, constituting a derogation from the ordinary law."[48] This being so, in case of doubt texts should be "construed in the manner most favorable to the sovereignty of the Albanian State."[49]

The particular issue addressed by the court was whether the treaties guaranteed simply nondiscrimination or whether they guaranteed treatment for those protected by treaty provisions better than the treatment received by nationals in general. The advisory opinion elaborated the point that the central purpose of the Minorities Treaties was to protect group rights, and that this meant that a neutral principle of nondiscrimination would not be adequate:

The idea underlying the treaties for the protection of minorities is to secure for certain elements incorporated in a State, the population of which differs from them in race, language or religion, the possibility of living peaceably alongside that population and co-operating amicably

[45] Ibid., 364.

[46] Ibid. Pomerance notes that the "repeal of the controversial provisions in the Albanian Constitution in accordance with the Court's guidelines effectively removed the grievance out of which the petition to the Council had arisen." Michla Pomerance, *The Advisory Function of the International Court in the League and U.N. Eras* (Baltimore: John Hopkins University Press, 1973), 340.

[47] Advisory Opinion No. 49, 494–95.

[48] Ibid., 495.

[49] Ibid. The Greek government urged a construction in light of the historical existence of community rights in the region.

For a self-help manual on sovereignty, see Erwin S. Strauss, *How to Start Your Own Country,* 2d ed. (Port Townsend, Wash.: Loompanics Unlimited, 1984).

with it, while at the same time preserving the characteristics which distinguish them from the majority, and satisfying the ensuing special needs.

In order to attain this object, two things were regarded as particularly necessary, and have formed the subject of provisions in these treaties.

The first is to ensure that nationals belonging to racial, religious, or linguistic minorities shall be placed in every respect on a footing of perfect equality with the other nationals of the state.

The second is to ensure for the minority elements suitable means for the preservation of their racial peculiarities, their traditions and their national characteristics.

These two requirements are indeed closely interlocked, for there would be no true equality between a majority and a minority if the latter were deprived of its own institutions, and were consequently compelled to renounce that which constitutes the very essence of its being as a minority.[50]

A dissenting opinion urged that the state interest had to have equal weight. In interpreting the treaty, the dissent said:

[T]he question whether the possession of particular institutions may or may not be *important* to the minority cannot constitute the decisive consideration. There is another consideration entitled to equal weight. That is the extent to which the monopoly of education may be of importance to the State. The two considerations cannot be weighted one against the other: Neither of them—in the absence of a clear stipulation to that effect—can provide an objective standard for determining which of them is to prevail.

International justice must proceed upon the footing of applying treaty stipulations impartially to the rights of the State and to the rights of the minority, and the method of doing so is to adhere to the terms of the treaty—as representing the common will of the parties—as closely as possible.[51]

As Schwebel notes, from the point of view of modern human rights, this opinion involves what is today called affirmative action.[52] It also echoes, more obviously in the European than in the American context perhaps, the older system of estates and privileges in a world in which groups

[50] Advisory Opinion No. 49, 496.

[51] Ibid., 504–5.

[52] Stephen M. Schwebel, "Human Rights in the World Court," *Vanderbilt Journal of Transnational Law* 24 (1991): 945, 951.

and status dominated the political structure.[53] And it is possible to see the treaties as raising issues for the republican or democratic state, particularly in its modern unified form. But it is also possible to see that modern states had sometimes adopted the view taken by the treaties. Thus Clemenceau urged that "[t]he educational provisions contain nothing beyond what is in fact provided in the educational institutions of many highly organized modern States."[54] He believed that "[t]here is nothing inconsistent with the sovereignty of the State in recognizing and supporting schools in which children shall be brought up in the religious influences to which they are accustomed in their home."[55] And as to language, he thought that "[a]mple safeguards against any use of non-Polish languages to encourage a spirit of national separation have been provided in the express acknowledgment that the provisions of this Treaty do not prevent the Polish State from making the Polish language obligatory in all its schools and educational institutions."[56]

In fact, the precise delineation of control over the schools by the state was not accomplished in the treaties. Jacob Robinson and his coauthors cited a number of questions left open, particularly state control over the minority schools:

> The portions of the Treaties granting the minorities the right to establish, manage and control their own educational establishments also provoked many other questions. "Was the government free to prohibit or to close private minorities schools and associations?" "Was the state entitled to supervise such institutions?" "What was the relationship between those who established such schools and the state authorities, and what were the rights of the schools?" "In their schools and other institutions the minorities could use their language, but what was the extent of the right?" "Were the teachers obliged to know the State language?"[57]

The approach of the treaties to public support of minority education could raise a number of questions.[58] Americans, while of course they were not obligated to do anything under the treaties, might have noted that in the United States there are objections, and constitutional problems, with

---

[53] See R. R. Palmer, *The World of the French Revolution* (New York: Harper and Row, 1971) for a description of privileges in Europe. See discussion in chapter 5.

[54] Letter from Clemenceau to M. Paderewski, June 24, 1919, in Temperley, *Peace Conference of Paris,* 436.

[55] Ibid.

[56] Ibid.

[57] Robinson et al., *Minorities Treaties a Failure,* 68.

[58] See chapter 8, especially discussion of Mises.

public funding for sectarian schools, and in some quarters opposition to funding for any sort of private school.[59] And Clemenceau's reference to the children's learning only that which they are taught in their homes anticipates an emphasis the United Nations documents, as well as the focus of those who view the educational issues for a society as very close to family autonomy issues.[60]

Issues of minorities are closely connected to questions of claims to particular territories. Minorities are frequently made so by shifts in territorial boundaries, and national minorities are sometimes discussed in terms of their (assumed) desire to either constitute or reconstitute a state or to join an existing state. The matter, however, is complex, on, for example, the issue of knowing what the group is and what it wants.

The problems intensify when one considers minorities that are not national but rather religious, or finally "other," that is, groupings other than the traditional religious ethnic or racial groups. On the one hand, we might say that it is not clear that a (sovereign) territory is, for example, a characteristic demand of gays and lesbians, or persons with physical disabilities. On the other, we might conclude that issues of territory are involved, precisely because such groups, as much as ideological or political groups, may want to found communities or towns, or concentrate themselves in neighborhoods as an expression to their autonomy.

The current United Nations documents do not limit the rights of parents to issues of education organized on a religious basis.[61] They are

---

[59] Of course private schools have been very important in the United States. The history of intentional communities, as well as the history of psychological movements, reveals an interest in private education that is essentially derived from a structural underlay that relates subgroups and minorities to the issue of private education. See, for example, the discussion of educational radicalism in the chapter on the Ferrer Colony and the Modern School in Laurence Veysey, *The Communal Experience: Anarchist and Mystical Communities in Twentieth Century America* (Chicago: University of Chicago Press, 1978), 77–177.

[60] The family is often viewed as a unity. Of course it is not. It is an aggregation of individuals. See Lee E. Teitalbaum, "Intergenerational Responsibility and Family Obligation on Sharing," *Utah Law Review* 1992:765. It is also a foundation of various minority groups. See Stephen J. Roth, "Toward a Minority Convention: Its Need and Content," *Israel Yearbook of Human Rights* 20 (1990): 93. "For many minorities the family forms the nuclear group unit for their existence; the protection of the family is therefore of existential importance to minorities, just as the rights of the child are vital assurance of their continuity" (109).

[61] For example, article 18 or the International Covenants on Civil and Political Rights reads: "Everyone shall have the right to freedom of thought, conscience and religion. This right shall include freedom to have or to adopt a religion or belief of his choice, and freedom, either individually or in community with others and in public or private, to manifest his religion or belief in worship, observance, practice and teaching" (International Covenant on Civil and Political Rights, December 19, 1966, art. 18, par. 1, 999 *United Nations Treaty Service* 999: 171, 178).

broader than some of the coverage in the Minorities Treaties. At the same time, however, they do not much reflect the issues involving the definitions of parents (in view of the issues raised by new birth technologies) or family (a subject discussed in law review writing) or possible limits the state might want to impose of family autonomy, whether expressed through a formula relating to the best interests of the child or another formula (common in religious liberty provisions) relating to public welfare and good morals. And of course the current guarantee clauses do not much address the possibility of tensions between various aspirations expressed.[62]

Thornberry comments on the issue of religious education that "[a]ccess to religious education in accordance with parental wishes implies a duty on the State to remove any obstacles to this, as well as, on a reasonable reading of the paragraph, to provide facilities for such education if the right of access is to be an effective right" (*Rights of Minorities,* 194, commenting on article 5, paragraph 2 of the International Declaration on the Elimination of All Forms of Intolerance). Francesco Capotorti believes that "the more a religious community lacks resources, the more the State is bound to take steps to ensure its survival." "The Protection of Minorities under Multilateral Agreements on Human Rights," *Italian Yearbook of International Law* 2 (1976): 23.

On another point, Krishnaswami thought that religion and belief must be defined very broadly ("Study of Discrimination," 1 n. 1). Compare United States discussions on definitions and religion, especially *Torcaso v. Watkins,* 367 U.S. 488 (1961).

The forms of necessary encouragement would have to be developed. As already noted, the Minorities Treaties viewed the internal minorities as part of the state, entitled even to state funding for their separate schools including religious schools. This is of course inconsistent with some domestic law, but we are not concerned here with problems raised by inconsistency with domestic law. Rather, the suggestion is made that such policies have reasons, history, and experience behind them, and that the international discussion might well consider those reasons before flatly adopting the position that funding is a desirable or even necessary component of a human right, or the alternative position that funding always raises religious liberty issues.

[62] Consider the text of article 5 of the International Declaration on the Elimination of All Forms of Intolerance and of Discrimination Based on Religion or Belief:

1. The parents or, as the case may be, the legal guardians of the child have the right to organize the life within the family in accordance with their religion or belief and bearing in mind the moral education in which they believe the child should be brought up.

2. Every child shall enjoy the right to have access to education in the matter of religion or belief in accordance with the wishes of his parents or , as the case may be, legal guardians, and shall not be compelled to receive teaching on religion or belief against the wishes of his parents or legal guardians, the best interest of the child being the guiding principle.

3. The child shall be protected from any form of discrimination on the ground of religion or belief. He shall be brought up in a spirit of understanding, tolerance, friendship among peoples, peace and universal brotherhood, respect for freedom of religion or belief of others.

International Declaration on the Elimination of All Forms of Intolerance and of Discrimination Based on Religion or Belief, November 25, 1981, art. 5, 21 I.L.M. 205, 207 (adopted by the U.N. General Assembly January 18, 1982, G.A. Res. 36/55, U.N. GAOR, 36th Sess., Agenda item 75). Compare Universal Declaration of Human Rights, art. 26, par. 3, G.A. Res. 217A, U.N. GAOR, 3d Sess., pt. 1, U.N. Doc. A/810 (1948) (adopted December 10, 1948) ("Parents have a prior right to choose the kind of education that shall be given to their children."). See generally Elizabeth Odio Benito, *Elimination of All Forms of Intolerance and Discrimination Based on Religion or Belief. Sub-commission on Prevention of Discrimination and Protection of Minorities,* U.N. Sales No. E.89.XIV.3 (1989).

In theory, nonstate education could be organized on the basis of almost any identification.[63] The focus would then be on some kind of minimal regulation, minimal core content, and maximal room for complex group life. The world might look like something John Stuart Mill would have appreciated, in which the state involvement with education would be limited, as he suggested, to the administration of a national examination, limited perhaps, as he suggested, to an inquiry into facts rather than opinions.[64] The problem as he saw it was the risk of state power, and so on disputed questions Mill wanted taught only the information that some thought x while others thought y.[65] On this view, a framework that allows maximal choice for individuals (in their groups) works best. The home education movement offers a clear illustration of how small the tribe can finally be.[66]

It is in the educational context that we see an interesting illustration of a shift from one group to another as the status category. In 1988, Quebec replaced confessional school boards with language-based boards, arguing that this system "would better reflect the province's religious diversity and natural division in linguistic lines."[67] A lawyer arguing for the Protestant boards noted that the new linguistic boards would not have the constitutional protections of the old denominational boards (under the British North America Act) and that "without constitutional protection, they could turn around and replace linguistic boards with boards for left-handed people or for people who wear shorts."[68] We are at a point in history in which language difference and religious difference in Canada count for public purposes, while handedness and short versus long pants do not. In the United States, diversity (viewed as desirable) is measured

---

See on such tensions Jack Greenberg, "Race, Sex, and Religious Discrimination in International Law," in *Human Rights in International Law: Legal and Policy Issues,* ed. Theodor Meron (Oxford: Clarendon Press, 1984), 307, 331.

[63] "Almost" is a qualification relating to those problems understood to be opposed to central and strongly held social norms, whatever they are. But we can imagine—or can't we?—schools built on race, gender, class, ideology, all required to meet certain standards, including the teaching of tolerance and respect.

[64] John Stuart Mill, "On Liberty," in *On Liberty and Other Essays,* ed. John Gray (Oxford: Oxford University Press, 1992), 118 ff.

[65] But when is an issue "contested," as against seen as "we know" but "they think"?

[66] The question of state and group can equally be pursued through the issue of exemption to programs within the public schools. It is in the answers provided to these very specific problems that we get some sense of the ranges of tolerance in particular societies. Consider also the impact of universal dress codes on subgroups, for example, in the headdress controversy in France. See Martha Minow, "Identities," *Yale Journal of Law and the Humanities* 97 (1991): 122–26.

[67] Peggy Curran, "Protestant Boards Say Court Case Is Fight for Survival," *Gazette* (Montreal), December 8, 1992, A1.

[68] Ibid.

by ethnicity, gender, and race, more perhaps than by region of residence or birth or by religion, all of which were once prominent differentials. Sexual orientation is often viewed as relevant in a context forbidding discrimination, but not (yet) relevant in the context of diversity or affirmative action.

This discussion is not intended to outline or endorse any particular form of educational structure, though many proposals relating to such forms, and many discussions of such proposals are available.[69] For some the emphasis will be on the alternatives to public education, for others the content of a basic public education, often minimal and with the development on institutions for diverse opportunities for education undertaken later on. These discussions assume that differences will remain between people, even after the issues that we intend by such terms as racism, sexism, and discrimination have disappeared.

[69] E.g. McCarthy et al., *Society, State, and Schools;* John E. Coons and Stephen D. Sugarman, *Education by Choice: The Case for Family Control* (Berkeley and Los Angeles: University of California Press, 1978); Michael Walzer, *Spheres of Justice: A Defense of Pluralism and Equality* (New York: Basic Books, 1983), 181 ff.

CHAPTER 8

The Debate over Education: Truth, Peace, Citizenship

> [S]ince wars begin in the minds of men, it is in the minds of
> men that the defenses of peace must be constructed.
>
> —UNESCO Constitution, preamble

✦ THE DISCUSSION of the Amish and other religious groups up to now has
raised a substantive point about toleration. Specifically, the problem is that
religious liberty intrinsically includes liberty for highly specific ideas of excellence, worthiness, and sanctity. These ideas are in place even in the absence
of consequent behavior. That is, if freedom to believe is absolute, these ideas,
like all others, are absolutely beyond the reach of the government.

Education, however, deals with ideas, and education is finally about the
impact of new ideas on preexisting ideas. Children do not, in fact, come
to school thinking nothing, believing nothing. It is possible that children
are born thinking something,[1] but certainly they have received serious
socialization by the time they go to school. The objection raised by fundamentalist families—that school creates an environment that deprecates
their beliefs[2]—is a problem that might, under particular circumstances,
be experienced by any child. The question is then to define an appropriate
role for the state.[3]

In order to open a range of opinion on this subject, this chapter reviews
the work of three thinkers who addressed these questions from very differ-

---

[1] Two experiments on hard-wiring of infants regarding language are cited in Robin Fox,
"The Cultural Animal," in *The Search for Society* (New Brunswick, N.J.: Rutgers University
Press), who discusses experiments by the pharaoh Psammetichus in ancient Egypt and by
James IV of Scotland. See also Antoni Sulek, "The Experiment of Psammetichus: Fact, Fic-
tion, and a Model to Follow," *Journal of the History of Ideas* 50 (1989): 645–51.

[2] The well-known Mozert litigation rejected the claim that this was an unconstitutional
burden on religion. *Mozert v. Hawkins County Bd. of Ed.*, 827 F.2d 1058 (1987) (no injunctive relief for parents arguing that their children should not be exposed to offensive ideas.)

[3] See Matthew Arnold, *Culture and Anarchy and Other Essays* (Cambridge: Cambridge
University Press, 1993), 117: "The Sovereign, as his position raises him above many preju-
dices and littlenesses, and as he can always have at his disposal the best advice, has evident
advantages over private founders in well planning and directing a school; while at the same
time his great means and his great influence secure, to a well-planned school of his, credit
and authority."

ent orientations. One was known as a scientist, another as an economist, the third as a political theorist. While all are Western, none of them is taken to represent the point of view of a single national or cultural background. The English scientist Julian Huxley taught for a time in the United States and spent two years as head of UNESCO. Much writing by Ludwig von Mises and Hannah Arendt was done in the United States. Julian Huxley is used to represent the advocate of maximal state intervention, Ludwig von Mises the classical liberal position in which the state does (because it can do) very little, and Hannah Arendt a position in which the state does some things but not others, based on her own categories of public, private, and social. The chapter then explores *Pierce v. Society of Sisters.*

JULIAN HUXLEY

Let us consider, to begin with, the universalist efforts of Julian Huxley. Huxley served for two years as director of UNESCO. Perhaps he was led to his approach because he was overwhelmed as UNESCO's director by the practical problems of doing what he had in mind. And perhaps he saw, as others came to, that UNESCO had itself a political dimension and was a political organization. Just before his death in 1975 he criticized UNESCO for ostracizing Israel.[4] The grandson of T. H. Huxley, the grandnephew of Matthew Arnold, and the brother of Aldous Huxley, the first director of UNESCO was distinguished as a scientist and a humanist. Interested always in large issues of human development, Huxley was a well-known writer on many subjects, including evolution and humanistic religion. His appointment was indeed controversial because of his position on revealed religion.[5] But he also had a great vision for mankind based on an evolutionary humanism.

Huxley wanted a universal world philosophy. "[I]n order to carry out its work," he said, "an organization such as UNESCO needs not only a set of general aims and objects for itself, but also a working philosophy, a working hypothesis concerning human existence and *its* aims and objects." This would "dictate, or at least indicate, a definite line of approach to its problems."[6] At the time or writing, at least, Huxley thought that such an overview was essential. Without it, "UNESCO will be in danger of undertaking piecemeal and even self-contradictory actions, and will in any case lack the guidance and inspiration which spring from a belief in a body of general principles."[7]

---

[4] "Julian Huxley, Scientist and Writer, Dies," *New York Times*, February 16, 1975, sec. 1, p. 1.

[5] Ibid.

[6] Julian Huxley, *UNESCO: Its Purpose and Its Philosophy* (Washington, D.C.: Public Affairs Press, 1947), 6.

[7] Ibid.

Huxley was essentially focused not on religion but on science. While he might have viewed his philosophy as a kind of religion, much of his discussion sees religion in one of its historical roles, as an opponent of science. UNESCO, he said, "cannot and must not tolerate the blocking of research or the hampering of its application by superstition or theological prejudice."[8] It must "disregard or, if necessary, oppose unscientific or anti-scientific movements." These movements included "anti-vivisectionism, fundamentalism, belief in miracles, [and] crude spiritualism." He called for "widespread popular education in the facts of science, the significance of the scientific method, and the possibilities of scientific application for increasing human welfare."[9]

But within a year or two Huxley had abandoned, if not the goal of a world philosophy, at least the belief that UNESCO could achieve it. By the time of a volume published in 1949,[10] Huxley had given up, as an initial project, UNESCO's formulating such a philosophy. It was not feasible. Presumably Huxley had come to see what is so obvious to us, that is, the necessary particularisms involved in his version of universalism.

LUDWIG VON MISES

Ludwig von Mises, the free market economist who urged the sovereignty of the consumer, addressed the issue of education in 1927 in a discussion of minorities,[11] and again in 1947 more generally in his work *Human Action*.

"Parents are obliged to send their to school for a certain number of years or, in lieu of this public instruction at school, to have them given

---

[8] Ibid., 37. The Minorities Treaties had already, at least implicitly, considered and rejected the universalism of Huxley's approach in the provisions on minority education. United Nations documents on education continue to assert, in the context of parental rights, values besides the values of the state philosophy.

[9] Ibid.

[10] Julian Huxley, "UNESCO: Its Purpose and Its Philosophy," in *Ideological Differences and World Order,* ed. F. S. C. Northrop (New Haven: Yale University Press, 1949):
[S]ince I wrote the pamphlet my views have somewhat changed. In the first place, I do not now feel that UNESCO, in the present stage of its career, should even aim at formulating an explicit philosophy. This would at best lead to interminable and on the whole pointless debate, and might promote serious ideological conflict. What the first conference of UNESCO and our subsequent years' work have taught us is that UNESCO can best achieve its aims by undertaking a program of concrete and limited projects, and that on such a program a remarkable degree of agreement can be reached among delegates with astonishingly different philosophical, racial, and cultural backgrounds.
  In the second place, although I still believe strongly in the need for the world to reach an eventual agreement on some basic creed or philosophy, I would now lay less stress on the urgency of this task and more on the immediate necessity of securing mutual comprehension between different and apparently alien or even hostile cultures, as the inevitable first step toward the later, unified "world philosophy." (305).

[11] Ludwig von Mises, *Liberalism* (1927; repr. Irvington-on-Hudson, N.Y.: Foundation for Economic Education, 1996).

equivalent instruction at home," he wrote in 1927."[12] He saw no point in reviewing the general debate on compulsory education, important when that question was alive, but of no current interest. "There is only *one* argument that has any bearing at all on this question, viz., that continued adherence to a policy of compulsory education is utterly incompatible with efforts to establish lasting peace."[13] (Writing under the impact of the First World War and its aftermath, Mises was still intensely concerned with nationality and language. That social and political context is critical for his discussions.) "The inhabitants of London, Paris, and Berlin will no doubt find such a statement completely incredible. What in the world does compulsory education have to do with war and peace?" But, he cautioned, "One must not judge this question, as one does so many others, exclusively from the point of view of the peoples of Western Europe."[14] In those places he thought one could solve the problem easily: There was no serious issue about which language should be used in teaching, since even the newcomers, he thought, would find that, living in London, for example, it would be "in the obvious interest of their children that instruction is given in English and in no other language." Things were not thought to be different in Paris and Berlin.[15]

> However, the problem of compulsory education has an entirely different significance in those extensive areas in which peoples speaking different languages live together side by side and intermingled in polyglot confusion. Here the question of which language is to be made the basis of instruction assumes crucial importance. A decision one way or the other can, over the years, determine the nationality of a whole area. The school can alienate children from the nationality to which their parents belong and can be used as a means of oppressing whole nationalities. Whoever controls the schools has the power to injure other nationalities and to benefit his own.[16]

Mises urged that it was no answer to say that each child be sent to the school in which the language of his parents is spoken. To begin with, some children were of mixed linguistic background. Moreover, it was sometimes difficult to decide which language was the parents'. In polyglot areas, many people use, in the course of their professional activities, all the country's languages. "Besides, it is often not possible for an individual—again out of regard for his means of livelihood—to declare himself

[12] Ibid., 114.
[13] Ibid.
[14] Ibid.
[15] Of course his argument looks different now, even as to the European capitals.
[16] Ibid., 114–15.

openly for one or another nationality. Under a system of interventionism, it could cost him the patronage of customers belonging to other nationalities or a job with an entrepreneur of a different nationality." Another argument is that "many parents . . . would even prefer to send their children to the schools of another nationality than their own because they value the advantages of bilingualism or assimilation to the other nationality more highly than loyalty to their own people." Parental choice has its own problems: "If one leaves to the parents the choice of the school to which they wish to send their children, then one exposes them to every conceivable form of political coercion. In all areas of mixed nationality . . . [the school is of a] political character as long as it remains a public and compulsory institution."[17]

Mises's conclusion is that "[t]here is, in fact, only *one* solution: the state, the government, the laws must not in any way concern themselves with schooling or education. Public funds must not be used for such purposes." Education "must be left entirely to parents and to private associations and institutions." It is better that a number of boys grow up without formal education than that they enjoy the benefit of schooling only to run the risk, once they have grown up, of being killed or maimed.[18]

In 1949, Mises conceded that "[i]n countries which are not harassed by struggles between various linguistic groups there might be a role for public education, and only if it is limited to reading, writing, and arithmetic. With bright children it is even possible to add elementary notions of geometry, the natural sciences, and the valid laws of the country." But that was the limit. "[A]s soon as one wants to go farther, serious difficulties appear." These are objections that take this form: "Teaching at the elementary level necessarily turns into indoctrination." One cannot "represent to adolescents all the aspects of a problem and to let them choose between dissenting views." And similarly, "It is no less impossible to find teachers who could hand down opinions of which they themselves disapprove in such a way as to satisfy those who hold these opinions." Thus, "The party that operates the schools is in a position to propagandize its tenets and to disparage those of other parties."[19]

The history of church-state relations offered a limited solution in the form of the doctrine of separation of state and church. Thus, in liberal countries "religion is no longer taught in public schools. But the parents are free to send their children into denominational schools supported by religious communities."[20] But this is not a complete solution.

---

[17] Ibid., 115.

[18] Ibid.

[19] Ludwig von Mises, *Human Action,* 4th ed. (San Francisco: Fox and Wilkes, 1963), 876.

[20] Ibid.

"[T]he problem does not refer only to the teaching of religion and of certain theories of the natural sciences at variance with the Bible. It concerns even more the teaching of history and economics." Mises noted that "[t]he public is aware of the matter only with regard to the international aspects of the teaching of history." And thus, "There is some talk today about the necessity of freeing the teaching of history from the impact of nationalism and chauvinism."[21] Again, the solution appears as a very limited involvement in the field of education.

In general, by 1949, Mises was not persuaded of the great significance of education. To begin with "creative geniuses cannot be reared in schools,"[22] and further the impact of the media and "environmental conditions" will be "much more powerful than that of teachers with text books."[23] (Among such environmental conditions he includes "propaganda" of churches, political parties, and pressure groups.) The influence of public education will be minor.

HANNAH ARENDT

Hannah Arendt's reputation as a controversial thinker is based in part on the public debate over her analysis of two of the most well known legal events of her time.[24] The first was the integration of the public schools in the United States following the Supreme Court decision in *Brown v. Board of Education*[25] and the second, the trial by an Israeli court of Adolph Eichmann for war crimes committed during the Holocaust.[26] In both instances, her analyses were based on categories and approaches that ex-

[21] Ibid.

[22] Ibid., 314.

[23] Ibid., 877.

[24] Writing in 1982, in a review of Elizabeth Young-Bruehl's biography of Hannah Arendt, Alasdair MacIntyre suggested that "the chief interest of Hannah Arendt's life arises not from the successes or failures of her arguments but rather from the largely unique role that she played in American intellectual life." MacIntyre believed that "in a period of great and appalling events there was a large and intelligent public which hungered for understanding, an understanding which the professionalized academic theorists of politics and society did all too little to supply." Arendt, he concluded, "seemed to give what they withheld." In the end, he thought, the material would be of interest to the "future sociologists of culture, rather than to the historian of ideas." "Hannah Arendt as Thinker," *Commonweal,* September 10, 1982, 471.

[25] For an extended discussion, see Marie Failinger, "Equality versus the Right to Choose Associates: A Critique of Hannah Arendt's View of the Supreme Court's Dilemma," *University of Pittsburgh Law Review* 49 (1987):149.

[26] See Seyla Benhabib, "Arendt's *Eichmann in Jerusalem,*" in *The Cambridge Companion to Hannah Arendt,* ed. Dana Villa (Cambridge: Cambridge University Press, 2001), 65; also Pnina Lahav, "The Eichmann Trial, the Jewish Question, and the American Jewish Intelligentsia," *Boston University Law Review* 72 (1992): 555.

isted outside the framework of the legal systems involved.[27] In both instances, her analyses were the basis of a critical judgment of the events that was quite different from those of many of her contemporaries in the public intellectual world. While *Eichmann in Jerusalem* is widely recalled, the essay on Little Rock seems to have been largely forgotten, at least outside the academic community.

"Reflections on Little Rock" was a "topical essay" published in *Dissent* (winter 1959) after *Commentary*'s reluctance to publish it had become plain. Arendt introduces the essay with a section addressing the controversy over publication. This preliminary material makes three points: (1) Rights are to be "determined by the Constitution, and not by public opinion or by majorities."[28] Thus it is irrelevant that the black community was uninterested in the issue of miscegenation, which she considered central. (2) Arendt was criticized for failing to consider the specific role of education in America. This was a just criticism, she said, but she had also written "Crisis in Education." The reader, in effect, was referred to that essay, published in the *Partisan Review.*[29] (3) Arendt takes for granted sympathy for the cause of Negroes as for all oppressed peoples and hopes the reader will do the same.

The central concepts in "Reflections on Little Rock" involve Arendt's three-part categorization of human life (public—social—private), the distinction between parvenu and pariah (developed in her writing on the history of the German Jews), and the distinction between education and indoctrination.

Arendt bases the essay on the analytic structure that she had developed in *The Human Condition*. Initially, the realm of the public is distinguished from the realm of the social.[30] "In the public realm, . . . nothing counts that cannot make itself seen and heard." Thus, the permanent visibility of the Negro, which is "unalterable and permanent," counts.[31] "Segregation is discrimination enforced by law, and desegregation can do no more than abolish the laws enforcing discrimination; it cannot abolish discrimination and force equality upon society [the social sphere], but it can and indeed must enforce equality within the body politic."[32]

---

[27] Although in *Eichmann in Jerusalem* she addresses specifically legal issues, and in effect, offered a specific structural proposal.

[28] Arendt, "Reflections on Little Rock," *Dissent,* winter 1959, 46.

[29] Arendt, "Crisis in Education," *Partisan Review* 177–78 (1958): 493–513.

[30] Seyla Benhabib suggests that "the distinction between the social and political makes no sense in the modern world." This is because "the struggle to make something public is a struggle for justice." "Hannah Arendt and the Redemptive Power of Narrative," *Social Research* 57 (1990): 167–96.

[31] "Reflections on Little Rock," 47.

[32] Ibid., 50.

She summarizes in the striking sentence: "What equality is to the body politic—its innermost principle—discrimination is to society." And "discrimination is as indispensable a social right as equality is a political right. The question is not how to abolish discrimination, but how to keep it confined within the social sphere, where it is legitimate, and prevent its trespassing on the political and the personal sphere, where it is destructive."[33]

The third realm is private. This realm is "ruled neither by equality nor by discrimination but by exclusiveness."[34] Here we choose as individuals, in our uniqueness. Social standards are different from legal standards. Government has to ensure that social discrimination never curtails political equality and must safeguard the rights of every person to do as he or she pleases within the four walls of home.

When social discrimination is legally enforced, it becomes persecution. When social discrimination is legally abolished (meaning when it is illegal, since it cannot in fact be abolished), the freedom of society has been violated. Arendt believes that thoughtless handling of civil rights would cause this violation. The government "can legitimately take no steps against social discrimination because government can act only in the name of equality—a principle that does not obtain in the social sphere."[35] Churches are the only public forces that can fight prejudice, in the name of the uniqueness of persons and souls on which religion, and especially Christianity, is based.

Arendt examines education in light of the theory she has advanced on the three realms of human life. Children are first part of family. The family atmosphere is that of idiosyncratic exclusiveness. It shields the young against the demands of the social and the responsibilities of the political. The right of parents is a right of privacy. Since the introduction of compulsory education, the right is restricted but not abolished by right of the state to prepare children to fulfill future duties. The stake of government is undeniable. Because of individuals' financial limitations, private education is no way out of this dilemma.[36]

Parents' rights over their children are legally restricted by public education "and nothing else."[37] The state has an unchallengeable right to prescribe minimum requirements, and beyond that to the teaching of subjects

[33] Ibid., 51.

[34] Ibid., 52.

[35] Ibid., 53.

[36] Ibid., 55.

[37] Ibid. She omits discussion of child abuse laws and neglect statutes, as well as intervention in the context of marital breakdown. On Arendt's "Eurocentrism" see Shiraz Dossa, "Human Status and Politics: Hannah Arendt on the Holocaust," *Canadian Journal of Political Science* 13 (1980).

"necessary to the nation." The state concern is only with content, however, and not the context of association and social life that invariably develops out of his attendance at school. "Otherwise one would have to challenge the right of private schools to exist." The school is the "first place away from home where child establishes contact with public world that surrounds him and his family. This version of the public world is not political but social, and school is to child what a job is to adult."[38] Free choice, however, lies not with child, but with parents.

Early in the essay Arendt characteristically turns to Tocqueville on American law and values. He saw that equality of opportunity as well of equality of rights constituted the basic law of American democracy. "In its all-comprehensive typically American form, equality possesses an enormous power to equalize what by nature and origin is different—and it is only due to this power that the country has been able to retain its fundamental identity against the waves of immigrants who have always flooded its shores."[39]

According to Arendt, "Since the Supreme Court decision to enforce desegregation in public schools, the general situation in the South has deteriorated."[40] She urges that while the country cannot avoid federal enforcement altogether, we should take this step only when the law of the land and the principle of the republic are at stake. The question was, then, were the public schools such a case?

The administration's civil rights program covered two points, the franchise and segregation. On the franchise, there was no doubt of a federal role.[41]

Arendt notes that it is not the social custom of segregation that is unconstitutional but its legal enforcement. "To abolish this legislation is of great and obvious importance."[42] But she sees, perhaps, that the public discussion does not go far enough, because abolishing antimiscegenation laws would be even more important. "The right to marry whomever one pleases is an elementary human right,"[43] compared to which schools, or public accommodations, are secondary. But if the Court had somehow

---

[38] Arendt, "Reflections on Little Rock," 55. "Crisis in Education" offers a similar description of the school as a place of security for the child (504).

[39] Arendt, "Reflections on Little Rock," 48.

[40] Ibid.

[41] Ibid.

[42] Ibid., 49.

[43] Arendt's treatment of marriage is instructive. Her discussion assumes conventional heterosexual monogamous marriage. Her proposal is that marriage/miscegenation should be the focus of civil rights activity. Her discussion, places marriage in the private (exclusive) sphere. But this ignores the American/English understanding of the strong connection between marriage and the state.

dealt with the issue of antimiscegenation laws, "it would hardly have felt compelled to encourage, let alone enforce, mixed marriages."[44]

For Arendt, the "most startling part of the whole business was the federal decision to start integration in of all places public schools."[45] The process placed an unacceptable burden on children. She cited the photograph of the Negro girl at the Little Rock High School. It was a caricature of progressive education, which "by abolishing the authority of adults, implicitly denies their responsibility for the world into which they have borne their children and refuses the duty of guiding them into it."[46] She concludes that "[t]o force parents to send children to an integrated school against their will" is to deprive them of the "private right over their children and the social right to free association."[47] Finally, forced integration, for the children, presents a conflict between home and school that children cannot handle, and this will result in power of peer group and mob rule.

In her "Reply to Critics," Arendt suggests that voluntary integrated private schools would be the way to solve the problem of segregated education. If the state refused such schools legal status, then the federal government should intervene.[48] Arendt came to the Little Rock issue through the categories pariah/parvenu that she had developed in working on the German Jews. The pariah was the individual who was outside, but who would be stronger in that status than if the strategy of accommodation and social integration of the parvenu were adopted.[49] She thought the Negro children were being used to pursue a parvenu goal.

It is only on the pariah point that Hannah Arendt pulled back. She indicates, in her response to Ralph Ellison, that she had not understood the concept of the ideal of sacrifice in the context of Little Rock.[50]

The controversy over public schools assumes not just the existence of schools but communal experiences, intermediate points between home and family, as Walzer describes them.[51] But Arendt insists that the state has no interest in the associational aspects of education.

[44] Arendt, "Reflections on Little Rock," 49–50.

[45] Ibid., 50.

[46] Ibid.

[47] Ibid., 55

[48] Hannah Arendt, "Reply to Critics," *Dissent,* spring 1959, 180–81.

[49] Judith Shklar described Arendt herself as an arrogant pariah who, though knowing little about the specific American situation, nonetheless assumed that the parents of the Negro children were acting like parvenus, trying to enter situations in which they were not wanted. Judith Shklar, "Hannah Arendt as Parvenu," *Partisan Review* 50, no. 1 (1983): 64–77.

[50] Elisabeth Young-Bruehl, *Hannah Arendt, for Love of the World* (New Haven: Yale University Press, 1982), 316.

[51] 309–23. See also Walzer, *Spheres of Justice.* Walzer's argument is that, assuming that private schools and options exist around the margins of a public school system, there is no

As to the burden that forced integration placed on the students themselves, Arendt was apparently right. A book by a young woman who was
one of the nine black students who integrated the Little Rock high schools
makes plain the constant danger for the children and refutes the assumption that the presence of troops was an effective deterrent to violence.
Rather like Arendt's arguing that she would not have sent a child into
that situation, Melba Beals writes, "When . . . on September 23, 1957,
the NAACP officials and ministers dropped us off to go to Central for the
second time under court order, I wonder how in their minds they justified
such an act. As an adult, I believe had it been me driving, I would have
kept going rather than allow my children to face that rampaging mob."
And yet, Beals adds, "had we students not gone to school that day, perhaps the integration of Central . . . would never have taken place."[52]

In the same way that the discussion in "Reflections on Little Rock"
proceeds against the background of a scheme that separates human existence into three spheres, each with a function, the piece goes on against a
set of ideas about education some of which are alluded to, and some of
which hardly appear directly. For example, as her biographer notes, even
after the debate over Little Rock, Arendt "remained convinced that education could not be the sole or even the most important source of social or
political change."[53] Arendt had a specific version of the history of education or at least ideas about education. She distinguished between possible
different purposes of education in the eighteenth, nineteenth, and twentieth centuries. In the theory of the eighteenth century, education was for
the public good, assuming a broad distinction between educated and la-
boring men. She notes the nineteenth-century liberal ideal of pursuits
open to talent, and a concern with the injustice involved in limits on talent. But the present orientation, she says, is different from either of these,
since the current argument is that people have a right to social advance-
ment and hence to education, as a method of improving status.[54] The
American story was also deeply connected with issues of immigration.
The historic function of education in America, as she saw it, related to
the absorption of immigrants, and the teaching of language (at least) to
children and also their parents.

"Education," she says, "can play no part in politics, because in politics
we always have to deal with those who are already educated. Whoever
wants to educate adults really wants to act as their guardian and prevent

---

reason to oppose them because they simply add ideological diversity. The real point, he says,
is to provide for the encounters between children from different groups.

[52] Melba Patillo Beals, *Warriors Don't Cry* (New York: Pocket Books, 1994), 309.

[53] Young-Bruehl, *Hannah Arendt,* 377.

[54] Hannah Arendt, "The Social Question," in *On Revolution,* 72–73.

them from political activity. Since one cannot educate adults, the word 'education' has an evil sound in politics; there is a pretense of education when the real purpose is coercion without the use of force."[55]

Although the existence of private schools is noted in both of her educational essays, Arendt does not discuss—and perhaps did not know—significant language from *Pierce v. Society of Sisters,* upholding the constitutional status of private and religious schools. Thus we are left with doubts as to the implications of Arendt's position for private schools that are not necessarily racially segregated but particularistic on some other basis.[56]

PIERCE V. SOCIETY OF SISTERS

The strongest statement of the danger posed by the radical decentralization possible under either the limited approach of the Minorities Treaties or the broader concepts of family autonomy in the later U.N. statements is perhaps found in Homer's description of the social order of the Cyclops, who had "no muster and no meeting, no consultation or old tribal ways, but each one dwells in his own mountain cave dealing out rough justice to wife and child, indifferent to what others do."[57] But this particular danger seems remote in our present context, in which the greater threat seems to come from the powerful centers, governmental and nongovernmental, of mass societies. The state's responsibility to make room for and even assist minority schools is central to the approach of the League of Nations and has a parallel (with a significant difference on the issue of subsidy) in American law.

Pierce v. Society of Sisters[58] is a leading case on free exercise issues, involving a Roman Catholic school and a military academy. *Pierce* is a

[55] Arendt, "Crisis in Education," 496.

[56] Do we agree with Scalia, Rehnquist, and Thomas in dissent in the Kiryas Joel case? "The creation of a special one culture school district for the benefit of [children whose] parents were nonreligious commune dwellers or American Indians or gypsies [would] pose no problem. . . . The neutrality demanded by the religious clauses requires the same indulgence towards cultural characteristics that are accompanied by religious belief." *Board of Education of Kiryas Joel Village School District v. Grumet,* 114 S.Ct. 2481 (1994). Cf. *Plessy v. Ferguson,* 163 U.S. 527 (1896).

[57] *The Odyssey,* trans. Robert Fitzgerald (New York: Vintage Classics, 1990), bk. 9, ll. 1220–24, p. 148. Arendt had written on the Minorities Treaties of the League of Nations, largely in terms of their challenge to the conventional European idea of sovereignty. The center of the problem is Arendt's insistence on the point that a national state—a form she believed, despite its obvious resurgence in her lifetime, to be dead—must inevitably deal with minorities either through assimilation or liquidations. Mises criticized the efforts of the League of Nations for inattention to economic issues. "The Political Economy of International Reform and Reconstruction," in *Selected Writings of Ludwig von Mises,* ed. Richard M. Ebeling (Indianapolis: Liberty Fund, 2000), 12–13.

[58] 268 U.S. 510 (1925).

critical case in the history of American pluralism, as essential for the possibility of multiple systems as *Reynolds v. United States*,[59] the Mormon polygamy case, is for common values. *Pierce* stands for the proposition that the state does not own children, and that the state cannot have a monopoly in the education of children. *Pierce* makes room for alternative educational systems within the state, and by extension for multiple communities within the state.

The *Pierce* Court wrote, "The fundamental theory of liberty upon which all governments in this Union repose excludes any general power of the state to standardize its children by forcing them to accept instruction from public school teachers only."[60]

The state's argument in *Pierce* was similar to the argument of the dissent in the case on minority schools in Albania to the extent that it stressed first that a substantial state interest was involved, and second that the particular state interest was in effect patriotic universalism.

> If the governments of the several states have no power to provide for the education of the children within its limits, and if the character of the education of such children is to be entirely dictated by the parents of such children, or by those persons by whose influence the parents are controlled, it is hard to assign any limits to the injurious effect, from the standpoint of American patriotism which may result.[61]

A pamphlet quoted in an amicus brief offered some detail: "Our children must not under any pretext, be it based upon money, creed or social status, be divided into antagonistic groups, cliques, or *cults there to absorb the narrow views of life as they are taught.*"[62]

The *Pierce* case is understood by American constitutional lawyers to have in its most technical readings not much to do with First Amendment rights.[63]

---

[59] 98 U.S. 145 (1878).

[60] 268 U.S. at 535. The Hill Military Academy was a private school for boys.

[61] Appellant's Brief at 62, *Pierce v. Society of Sisters*, 268 U.S. 510 (1925) (No. 583) (No. 584).

[62] The pamphlet is quoted in the Brief of Louis Marshall, Amicus, Curiae, *On Behalf of Appellates*, at 16, *Pierce v. Society of Sisters*, 268 U.S. 510 (1925) (No. 583) (No. 584) (emphasis added).

[63] Justice Black wrote of the technical holding in *Pierce*: "Mr. Justice McReynolds said that a state law requiring that all children attend public schools interfered unconstitutionally with the property rights of private school corporations because it was an 'arbitrary, unreasonable and unlawful interference' which threatened 'destruction of their business and property.' 268 U.S., at 536. Without expressing an opinion as to whether either of those cases reached a correct result in light of our later decisions applying the First Amendment to the States through the Fourteenth, I merely point out that the reasoning stated in *Meyer* and *Pierce* was the same natural law due process philosophy which many later opinions repudiated, and which I cannot accept." *Griswold v. Connecticut*, 381 U.S. 479, 516 (1965) (Black, J., dissenting) (citation omitted).

The issue was ruled upon before the general understanding that the First Amendment, with its guarantees of religious liberty, bound the separate states as well as the federal government. Nonetheless, despite its technical irrelevance, the case has a clear role in constitutional development. *Pierce v. Society of Sisters,* in protecting the existence of religious education and non-state education in general, is widely understood as a powerful statement of group rights against the intrusion of state authorities.

The images of totalitarianism that are invoked by the Supreme Court in *Pierce* make plain that the limits on state authority are understood broadly. From the point of view of a pluralist structure, the critical participant in the *Pierce* case is perhaps the Hill Military Academy, precisely because it was not a religious institution and was not protected, and would not now be, by the First Amendment's free exercise clause. Further, the military academy, with all of the associations that can be brought to military structures and training, is precisely the example of the educational institution that was not open, not experimental, and not focused on individual autonomy. At least as we can imagine it, it is the secular analogue of the religious fundamentalist school involved in some current American litigation. *Pierce* allows schools of quite different character to exist within a state-authorized school system.

The International Court of Justice case on the minority schools in Albania was curiously parallel to *Pierce v. Society of Sisters,* which, on the basis of principles peculiar to American constitutional law, reached a result similar to that reached by the international court. The constitutional question can be raised in the United States by asking: Is the term *United States* single or plural?

A general comment of the relation of the approach of the Minorities Treaties to the American scheme may at this point be in order. The comments of one contemporary academic observer are illustrative. Arthur Scott, assistant professor at the University of Chicago in 1920, attempted to explain why certain approaches were properly imposed on Eastern Europe but would not be proper in the United States. The minorities in America, he said, came voluntarily, presumably knowing what our institutions are and by implication accepting them. "If they find them unsatisfactory, they may go elsewhere."[64] By contrast, in central Europe, "the mi-

---

[64] Arthur Pearson Scott, *An Introduction to the Peace Treaties* (Chicago: in the Chicago Press, 1920), 206. Of course the omission here of the history of Native Americans or the institution of slavery not only distorts the American experience but also makes comprehensible the grievance one might attribute, for example, to the Roumanians, who could easily have said that one state that had abolished slavery only in the nineteenth century (Roumania enslaved the Gypsies until 1848 and refused civil rights to Jews much later) was being dictated to by another state that had only abolished slavery in the middle of the nineteenth century and had a problematic record on civil rights for Jews and Catholics through the nineteenth century that continued into the twentieth century. See Borden, *Jews, Turks, and Infidels.*

norities are in few instances recent and voluntary immigrants."[65] Rather, they are people "settled in their districts for centuries," many "detached from the main body of their fellows by political events which they could not control."[66] Many of them, Scott wrote, "are given a citizenship which they do not desire."[67] For these reasons, "to reconcile them to the situation, it is necessary, as a measure of practical statesmanship, to grant them privileges which are entirely unnecessary in the United States."[68]

In fact the treaty provisions relating to education were not identical to American law on the subject of private education, and, in fact, in one respect they were opposed to that law. Thus, as Arthur Scott pointed out in his *Introduction to the Peace Treaties,* the United States did not permit public funding of religious education. "While we permit any privately supported school, notably the Roman Catholic parochial system, to teach any religion, in any language, we are opposed on principles to giving them any support from public funds."[69] (Scott's word "any" is perhaps too strong, but certainly the history of the parochial school funding issue over several decades indicates strong sensitivity on the question.)

On the use of languages other than English, the American position was (and continues to be) ambiguous. Scott in 1920 saw that while "[i]n some country districts a considerable part of the instruction in the elementary public schools was given in some other language than English," when this fact came out during the war, "it was regarded with distinct disfavor."[70] The American point of view, Scott wrote with assurance, "is that we do not want permanent communities in this country that are not able and willing to speak our language."[71]

The American discussion, perhaps not surprisingly, is focused on religious groups as much as ethnic or linguistic groups, particularly when the focus is normative diversity.[72] Ethnicity itself may not have the role in the American setting that it has had in Europe. Race may have that role.

[65] Scott, *Introduction to Peace Treaties,* 206.

[66] Ibid.

[67] Ibid. The Coles suggest unqualifiedly that the First World War resulted in states having minority populations with "no loyalty" to the larger state (*Guide to Modern Politics,* 32).

[68] Scott, *Introduction to Peace Treaties,* 206. Scott included a discussion of the Jewish minority in Poland, noting that Sunday closing laws were not forbidden by the treaties, and also were to be found in a number of American states (207).

Jewish organizations were represented at the peace conferences by a number of delegations from various countries, among them the United States. See generally Oscar I. Janowsky, *The Jews and Minority Rights (1898–1919)* (New York: Columbia University Press, 1933; rpt. New York: AMS Press, 1966).

[69] Scott, *Introduction to Peace Treaties,* 205.

[70] Ibid., 205–6.

[71] Ibid., 206.

[72] See Philip Hamburger, "Equality and Diversity: The Eighteenth-Century Debate about Equal Protection and Equal Civil Rights" *Supreme Court Review* 1992:295.

The Minorities Treaties, for entirely understandable reasons, focused on groups limited to the familiar categories created by the historical conditions under which they were developed. But the possible groups that might be entitled to the positive support of the state are highly various.

Thus, the community of the deaf, having a distinctive language called sign, is brought forward as a linguistic community rather than a subgroup of the handicapped or disabled (or differently abled). Daniel Bell's list of groups[73] ranges from groups based on occupations, to age, to sexual orientation. Each of these might want (and be entitled to) schools, and even under some systems, public support for schools.[74] Each might at least for a time constitute a social context for associated individuals, and some might be judged (by someone) to be better than others. "[E]specially in the case of very small linguistic groups and in the case of obscurantist religious groups," Van Dyke writes, "to assure a right of group survival is to restrict the opportunities of individual members for full self-realization. Assimilation, involving the disappearance of the group, is sometimes desirable."[75]

One question, then, is what range of private (meaning nonstate) institutional life should be encouraged, or even tolerated. Another discussion focuses on the educational policy of the central state.[76] In the context of education, one might say that this requires a system of vouchers given to

---

[73] See the introduction to part 2.

[74] The issue of subsidy is complicated by the economic inequalities in particular societies, as well as by the problem created if the state decides which enterprises to fund (presumably those that suit state purposes), and it raises issues of free development versus fostered development. For a recent discussion, see Douglas Sanders, "Collective Rights," *Human Rights Quarterly* 13 (1991): 368–86. For an earlier discussion, see Chafee, "Associations Not for Profit."

[75] Vernon Van Dyke, "Justice as Fairness: For Groups? *American Political Science Review* 69 (1975): 613. But how is one to know what groups are to be assimilated? Who is to decide this? Isn't this exactly the power that we do not want the state to have? Certainly American courts, operating under the constraints of the First Amendment, would have to be cautious about the consequences of any possible "obscurantism" in a religious group.

[76] See Amy Gutmann, *Democratic Education* (Princeton: Princeton University Press, 1987), 64 ff. (discussing especially arguments against an understanding of a minimal state-enforced standard with maximum decentralization of decision-making authority through ideas of family sovereignty). On family sovereignty, see Coons and Sugarman, *Education by Choice*.

J. A. Laponce, in *The Protection of Minorities* (Berkeley and Los Angeles: University of California Press, 1960), 181, distinguishes generally between minorities by force and minorities by will and suggests that certain latitudes ought to be allowed minorities by will in the area of education. He sees the central problem of the Doukobors as that of whether the government can tolerate a certain number of uneducated children. This, however, misses the issue of the claims of the children as citizens (members of the state) or the claim of the state to protect the rights of the children even when they do not assert those rights. See Justice Douglas's opinion in *Wisconsin v. Yoder*, 406 U.S. 205, 240 (1972).

parents of children who want to attend any school for any reason, subject to state regulation of minimum content. Or one might want to say that state funding is required for state schools only (what does the state school teach about which groups?), but individuals who can afford the cost can send their children to private schools.[77]

Once we get an image of the chaotic array of educational options, run by a theoretically unlimited number of groups, the question of the center reemerges powerfully. What is holding all of this together?

Some in the United States have been concerned with symbolic answers to this question.[78] Others are concerned with minimal educational content,[79] and controversies continue to arise as to the substance of public education in the United States.

While the minimal content of an educational program might be debated, one can usefully recall the language of Justice McReynolds writing for the Court in *Pierce:*

> No question is raised concerning the power of the State reasonably to regulate all schools, to inspect, supervise and examine them, their teachers and pupils; to require that all children of proper age attend some school, the teachers shall be of good moral character and patriotic disposition, that certain studies plainly essential to good citizenship must be taught, and that nothing be taught which is manifestly inimical to the public welfare.[80]

There is an argument that even the most minimalist state-sponsored education[81] contains normative judgments and requires agreement among those who generally do not agree. Undoubtedly such proposals do, but perhaps they are usefully seen as normative in the same sense that the teaching of language to infants normatively judges language to be better than no language, and the mother tongue to be better than others not (yet) taught. The basic point here is that minimalist goals are different

---

[77] The focus here has been on education because it is so central for group life. Related issues concern group libel, treated in the American literature in the 1950s and again a subject. See Calvin R. Massey, "Hate Speech, Cultural Diversity, and the Foundational Paradigms of Free Expression," *UCLA Law Review* 40 (1992): 103.

[78] See a reworking of the language of the Pledge of Allegiance in George P. Fletcher, "Update the Pledge," *New York Times,* December 6, 1992, sec. 4, p. 19.

[79] One aspect of the parental choice solution advanced by Coons and Sugarman is perhaps most clearly addressed in detail by E. D. Hirsch Jr. in *Cultural Literacy: What Every American Needs to Know,* rev. ed. (New York: Vintage, 1988), and *A First Dictionary of Cultural Literacy: What Our Children Need to Know* (New York: Houghton Mifflin, 1991).

[80] *Pierce v. Society of Sisters,* 268 U.S. 510, 534 (1925).

[81] The arguments for state control put forward by Matthew Arnold (see *Culture and Anarchy and Other Essays*) presumably kept some level of state activity in the educational area.

from maximalist goals, and that agreements on minimum frameworks might be possible where agreements on the good life might not be.

The difficulties in this area have been well understood for some time, and the tensions between the goals of various entities involved have been clear to those advocating the importance of group life and institutions. Thus it was said in 1920: "The educational process alone is the instrumentality properly responsible in a democracy for maintaining the national identity of minority communities.[82]

Because that minimal ordering which makes peace possible has to include some sort of education, the discussion in the United States has focused very explicitly on education in a world of conflicting values and cultures. Some of the discussion has been by representatives of groups that have insisted that the public narrative include some telling of their story.[83] The Minorities Treaties approached the enterprise by protecting minority schools and also insisting, for example, on the right of the central state to teach the national language as part of the basic state program. Many today do the same. The educational arena continues to be a critical forum for the pluralist conversation. It is in this area that we find thinking about voucher plans, decentralization of educational authority, and a multiplicity of approaches to the subject matter itself. Pluralism provides one way to cut through the grammar of epithets in which, as Gellner suggests, "I am a patriot, you are a nationalist and he is a tribalist."[84] Thus the historian John Hingham has noted that "pluralism in all its forms is a philosophy of minority rights."[85]

Education is one of the critical contexts for the application of any political idea. Through education, whether in the home[86] or in private (non-

[82] Isaac Berkson, *Theories of Americanization: A Critical Study* (1920; Arno Press and the New York Times, 1969), 147. This is because "[n]either local segregation nor governmental separatism would allow the undisturbed interchange of social forces with democracy demands. On the other hand communal organization with the school as the centre would make possible to continue the ethnic loyalty and to preserve the cultural and spiritual personality of the group without of necessity interfering with the free play of currents demanded by the unity of American life" (147). Berkson was thinking largely of supplementary schools. See Gutmann, *Democratic Education*, 64 ff. (discussing especially arguments against an understanding of a minimal state-enforced standard with maximum decentralization of decision-making authority through ideas of family sovereignty). On family sovereignty, see Coons and Sugarman, *Education by Choice.*

[83] Gypsies are still, for example, working to get their story told. On their history, see Ian Hancock, *The Pariah Syndrome*, rev. ed. (Ann Arbor, Mich.: Karoma, 1988).

[84] Ernst Gellner, *Nations and Nationalism* (Ithaca, N.Y.: Cornell University Press, 1987), 86.

[85] John Hingham, *Send These to Me: Immigrants in Urban America*, rev. ed. (Baltimore: Johns Hopkins University Press, 1984), 200.

[86] Jean Bethke Elshtain has noted that the family is often attacked as "the example par excellence of imbedded particularly." "The Family and Civic Life," in *Rebuilding the Nest,* ed. David Blankenhorn et al. (Milwaukee: Family Service America, 1990), 119, 121.

state) schools, minorities of all kinds create new generations of people identifying themselves as members of that minority. It is through the family as well as publicly enforced norms of education that the central structure asserts its values. Thus it has been noted that "[t]he autonomy of the family defines an often unrecognized condition for the transmission of religious and ethnic pluralism from one generation to the next."[87] Chapter 9 turns to some additional issues about children, particularly focused on child rearing and identity formation.

---

[87] James S. Fishkin, *Justice, Equal Opportunity, and the Family* (New Haven: Yale University Press, 1983), 59. But autonomy can mean different things. Compare the approach in *Kilgrow v. Kilgrow* with a Mexican statue that reads, "Husband and wife shall enjoy equal authority and privileges regarding the household and shall, therefore, resolve by agreement all matters relating to its operation, the upbringing and education of the children and the management of the latter's assets. In the event of disagreement between them, the Family judge shall resolve such conflicts" (C.C.D.F. art. 168, 1996 WL 915540).

CHAPTER 9

Children and Groups: Problems in Fact and in Theory

> Though I have said . . . *[t]hat all Men by Nature are equal* . . .
> Children, I confess are not born in this full state of *Equality,*
> though they are born to it. Their Parents have a sort of Rule
> and Jurisdiction over them when they come into the World,
> and for some time after, but 'tis but a temporary one.
>
> —JOHN LOCKE, *Essay concerning the True Original, Extent,*
> *and End of Civil Government*

✦ "WE are all born uncivilized," James Robinson remarked in 1929, "and would remain so through life were we not immersed in civilization. There is a long time in which we may, according to the place where we are born, be moulded into a well authenticated Papuan, Chinaman, or Parisian. We cannot choose whether we shall find ourselves talking like a Hottentot, a Russian or a German. And we learn to do in all things as those do among whom we are brought up. We cannot but accept their respective customs, scruples, and ideas, for all these are imposed upon us before we have any choice or discretion."[1]

It is for these reasons that the issue of children and groups requires special attention.

And of course, the subject is of more than theoretical interest. The *New York Times* of May 27, 1998, ran several items that, while apparently unrelated, all reach aspects of group issues. One was a long piece on bilingual education and the problems of the assimilation of foreign language groups. Another was on an abused child who was being returned, in accordance with his wishes, to his abusive parents. Another was not an article, but simply the announcement of a film from 1978 on the treatment of the Dionne quintuplets. The last was a large photograph of an aboriginal child with a caption reading, "Australia held its first Sorry Day yesterday[2] to commemorate the thousands of Aboriginal children taken from

---

[1] James H. Robinson, *Civilization* (New York: Britannica, 1929).

[2] On the issue in general, see Martha Minow, *Between Vengeance and Forgiveness* (Boston: Beacon Press, 1998).

their families under former policies of forced assimilation." All of these stories implicate questions of children and groups.[3]

This chapter reviews problems associated with the child in discussions of group rights.

It begins with the point that the idea of groups is often thin, reflecting the idea of groups within liberal political culture. The chapter then sets up a spectrum of cases that bring to the fore the relations between groups and children. These cases range from historical examples to those that are quite typical today but not necessarily understood as raising group issues. The argument is that our tendency to identify cases in terms of individuals blinds us to important group interests, as well as questions of group claims and strategies. Liberalism, as has already been noted, has very little to say about groups generally, placing its emphasis on the individual and the state. Where it does consider groups, it does so within the context of individualism, so that the group is a product, for example, of the exercise of an individual's rights to association or free exercise. Additionally, liberal thought often perceives groups in the context of discriminatory behavior against group members because of group membership. Again, the emphasis is on an individual claim, that of the individual to be free of invidious discrimination because of group membership.

Alternative views might invoke the idea of groups within the group's own culture or the idea of groups as it may exist within a variety of disciplines.

The emphasis here will be on the group claim itself—particularly with reference to children. "Itself" means that the attempt is to set out the group's claim not with reference to some particular state benefit in litigation[4]—so that we do not begin, for example, with the claim to state support for some group behavior or other—but rather the group position without reference to the state at all. The claim when asserted in a state lawsuit can then be seen as a group might see it, as part of a much larger story.

What do we really mean by group claims? We might mean that the group right displaces any right of individuals (as it might under fascism, for example) or that the group has received the individual right through contract.[5]

---

[3] Frank Bruni, "Bilingual Education Battle Splits Santa Barbara," *New York Times,* May 27, 1998, A12; Rachel L. Swarns, "Despite Abuse, Boy Getting Wish to Go Home," *New York Times,* May 27, 1998, A1; "Dionne Quintuplets," *New York Times,* May 27, 1998, E10; "Australia Says It's Sorry," *New York Times,* May 27, 1998, A3.

[4] This is consonant with the view of "interest group pluralism."

[5] Does inalienable right mean only a right that others cannot take away? Does it include the idea that individuals or groups cannot alienate it? There was an attempt in at least one case to renounce rights provided by the League, when minorities in Turkey said that they

If we ask whether it matters if we address these issues in terms of something called an individual right or something called a group right, we might say that the difference would be revealed in the attitude of the outside state toward decisions made by the group over its own members. That is, the group issue is tested by the deference given by the state to, for example, the claims of the group to decide membership, discipline, or educational issues. Related to this deference is the issue of representation and the question, "Who speaks for the group?" This is clearly difficult to answer in the case of disorganized groups and is equally difficult, although different, in the case of highly organized groups.

With these as the general matters at hand, what can we say about children? It is conventionally assumed that children do not choose their groups and that the ordinary contact/consent analysis will not work.[6] Many of the illustrations here will involve religious groups, because they have a clear and long-standing discussion of these problems.[7]

Liberal thought tends to look at religious affiliation as voluntary and based on belief and commitment rather than status by birth (and the liberal state is often constitutionally obliged to look at it this way). Religious groups see the situation quite differently at times. A religion may be based on a fact, a narrative rather than a belief. One is chosen rather than choosing. Affiliation is thus sometimes not voluntary to begin with and further cannot necessarily simply be abandoned. Religions may be groups one can join but not leave. Moreover, a church might consider itself tolerant (or universal) because it contrasts its own idea—that all who accept its truth can be saved—with a belief that only those linked to the group by blood will receive the benefits of group membership.

We can consider the issues raised by three specific historical situations and then consider a fourth case that illustrates the problem in the setting of custody and adoption in the United States:

1. The Mortara case, a late-nineteenth-century event, involved the taking of a child from a Jewish family by agents of the Papal States. In this case a church-as-state[8] makes a group claim on a child said to be a member of that group, against the wishes of the parent and possibly the child.[9]

---

did not want to be protected by the Minorities Treaties. See Robinson et al., *Minorities Treaties a Failure,* 81, 288.

[6] Cf. Samuel Butler in *Erewhon,* which offers a contract signed by the individual seeking birth, absolving others from responsibility.

[7] See Weisbrod, "Family, Church, and State," on which some of this analysis draws.

[8] The Mormons in the early period used a theocratic form, as did the Puritan commonwealths.

[9] For an alternative reading, emphasizing the choice of the child, see below.

2. The next narrative is like the first, except that the actor is a secular state that chooses to remove a child in the interests of the child, against the claims of the parent. Here we again see a group claim trumping an individual (parental) claim, but the group is the state itself.[10] Here the events relate to the Dionne quintuplets.

3. The third case, in which a state reassigns a child in the involuntary absence of one or both parents, arose out of the tragedy of the Dutch orphans after the Second World War. Here the question becomes what the strength is of a possible group claim in the background.[11]

4. These themes continue in issues involving religious placement in the context of custody and adoption. These cases arise on a wide variety of facts. They are of interest here because they provide a context in which the state can express itself on the question of group identification.

Here the group is a religious group. The questions relate to any group. Is group identification important or not? Are the practices of a particular group acceptable or not? These questions are continually involved in decisions concerning the placement of children. Sometimes questions involving the medical treatment of children are also involved to the extent that groups have distinctive positions on medical treatment. While the underlying facts in case 4 may overlap the other cases—parents may be missing for example, or children may have been removed from homes—there is a separate treatment because we can here review the general issue of matching, with an emphasis here on religious matching, over time in one country.[12]

CASE 1: THE *MORTARA* CASE

Orestes Brownson, an American convert to Catholicism, gave the facts this way in 1859:

> A child of Jewish parents living at Bologna, in the Roman States, who was baptized in infancy, in the presumed danger of death, by a Christian

[10] Note that one can collapse cases 2 and 3 by finding that in case 2 the unfitness of the parents results in their "constructive" absence and that the state has really been "forced" to act.

[11] There may be group claims in the background of controversies between parents, both of whom are present in the family. See discussion of *Kilgrow v. Kilgrow* in Carl E. Schneider and Margaret F. Brinig, *An Invitation to Family Law Teacher's Manual* (St. Paul: West, 1996).

[12] See Fadiman, *The Spirit Catches You.*

domestic, without the knowledge of the parents, has been recently taken by legal process from their custody, and transferred to Rome, that he may be instructed in the Christian faith, in a public institution devoted to the use of Jewish converts. The age of the child is variously stated, at eight or eleven years. The actual state of his mind is reported by all to be that of happiness in his new position. His father has visited him, and has been graciously received by the Sovereign Pontiff. He is said to acquiesce in the detention of his son. What his wishes are it is not difficult to divine.[13]

A new book on the Mortara case provides some detail on the facts. A review of that book offers a useful summary:

Though nearly forgotten today, Edgardo Mortara's abduction was a cause celebre in its time. The struggle between Edgardo's parents and police on the night of June 23, 1858 in Bologna, as David I. Kertzer recounts in his fascinating new history, ended up drawing in kings, prelates, revolutionaries, intellectuals, and ordinary citizens around the world. That night, a police marshal knocked at the Mortaras' door. Once inside, he took a list of names from his pocket and proceeded to check off the members of the Jewish household one by one: husband, wife and eight young children. Then he announced the purpose of his errand. "Signor Mortara," the officer said, "I am sorry to inform you that you are the victim of betrayal. Your son, Edgardo, has been baptized. I am ordered to take him with me.

The description of the dramatic events continues, as the parents watch the child taken away by papal authorization. "A few days later, Edgardo, still under police escort, rode through the gates of the city in a coach bound for Rome. The authorities had decreed that he was never to return to his family again."[14]

In fact, the wishes of the child were not altogether clear. According to other sources, "He cried out quite loud that he wanted to go home with his parents to his brothers and sisters.[15]"

---

[13] Orestes Brownson, "The Mortara Case," *Brownson's Quarterly Review,* April 1859, 226.

[14] Adam Goodheart, "The Soul of the Matter," review of David Kertzer, *Kidnapping of Edgardo Mortara* (New York: Knopf, 1997), *Washington Post,* August 10, 1997, X10. See also Brownson, "The Mortara Case," 230. Brownson was defending the position of the pope in relation to the taking of the child, in the Papal States.

[15] Bertram Wallace Korn, *American Reaction to the Mortara Case* (Cincinnati: American Jewish Archives, 1957), 9.

But as Brownson presents the case,

> [T]his child is firm in the faith, like an apostle. His father begged him to go back with him to Bologna, saying to him, "Why don't you come with me? Have you forgotten God's commandment, 'Honor thy father and mother'?" The child remained pensive for a moment, and then replied—"The Pope knows the commandments better than you or I. I shall do what the Pope says."[16]

One reading of the case would stress the authority of the church over the baptized. Once that authority was established, a range of specific results might be possible, including returning a child to his or her birth parents.

Orestes Brownson's argument stresses that Edgardo's choice is important.

> The dispositions of the child himself are not entirely to be overlooked in this investigation. From all the testimony that can be obtained it appears that he is contented and happy. Some may give little importance to the assent which a child of tender years gives to the Christian doctrine; but the Church recognizes the capacity of all who have attained to the use of reason, to conceive divine faith. The control of parents in matters of religion is necessarily confined to the inculcation of divine truth and the laws of God. Our courts of law seem to acknowledge in them a religious guardianship over their children until these attain to full age; but the ecclesiastical tribunals, with St. Thomas of Acquin,[17] hold, that the child is free from his earliest use of reason, to submit his mind to God, without regard to the views or wishes of his parents, and is bound to embrace the faith, when propounded to him in a manner corresponding to his capacity. He owes obedience to his parents in domestic discipline; he must obey God in things divine. Since, then, the child Edgar, under the instruction which he has received, assents to the Christian faith, it would be wrong for the Pope, who has legal control over him, to place him with his parents, whose prejudices dispose them to train him in contrary principles.[18]

---

[16] Ibid., 10.

[17] Aquinas said, "[I]f children without the use of reason were to receive baptism, then after reaching maturity they could easily be persuaded by their parents to relinquish what they had received in ignorance. This would tend to do harm to the faith." Summa of Theology, II, 10, 12, in *The Pocket Aquinas,* ed. Vernon J. Bourke (New York: Pocket Books, 1960), 253. And also: "Now, after he begins to have the use of free choice, he then begins to be in charge of himself and, as far as things that come under divine or natural law are concerned, he is able to manage these for himself. And at that time, he is to be brought to the faith not by force but by persuasion. He can, then, even consent to the faith and be baptized against the will of his parents; but not before he has the use of reason" (253–54).

[18] Brownson, "The Mortara Case," 234.

A reviewer noted, "From the vantage point of more than a century later (and to some contemporary observers as well) the Mortara case reads as a conflict between modernity and medievalism, between secular liberalism and the last remnants of rule by divine right." But in fact "last remnants" is probably not quite right since, if not divine right, at least a claim to religious authority is precisely what is involved in claims of free exercise.

"Rather than a flickering vestige of the dark days of the Counter-Reformation, the taking of Jewish children was a common occurrence in nineteenth-century Italy,"[19] Kertzer writes.

The clear assertion of a claim by the church to a stance that is today adopted by the state brings us to case 2.

CASE 2: THE DIONNE QUINTUPLETS

The second case here relates to a quite famous group of children, the Dionne quintuplets. The account here is quoted from *The Canadian Encyclopedia*.

> Dionne quintuplets, Annette, Emilie, Yvonne, Celine and Marie aroused worldwide attention after their birth at Corbeil, Ont. to Oliva and Elzire Dionne on 24 May, 1934. A sport on the human species (only 2 previous cases are on record), they were the only quintuplets to survive for more than a few days. This miracle, plus their baby cuteness, the poverty of their French Canadian parents and the controversy over their guardianship, made them the sensation of the 1930s.

The article goes on to describe the actions of the Ontario government, which removed the children from their parents. A hospital was built for them, and they were cared for by the doctor who delivered them. "Olivia Dionne fought a 9-year battle to regain them. In the interval, they became the country's biggest tourist attraction and a $500 million asset to the province. Three million people trekked to 'Quintland' to watch the babies at play behind a one-way screen."[20]

The surviving quints were recently awarded a large settlement.

The removal of children from the Gypsies and aboriginals is well known. Less familiar is the raid on the Mormon polygamous communities in Short Creek, Arizona, in 1953, seen by officials as an effort to save 263 children.[21] Some of the examples we see have to do with an exercise of state power, widely denounced at the time of the events. These, we might

---

[19] Kertzer, p. 34. Mortara, a Catholic priest as an adult, died in 1940.

[20] *The Canadian Encyclopedia,* s.v. "Dionne Quintuplets." See Anthony DePalma, "3 Dionne Survivors Accept a $28 Million Settlement," *New York Times,* March 7, 1998, A4.

[21] Martha Bradley, *Taken from the Land* (Salt Lake City: University of Utah Press, 1996).

say, are the Nazi cases. We like to see these as aberrations, both in terms of the history of a single nation and the history of the world.

But a more troubling fact is that other examples seem to reveal state behavior uncontested at the time, and seen as abusive only several decades later. In this category, we see the current discussions of the Swiss treatment of the Gypsies, the Canadian treatment of the First Nations children (residential homes) and the Canadian government's response to the Dionne quintuplets. These, often involving legal settlements decades after the events, suggest that something has changed in the standard that is applied. Or perhaps it is that more people are included in the concept of "people." Things that would always have been abusive against the privileged group are seen now as abusive also against the pariahs. These are examples of the phenomenon that J. S. Mill considered a fairly standard piece of the history of social progress:[22] "The entire history of social improvement has been a series of transitions, by which one custom or institution after another, from being a supposed primary necessity of social existence, has passed into the rank of an universally stigmatized injustice and tyranny." But knowledge of the history seems to suggest that we must always be at least a little uncertain about one's conclusions in the best interests of the child.

CASE 3: THE DUTCH ORPHANS

A recent book on Fermat's Last Theorem contains the following biographical information about the author: "Alfred Jacobus van der Poorten was born in Amsterdam in 1942 and spent the war as 'Fritsje Teerink,' believing himself to be the youngest child of a family in Amersfoort. His true parents, David and Marian, were among the few who returned from the camps. His family migrated to Sydney, Australia when he was eight years old."[23]

His "true parents," his "family," are understood to be his birth parents.

Here, some will argue the issue of placement in terms of the group claims, while others, notably Freud, Goldstein, and Solnit,[24] will tend to see the question more as a matter of the welfare of the child and need of the child for continuity.

---

[22] J. S. Mill, *Utilitarianism,* ed. Roger Crisp (Oxford: Oxford University Press, 1998).

[23] Alf Van der Poorten, *Notes on Fermat's Last Theorem* (New York: John Wiley and Sons, 1996), xiii. I am grateful to Mark Sheingorn for providing this reference. The material in this section is adapted from Weisbrod, "Family, Church, and State."

[24] See Joseph Goldstein, A. Freud, and A. Solnit, *Beyond the Best Interests of the Child* (New York: Free Press, 1973), 107–8, offering guidelines on child placement using psychoanalytic theory.

"Where abandonment by the biological parent is wholly involuntary, the judge, notwithstanding the child's need, may respond entirely differently. He will judge the parents as innocent victims of war, illness, or any other form of 'force majeure.'" Goldstein, Freud, and Solnit use the example of the Dutch Jewish orphans as a particularly difficult test of their theories of the psychological parent. "The choice in such tragic instances is between causing intolerable hardship to the child who is torn away from his psychological parents, or causing further intolerable hardship to already victimized adults who, after losing freedom, livelihood, and worldly possessions, may now also lose possession of their child."

The Dutch Parliament ruled that "the children would be returned to their biological parents, thereby not leaving the outcome to case-by-case determination by the courts."[25] "Nevertheless, there are many situations of similar impact, no less tragic, though with less world appeal, confronting the decision makers in contested child placements. The guidelines clarify for such decision makers the range, complexity, and nature of the choices that confront them."

Judge Baltimore, the fictitious judge deciding the case, issues a statement of his opinion based on the psychological parent guidelines:

Despite my sympathetic concern for adults faced with tragedy, the choice before the court is no different, though apparently more difficult, than it often seems in foster parent–common-law adoption cases. Whatever the court decides, inevitably there will be hardship. It may be the biological parents, already victimized by poverty, poor education, ill health, prejudice, their own ambivalence, or other circumstances, who are denied their child. It may be the child who is torn away from his psychological parents. It may be the psychological parents who are deprived of the child for whom they have long and faithfully cared. It may be all of them.

If I, in accord with my oath, am to implement the state's preference for serving the child's interests, my choice and decision are clear, though not, as they seldom are, easy. I must decide not to disturb the child's relationship with his common-law parents. More precisely, I must even

---

[25] A footnote quoting a 1972 letter from a Dutch official reads, "At the end of the war some 4500 Jewish children were in hiding in this country. As regards about 2500 of them one parent or both parents survived the war and in these cases the children concerned were returned to their parents, as was prescribed by law. As regards the remaining 2000: most of them were entrusted to members of their Jewish families, but some 360 were left in the care of non-Jewish foster-parents and these cases led to violent disagreements, some of which were protracted over many years. There were therefore no conflicts 'between the two sets of parents.' Of course, there were emotional difficulties when the children were returned to their natural parents" (Goldstein, Freud, and Solnit, *Beyond the Best Interests,* 108).

deny the biological parents an opportunity to call into question the existing placement of "their" child unless they could introduce evidence that "their" child is neglected or abandoned. Harsh as it is and as it must seem to the biological parents, their standing in court is no greater than that of a stranger.[26]

A group claim here might have involved the idea that if the birth parents were unavailable, other members of the group should have been given a priority over the claims of any of the "foster" parents.[27] Often, and on less tragic facts, the group claim is represented by a parent-claimant, or by a person seeking parental status. This problem is the general issue of religious matching, treated here as case 4.[28]

CASE 4: RELIGIOUS MATCHING

Religious matching of children placed by the state in homes or in institutions has to some degree been a characteristic of the American legal system from an early period. But religious matching statutes do not seem to be best understood as a vestige of the early religious establishments. Rather, some of the statutes were adopted as a response by immigrant groups to problems they faced in the American environment. Thus, in 1916, Lee Friedman noted in the *Harvard Law Review*, "In recent years, as the minority religious groups have strengthened themselves they have more aggressively asserted a right to protect from proselytism the children of their faith who come before the courts for disposition usually as dependent, delinquent, or neglected children."[29]

In fact, the issue went back some time. Writing in 1859, Orestes Brownson indicated some of the grievances of nineteenth-century Catholics in America relating to the placement of children:

In our country although the Constitution and laws give no preference to any doctrine or form of worship, public prejudice prevails to such a

---

[26] Ibid., 107–8. The amplifying statement by Dr. Madzy Rood-de Boer, in the Dutch translation of *Beyond the Best Interests of the Child* (*De Toverformule: in Het Belang Van Het Kind*) (1979) makes the point that under Dutch law the birth parents had never lost their parental rights.

[27] See Joel S. Fishman, "Jewish War Orphans in the Netherlands—the Guardianship Issues, 1945–50," *Wiener Library Bulletin* 27 (1973–74): 31–36.

[28] Racial matching and interracial adoption raise similar questions.

[29] Lee Friedman, "The Parental Right to Control the Religious Education of a Child," *Harvard Law Review* 29 (1916): 485, 498. See generally Leo Pfeffer, "Religion in the Upbringing of Children," *Boston University Law Review* 35 (1955): 333, 341. Some of the controversy over religious upbringing of children relates to the enforceability (in the state system) of contracts dealing with the issue.

degree, that the children of Catholics are very frequently withdrawn from their parents, if poor and destitute, and placed under Protestant influence in public institutions. . . . In most States the magistrates can bind out such children, and in some places, as in St. Louis, preachers are employed as paid agents, to enter the houses of the poor, and snatch away their children in the name of the law. Their names are sometimes changed, and they are soon sent away and bound out far from the reach of their parents, whose natural rights are most unfeelingly disregarded.[30]

Similarly, Levi Silliman Ives wrote in 1857 of the problem of Catholic children committed to private asylums run by Protestants.[31] Like Brownson, Ives referred to a constitutional mandate of the state to ensure "the sacred rights of conscience," and claimed the protection of this mandate.

The interreligious tension over children has been clear to historians. Billington called his chapter on school issues in New York (in *The Protestant Crusade*) "Saving the Children for Protestantism."[32] O'Grady wrote, "The history of Catholic charities in the United States is almost a history of the struggle of the immigrant for the preservation of the faith of his children."[33] This struggle involved legislative and political activity. Statutes were adopted ranging from those that gave a strong weight to religious matching, to those that simply included religion among the possible factors, and, finally, those that asked for matching "when practicable."[34] The statutory patterns could reach not only adoption, custody, and guardianship, but even abrogation of adoption. Thus, a New York statute authorized suits to abrogate an adoption because of any "attempt to change or the actual making of a change or the failure to safeguard the religion of such child."[35]

Judicial response to the issue of the religious group presence in individual adoption cases varied. In the 1907 Massachusetts case *Purinton v.*

[30] Brownson, "The Mortara Case."

[31] Levi S. Ives, "Against Sectarian Partisanship in Public Institutions," in *American Catholic Thought on Social Questions,* ed. Aaron Abell (Indianapolis: Bobbs-Merrill, 1965), 90–100.

[32] Ray Billington, *The Protestant Crusade, 1800–1860* (New York: Macmillan, 1938), 142. The reformers, while often religiously oriented, did not necessarily feel committed to the family, either natural or reestablished. See Paul Boyer, *Urban Masses and Moral Order in America, 1820–1920* (Cambridge: Harvard University Press, 1978) (discussion of Charles Loring Brace).

[33] John O'Grady, *Catholic Charities in the United States: History and Problems* (Washington, D.C.: National Conference of Catholic Charities, 1930), 147.

[34] For a review of the statutes, see Note, "Religion as a Factor in Adoption Guardianship and Custody," *Columbia Law Review* 54 (1914): 396–403.

[35] N.Y. Dom. Rel. Law, sec. 118(a) (repealed 1974).

Jamrock,[36] the lower court referred to the presence of religious groups, but rejected their right to a leading role in the proceedings. The Roman Catholic Church and the Baptist Church were the institutions involved. "[I]f members of either church have taken an interest in this case as sectarians and promoters of the interests of their church, they have no proper place before the court and will receive no recognition there."[37] (Other courts, sometimes in other contexts, have viewed the role of the group, and the law of the group, more sympathetically.[38] But a dominant role for sectarian placement agencies remained obvious in the adoption process as a whole.) Thus a symposium held in 1956 on adoption included separate papers on the attitudes toward adoption of Protestant, Catholic, and Jewish groups.[39] At that time it could still be said that "there [was] no area in adoption practice that [was] more sensitive or controversial" than the area concerning the "religious heritage" of the child. The "principal question" confronting agencies was this: "In which religion will a child be raised?" In deciding this issue, "[A]gencies are bound by law and judicial precedent which in turn are products of the mores of the community and the influence of religious groups that make up our population."[40] In the 1950s the possibility of religious groups using a state legislature as a vehicle still remained clear: "If a particular group feels that within the intellectual makeup of the men from which the judges in their community are drawn, there will not necessarily be found an appreciation of the value of religious training similar to that which they possess, they should have recourse to the legislature."[41]

Although by the mid-1950s states often had statutes regulating religious matching in adoptions, the critical point in practice was not the language of the statute but rather judicial interpretation and agency operations.[42] As to this, Monrad Paulson noted that "[r]eligion is employed as a criterion in adoption and child placement cases even where statutes [are silent], . . . [as] agency personnel are likely to match children and

---

[36] *Purinton v. Jamrock,* 195 Mass. 187, 8 N.E. 802 (1907).

[37] Ibid., 196.

[38] See e.g., *Ramon v. Ramon,* 34 N.Y.S.2d 100 (Dom. Rel. Ct. 1942).

[39] Michael Schapiro, *A Study of Adoption Practice,* vol. 1 (New York: Child Welfare League of America, 1956), 58.

[40] Ibid.

[41] Note, "Custody and Adoption of Children—Imposition of a Standard," *Notre Dame Law Review* 33 (1958): 457, 462.

[42] See, e.g., Dale W. Broeder and Frank J. Barrett, "Impact of Religious Factors in Nebraska Adoptions," *Nebraska Law Review* 38 (1959): 641–91. On recent Catholic approaches, see *New Catholic Encyclopedia,* "Adoption (U.S. Law of)." See also Leo Pfeffer, *Creeds in Competition* (New York: Harper, 1958), 127–31.

prospective custodians on a religious basis."[43] Writing in 1953, Leo Pfeffer suggested that while the law spoke in terms of right, status was involved and that judicial protection was sought not for the parent but for the religion.[44] A well-known case in the mid-1950s—*Petition of Goldman*—refused to allow an interreligious adoption even on facts indicating that the mother had consented to the adoption.[45] Clearly, some recognition of a group claim was involved.[46]

But there has been an interesting change in the nature of the discussion over time. By the mid-1950s,[47] the entire debate was seen to raise difficult questions regarding the definitions of group membership.[48] The *Goldman* court did not "attempt to discuss the philosophy underlying the concept that a child too young to understand any religion, even imperfectly, nevertheless, may have a religion."[49] But other commentators on the dramatic litigation of the 1950s did treat this sort of issue.[50] By the mid–twentieth century, it was seen clearly that religious matching statutes require knowledge of the religion of the child and that of the birth and adoptive parents,

---

[43] Monrad Paulsen, "Constitutional Problems of Utilizing a Religious Factor in Adoptions and Placement of Children," in *The Wall between Church and State,* ed. Dallin Oaks (Chicago: University of Chicago Press, 1963), 132.

[44] Leo Pfeffer, *Church, State, and Freedom* (Boston: Beacon Press, 1953), 589.

[45] Petitions of Goldman, 331 Mass. 647, 121 N.E.2d 843 (1954), cert. denied, 348 U.S. 942 (1955). The *Goldman* case involved twin, born to a divorced Catholic mother, who had been privately placed with a Jewish couple. A guardian *ad litem* urged that the adoption violated the Massachusetts religious protection statute under which the twins, having the religion of their mother, had to be placed when practicable with Catholic parents. Since Catholic parents were available, the adoption was not permitted. The Goldmans left the state with the twins. See Pfeffer, *Church, State, and Freedom,* rev. ed., 711–12. The twins here were not baptized. The precise issue of the *Mortara* case, as Orestes Brownson saw it in "The Mortara Case" (relating to the authority of the church over the baptized), was not involved. In the *Goldman* case, unlike *Mortara,* the religion of the natural parent (whether she was still a Catholic) was discussed.

[46] Pfeffer, *Church, State, and Freedom* (1953), 589. Both Pfeffer and Marc Galanter, "Religious Freedoms in the United States: A Turning Point," *Wisconsin Law Review* 1966: 217, 229 n. 69, suggest this.

[47] That is, shortly after the end of the Second World War. Comment, "A Reconsideration of the Religious Element in Adoption," *Cornell Law Review* 560 (1971): 180. Note that genocide is by definition the violation of a group right.

[48] For discussions of group membership, see Marc Galanter, *Competing Equalities: Law and the Backward Classes in India* (Berkeley and Los Angeles: University of California Press, 1984), 305–26. See also Bittker, *Case for Black Reparations.*

[49] Petitions of Goldman, 331 Mass. 647, 652, 121 N.E.2d 843, 846 (1954). See also *In re* Adoption of E., 59 N.J. 36, 279 A.2d 785 (1971). A law review comment characterized the 1950 lawsuits as "cases that graphically demonstrated the basic disharmony between public temporal concerns and religious considerations in the adoptive process." Comment, "A Reconsideration of the Religious Element in Adoption.

[50] See Paul Ramsey, "The Legal Imputation of Religion to an Infant in Adoption Proceedings," *NYU Law Review* 3 (1959): 649.

and thus require some way of discovering what that religion is. It was understood that even for religious groups, the religion of adults (let alone children) might be difficult to determine. Problems of imputation of religion to children,[51] so called multiple dedication,[52] and adult lapses[53] and commitments were seen to be filled with complexity.

The fourth "case" is less about individuals and groups than about some particular ways in which state policies on this subject have been and are expressed through statutes about custody and adoption. The placements may be through custody or adoption decisions, and parents may or may not be present. The problems concern religion, ethnicity, race, and sometimes politics. The discussions and debates are reflected in legal and cultural artifacts—the Indian Child Welfare Act and the film *Losing Isaiah* represent different aspects of the question.

Issues of children and groups are a special subset of questions about individuals and groups. The general problem is that we, as individuals, form groups and we as individuals are formed by groups, indeed understand ourselves often as having been born into groups. If this is rationalized in adults, so that more and more is seen as "choice," these same rationalizations cannot be adopted with respect to children, who are understood, quintessentially, to be "different." The consciousness and capacity of the adult is taken as given. That of the infant is understood to be unknown, and of the small child to be uncertain, malleable, easily influenced, and to be accorded therefore less respect.

Images of childhood cover a wide range. We have "Heaven lies about us in our infancy" and "Our birth is but a sleep and a forgetting" in Wordsworth, and the echo of these themes in writers like P. L. Travers. We have the discussions of the development of consciousness in Sartre (see his *Baudelaire*) and Richard Hughes's description of Emily's assertion of individuality and consciousness in *High Wind at Jamaica*. Negatively, we have work ranging from William Golding's *Lord of the Flies* to *Barbarella* suggesting that, far from being good, children, like human beings in general, are fallen, evil.

In their good or evil, children are like the rest of us. It was the evil of children that had to be restrained as the nineteenth century saw it (and earlier generations also) despite the coexistence of a romantic image of the innocence of the child, and particularly the child dying young. Another

---

[51] Ibid. See also "Religion in Adoption and Custody Cases," in *Institute of Church and State, Conference Proceedings,* vol. 1 (Villanova, Pa.: Villanova Press, 1957), 56–114.

[52] Involved in the *Mortara* incident. See also *In re* Glavas, 203 Misc. 590, 121 N.Y.S.2d 12 (1953). Regarding "belief": does this standard raise the inquiry into actual belief in such a way that a Catholic's "belief" may be Protestant for the purpose of matching a statute? See "Religion and Adoption," *Cornell Law Review* 56 (1971): 798 n. 90.

[53] Petitions of Goldman, 331 Mass. 647, 121 N.E.2d 843 (1954).

tradition that said children were essentially no different from adults.[54] Thus, Lysander Spooner argued for full presumptive capacity,[55] anticipating an argument made by children's liberationists.

Law, whether religious or secular, has separated the children from the grown-ups under the category of rules about status and capacity. The age of sin in the church was seven. The age of majority in secular law for any number of things was highly variable.

Edgardo Mortara eventually became a Catholic priest. There was some dispute as to his actual views as a child. A review of the Kertzer book says: "Kertzer skirts the crucial issue of whether his conversion was accomplished by those who abducted him at an impressionable early age or whether it came sincerely from within himself. Who can tell for sure?"[56] But why is this the crucial issue? It seems to assume that a child of six could make a choice of this kind, as Brownson says that the church holds. Is this what we think?[57] Paul Ramsey's critical comment on testimony to the effect that a child had been "born a Presbyterian"[58] suggests a theological context in which we have to decide something about the point at which a child has an independent right to claim a religious affiliation.

So, too, issues of the cults.[59]

We have seen "liberationist" ideas applied to children. John Holt wants children to have "[t]he right to do, in general, what any adult may legally do."[60] Farson holds a similar position in *Birthrights*.[61] Underlying these arguments is ordinarily a belief that the child's autonomy should be paramount and particularly in instances of abusive or inadequate parenting. But there are limits to our material resources. And another problem could exist even if we had all the money in the world and all the imagination to conceive of good solutions to the problems of the family. This problem maybe suggested by the fact—whether viewed as good or bad depends on the viewer—that younger and younger children are willing to invoke a "rights discourse" against their parents. To this degree, they invoke the

---

[54] See Philippe Aries's *Centuries of Childhood,* trans. Robert Baldick (New York: Knopf, 1962).

[55] Lysander Spooner, "Letter to Grover Cleveland," in *Collected Works,* vol. 1.

[56] Robert Finn, "Kidnapping Story a Fascinating Look at Papal Power," *Plain Dealer,* July 20, 1997.

[57] In 1944, a case (Finlay) arose in France on similar facts, and the children were returned. See Korn, *American Reaction.*

[58] Ramsey, "Legal Imputation of Religion," 654.

[59] Though these cases arise within a context in which an initial capacity may be defeated by fraud or duress.

[60] John Holt, *Escape from Childhood* (New York: E. P. Dutton, 1974), 19. For a quite different idea of the "rights" of the child, see discussed material in John Finnis, *Natural Law* (Oxford: Oxford University Press, 1980).

[61] Richard Farson, *Birthrights* (New York: Macmillan, 1974).

liberationist model. They will call a lawyer, they will call the police, they will threaten their parents, in effect, with state intervention. Some of these children, undoubtedly, believe that the state will be able to help them and that they would be better off without their families. These children, who may already have run away from home, are clear in their judgments and their calculations of the relative risks, or at least as clear as anyone a few years older, and thus above the age of majority. For other children, it may be that the threat of state intervention is rather like the phone call to the lawyer in the context of a spousal argument. It is intended not so much to lead to an immediate divorce as it is to clarify rights in the event of divorce, or even to operate as a threat. Thus, in the context of children and parents, we can imagine a parent saying: "Yes, call the police, and I hope you do well in foster care." Presumably not all the children who invoke their rights really want to leave their rooms. If this is true, the pervasive possibility of state intervention is only that, a possibility, and not a particularly good one, and the family negotiation is left roughly where it was before.[62]

Martha Minow locates in the history of children's rights the "entrance and exit of five legal frameworks for thinking about children: child protection, child liberation, children as potential adults, children in need of traditional authority, and social resource redistribution."[63] About the third of these frameworks, she remarks that "advocates for children's rights sometimes resolved the tension between protection and liberation through a conception of children as potential adults, deserving rights but needing care on the way to adulthood."[64] In 1977, Peter Edelman described a position that favored some rights for children but searched for a program responsive to children's needs. He explicitly resisted the goal of "total parity of rights for children" and instead argued that the proper goal would "extend some adult rights and improve government programs so that children will be assured protection and dignity and the chance to develop their maximum potential."[65] Unclear himself about which additional adult rights should be extended and which should be modified, Edelman lauded children's freedom of religion, racial equality, freedom of ex-

[62] The obituary of Nicole Maxwell, *New York Times,* May 24, 1998, reports that at the age of nine, in a household of Christian Scientists who did not call a doctor to treat her broken arm, she called a doctor herself.

[63] Martha Minow, "Whatever Happened to Children's Rights," *Minnesota Law Review* 80 (1995): 267, 268.

[64] Ibid., 277.

[65] Peter Edelman, "The Children's Rights Movement," in *The Children's Rights Movement: Overcoming the Oppression of Young People,* ed. Beatrice Gross (Garden City, N.Y.: Doubleday, 1977).

pression, procedural due process, and the right to privacy—adult-type rights—along with a right to education that would be unique to children.[66]

The question is what a child's right to such things looks like.

A recent casebook on family law offers a hypothetical problem involving these issues.[67]

"The parents of two of [the principal's] students who are finishing the eighth grade belong to the Old Order Amish Religion. They wish to withdraw their children from her school. Both children are 14 years of age, and both have said that they would like to continue in public school." Adolph is described as a "very fine student," with unusual strength in mathematics and science. He wants to work as a scientist. "Removal from school will make it impossible for him to realize that promise."

Rudolph is described as a good, but not outstanding, student. "He is, however, a very popular member of his class, although his beliefs seem odd to some of his classmates." He is so well liked that he was chosen to be class president. He basically wants to stay in school for social rather than academic reasons.

The problem concludes with a question about the advice to be given to the school principal.

The teacher's manual to the casebook offers some comments on the story. The comments stress the shunning issues that might arise between the child, his parents, and the community. Further, it raises the issue of religious identification. When is someone "Amish," and when is someone of Amish background? The comment concludes by noting the openness of the American educational system. "Perhaps we should say that withdrawal from school will make it 'impossible' for a student to fast track it to his future as a scientist but will not make it impossible to return to school when he is no longer subject to his parents' authority. He can become a scientist on a somewhat slower track."[68]

We often analyze this conflict in terms of tolerance.[69] But we also speak of the child's right to religion. The question of the belief may be quite different from what the liberal takes it to be. A familiar comment of Thomas Jefferson's exemplifies the current liberal version of religious belief: "It does one no injury," Jefferson said, "for my neighbour to say

---

[66] Minow, "Children's Rights," 278 (quoting Edelman, "The Children's Rights Movement," 203–4).

[67] From Leslie J. Harris, L. Teitelbaum, and Carol Weisbrod, *Family Law* (New York: Little, Brown, 1996), 932–33. Note that some former Amish are particularly focused on the group's attitude toward education. Ottie A. Garrett, *True Stories of the X-Amish*, revised by R. Irene Garrett (Horse Cave, Ky.: New Leben, 1998), 38.

[68] Gutmann, *Democratic Education*.

[69] Nomi Stolzenberg, "He Drew a Circle That Shut Me Out," *Harvard Law Review* 106 (1993): 106.

there are twenty gods, or no god. It neither picks my pocket nor breaks my leg."[70] This idea of course is underneath the action/belief dichotomy in the field of church and state. Time enough to intervene, we think, when action is involved. The corresponding freedom to believe is said to be absolute.

As to behavior, another issue here is that certain behavior is not acceptable, even when that behavior is justified by religious belief. A final example of a problem of groups and children and the difficulty of changing locally enforced customs was reported in India in 1991. Both sets of parents, supported by friends and neighbors, killed a young man and young woman for violation of the traditional caste system in their marriage. A similar killing was reported in the *Times* of London ten years later.[71] A discussion of the 1991 killings raised a number of difficult questions.

> This incident is important to reflect upon, suggesting more general concerns. It challenges an uncritical reliance on democracy at the local level. It questions whether deference to tradition and cultural diversity is appropriate under all conditions. It suggests that non-Western cultural traditions, as well as Western traditions, can be oppressive. It points to the difficult predicament raised by a need for metacultural norms, and it encourages all of us to engage in interrogations of our own cultural heritage and to engage in intercultural dialogues. Cultural reality is no more univocal than political reality, and one must resist the temptation, often inflamed by ethnic and racial prejudice, to reduce an alien culture to its most violent and literalistic traditions. Such a tendency is especially pronounced, at present, in the stereotyping of Islam in the West, and of the West in Islam. There are also Hindu/Muslim tensions evident on the Indian subcontinent, both in Indo-Pakistan relations, the conflict relating to Kashmir, and most of all, in the rise of Hindu extremism within India, with its strong anti-Muslim orientation.[72]

While we are deeply interested in the phenomenon of groups and their role in the society, we are also deeply distrustful of any notion of group characteristics, seeing this as step on the way stereotyping or racism.[73] In

---

[70] Thomas Jefferson, "Notes on the State of Virginia," in *Writings* (New York: Library of America, 1984), 283.

[71] See *London Times*, August 9, 2001.

[72] Richard Falk, *On Human Governance: Toward a New Global Politics*, The World Order Models Project Report of the Global Civilization Initiative (University Park: Pennsylvania State University Press, 1995), 65.

[73] Recently, on associations and groups generally, see Nancy Rosenblum, *Membership and Morals* (Princeton: Princeton University Press, 1998). European integration and international trade generally, however, has brought a certain immediacy to discussions of national

response to a form of argument that tends in the opposite direction and suggests that all deviation is major, dangerous, and a threat to the social order, we focus on the arguably normless middle range. One way or another it seems that the strongest conventional examples of religious behavior that might be condemned under and action-belief dichotomy have become problematic. Our leading example had been, traditionally, nineteenth-century Mormon polygamy. Under the impact of current events in the area of divorce and nonmarital living arrangements, it is relatively simple to say that nineteenth-century Mormon marriage was not given a fair hearing.[74] But what case has replaced that case on the spectrum? Other examples of free exercise problems seem relatively nonthreatening. The recently decided *Smith* case involved religious use of peyote.[75] The Sikh turban cases surely involve behavior we could live with. Jonestown, generally conceded to be horrible, is also a case understood in terms of pathology so extreme that it is out of the range of ordinary discussion.

Perhaps for this reason, to put back on the table the possibility of religious groups not of the middle range, we might recall Carthage.[76] Will we say that even here, the culture must be judged against its reasons, so that the infanticide of Carthage was perhaps merely on balance wrong, and that *Delenda est Carthago* was perhaps a somewhat excessive reaction?[77] Whatever the answer to the problem of the sources of our moral judgments, clearly we do not gain much, for example, by discussing the free exercise problems as though all our cases involved small and apparently innocuous deviations from standard dress codes (apparently, of course, because we live by symbols, and the smallest may invoke the largest). Clearly Carthage—or the question invoked, for example, in medical care for children or religious groups—presents rather different issues.

---

character in a commercial context. See, e.g., Gavin Kennedy, *Negotiate Anywhere!* (London: Arrow Books, 1987), 83 (discussing many cultural approaches to negotiation, including American approaches, under heading: "Have a good day in the US of A or wham, bam, it's a deal, Sam").

[74] On the current discussion, see Johnson, "Polygamists Emerge from Secrecy," *New York Times,* April 9, 1991, 22; Joseph, "My Husband's Nine Wives," *New York Times,* May 23, 1991, A31.

[75] *Employment Div. v. Smith,* 110 S. Ct. 1595 (1990).

[76] See Gilbert K. Chesterton, *The Everlasting Man* (1925; Garden City, N.Y.: Image Books, 1955), 145: "These highly civilized people really met together to invoke the blessing of heaven on their empire by throwing hundreds of their infants into a large furnace. We can only realize the combination by imagining a number of Manchester merchants with chimney-pot hats and mutton-chop whiskers, going to church every Sunday at eleven o'clock to see a baby roasted alive."

[77] See Plutarch, *Plutarch's Lives,* trans. John Dryden, ed. A. Clough (London: J. M. Dente and Sons, 1910). Note also that another Roman thought that Carthage should stand. The film director Jean Renois said, "You see, in this world, there is one awful thing, and that is

As to beliefs, Jefferson's perspective omits a rather critical issue. Beliefs if deeply held[78] do matter, do have social consequences. This is why we are so concerned about the socializing aspects of the education of children. We want them to learn tolerance, respect for others. Perhaps polytheism or monotheism is not important, as Jefferson indicates. But other beliefs, concerning eligibility for salvation, for example, may matter quite deeply.

Religious groups define themselves with reference to a truth and also a membership question. *We* is not the same as *all* or *them*. Karl Llewellyn addressed this by saying, "[W]e misconceive group prejudice when we think of it as primarily a prejudice *against* some one or more particular groups. . . . It is instead at bottom a prejudice *in favor* of 'My Own Group' as against *all* others, 'pro-us' prejudice eternal, live, and waiting, ready to be focused and intensified against *Any* Other Group."[79] We are saved and they are not. *Salus extra ecclesiam non est.*[80]

In this sense, issues of the relation between Christianity and the Holocaust would exist without a single anti-Semitic text in the New Testament. This powerful sense of the consequences of group membership is associated today often with particular dissenting churches, particularly those out of the left wing of the Reformation, whose exclusionary and deviant tendencies seem particularly obvious. Thus, *Quiner v. Quiner* describes the Plymouth Brethren in terms than make them seem profoundly odd.[81] But perhaps the group is in some ways not unusual.

The fundamental teaching of traditional religion seems to be that there is a truth, which is behind us. Associated with this may be the claim that a particular affiliation based on the acceptance of that truth is necessary to salvation. Even when there is development of doctrine that mitigates the impact of this idea, the issue must have a profound impact on children socialized within groups.[82] It is hard to see how this idea is "tolerant"—is it not "intolerant" to say that those outside your group are

---

that everyone has his reasons." Quoted in Aviam Soifer, "Complacency and Constitutional Law," *Ohio State Law Journal* 42 (1981): 382, 397.

[78] See Frank Knight, "Theology and Education," *American Journal of Sociology* 44 (1939): 649. He notes that freedom of religion only came "with the relative eclipse of religion by secular interests" (668).

[79] Karl N. Llewellyn, *Jurisprudence* (Chicago: University of Chicago Press, 1962).

[80] See the recent discussion in Austin Flannery, ed., *Vatican Council II* (Northport, N.Y.: Costello, 1996). Augustine, *De Baptismo Contra Donatistes,* bk. 4, chap. 17, sec. 24. Also: Cyprian, *De Ecclesiae Catholicae Unitate*, sec. 6, *Epistle ad Pomponius, De Virginibus*, sec. 4. Also commonly found as *Extra Ecclesiam Nulla Salus.*

[81] 59 *Cal. Rptr.* 503 (1967). See on Plymouth brethren Edmund Grosse, *Father and Son* (1912; Oxford: Oxford University Press, 1934); Garrison Keiler and discussions in Carl E. Schneider, "Religion and Child Custody"; Weisbrod, *Butterfly, the Bride.*

[82] Aren't even wild children socialized within animal groups?

not saved?—except on the older understandings in which tolerance gives those tolerated equal standing but only a right to existence and, of course, on the issue of potentially universal membership, at least for some groups.

The doctrinal problem is far deeper, more centrally connected to the core of religious belief, than the matters ordinarily considered under the heading reform of liturgy. It is the difference between those issues addressed by Vatican II concerning references to the Jews in John (which are explained and modified by the council, which offers an interpretation that reduces the anti-Semitic overtone) and the propositions, based on the Gospel accounts, concerning the necessity of baptism for salvation.[83] Considerable subtlety is involved in the question of the categories of membership, or the different ways we can stand "in relation" to the church.[84] It may be worth noting that the position outlined above, based on the accounts of the New Testament, is often called "anti-Judaic" or "religiously based anti-Judaism" to reflect both its theological basis and the fact that in theory, in some religions, the consequences of damnation could be avoided by conversion to the true faith. The contrast is to racially defined anti-Semitism, whose consequences cannot be avoided on the basis of religious belief or identification. It is clear that Edgar Mortara, a Catholic priest, would have been regarded by the Nazis, entering his Belgian town in 1940, as a Jew.

This chapter has set out a number of group claims, moving from the strongest to the relatively weaker ones that are in controversy today. We do not expect to see a Mortara case today.[85] We do, however, see the issues over education and child rearing that are the modern versions of that case, all over America and indeed all over the Western world. The problem becomes, then, not the issue of the classification of groups by a central authority but rather our sense of the role of the state and other groups. When we say "our sense" of the role of the state, we have reached the level at which one can argue not so much that the personal is political, as that the political is personal, a product of our deepest selves. This problem—the relations among the individual self, the group, and the state—is the subject of chapter 10.

[83] See Miikka Ruokanen, *The Catholic Doctrine of Non-Christian Religions* (New York: E. J. Brill, 1992); *New Catholic Encyclopedia*, s.v. "Salvation"; Maurice Eminyan, *Theology of Salvation* (Boston: St. Paul Editions, 1960). On the papal apology see Alessandra Stanley, "Pope Asks Forgiveness for Errors of the Church over 2,000 Years," *New York Times,* March 13, 2000, A1.

[84] See *New Catholic Encyclopedia.*

[85] A discussion of the Mortara case that offers some similar contemporary questions is Steven Lubet, "Judicial Kidnapping, Then and Now: The Case of Edgardo Mortara," *Northwestern Law Review* 93 (1999): 961.

CHAPTER 10

Negotiating the Frameworks: The Problem of the Sensitive Citizen

I am large, I contain multitudes.

—WALT WHITMAN, *Leaves of Grass*

Come over here, where the chancellor can't hear us.

—KO-KO TO POOH-BAH, *The Mikado,* W. S. Gilbert

✦ THE line from *The Mikado* is, of course, a joke. Ko-Ko is Lord High Executioner of Titipu. Pooh-Bah, to whom he speaks, is the Lord High Everything Else, including the chancellor. Pooh-bah, asked how much money Ko-Ko should spend on his wedding, responds serially in each of his roles. "[A]s First Lord of the Treasury, I could propose a special vote that would cover all expenses, if it were not that, as Leader of the Opposition, it would be my duty to resist it, tooth and nail. Or, as Paymaster General, I could so cook the accounts that, as Lord High Auditor, I should never discover the fraud. But then, as Archbishop of Titipu, it would be my duty to denounce my dishonesty and give myself into my own custody as first Commissioner of Police."[1]

These persons could each be squared by a large bribe. The passage is a description of role conflicts as elegant as any of those in the academic literature. But the public roles of Pooh-Bah reveal a certain complication. If ever there was a person whose individuality survives his roles, his memberships, and his professional affiliations, it is he. Even his family pride is not, we feel, the true center of his sense of importance. He does not after all, follow the guidance of this affiliation. He matters because he matters.

This final chapter takes up the themes outlined above. The first section discusses the "sensitive citizen" in the modern nation-state as seen by Henry James; the second deals with that citizen as a person affiliated with

---

[1] *The Mikado,* from *The Complete Plays of Gilbert and Sullivan* (New York: W. W. Norton & Company, 1997), 307.

different groups. The third deals with the complex self and the conclusion of the chapter addresses law and multiple selves.

THE SENSITIVE CITIZEN

The *sensitive citizen* is used here as a formula for an individual who is affiliated with persons and groups and who, at the same time, contains them as an aspect of his or her identity in a culture. The phrase is used by Henry James in an account of his visit to Ellis Island published in 1907. It is useful here because it allows us to discuss more than such figures as the rational maximizer, the communitarian, or the reasonable man. The sensitive citizen may be all of these at different times. The self, as developed in this chapter, senses, thinks, and feels, but without what has been called the "unity of the I think."[2]

The phrase *sensitive citizen* evokes identifications and cultural linkages that might be more fluid and convoluted than, for example, the gendered citizen or the religious citizen or the naturalized citizen.[3] The adjectives there are, finally, limiting. They define more rather than less precisely.

Pooh-Bah's role conflicts are, at one level or another, universal. Particularly common ones involve the double role of citizen and believer: as another example, a naturalized citizen has complex identifications to a former role and a present one.[4] These "roles" relate to standardized relations and often to institutional and group memberships.[5] In the case of the United States, the nation of immigrants, the issues were obvious in relation to the large question of national identity, since all of those who came to be American had been, at one time, something else.

Ellis Island is the image. From 1892 to 1924, some 22 million immigrants, passengers, and crew members passed through Ellis Island. "Now, thanks to the generous efforts of volunteers of the Church of Jesus Christ

[2] Milton Singer, "Signs of the Self," *American Anthropologist* 82 (1980): 485, 488. Singer describes Charles Peirce's idea of the self: "Peirce's starting point is the sensing, thinking, feeling, willing self of 19th century philosophy and psychology. That self, however, is no longer for him a permanent Cartesian mental substance with the powers of introspection, intuition and universal doubt, which is dispelled by clear and distinct ideas of its own existence, the unity of the 'I think.'"

[3] Of course, in referring to a "citizen," rather than a subject, we are immediately discussing something late in the development of Western political forms.

[4] Some roles are declared by a state's law to be incompatible with each other. A father cannot be his daughter's husband or lover. The law of incest, like the law of conflict of interest, is about state regulation of roles.

[5] On groups, see Aviam Soifer, *Law and the Company We Keep* (Cambridge: Harvard University Press, 1998).

of Latter-day Saints, these [passenger] manifests have been transcribed into a vast electronic archive, which you can easily search to find an individual passenger."[6] The Web site for Ellis Island makes plain the dimension of the immigration.[7]

Immigration to America and its relation to his own sense of self was one of the issues that confronted Henry James when he returned to the United States for a visit in 1907. He described Ellis Island, "the terrible little Ellis Island, the first harbour of refuge and stage of patience for the million or so of immigrants annually knocking at our official door.

> Before this door, which opens to them there only with a hundred forms and ceremonies, grindings and grumblings of the key, they stand appealing and waiting, marshalled, herded, divided, subdivided, sorted, sifted, searched, fumigated, for longer or shorter periods—the effect of all which prodigious process, an intendedly "scientific" feeding of the mill, is again to give the earnest observer a thousand more things to think of than he can pretend to retail.[8]

It is clear that James was completely dismayed by what he saw of Ellis Island. He thought that any sensitive citizen would react in the same way. "I think indeed that the simplest account of the action of Ellis Island on the spirit of any sensitive citizen who may have happened to 'look in' is that he comes back from his visit not at all the same person that he went. He has eaten of the tree of knowledge, and the taste will be for ever in his mouth."[9]

Ellis Island was to James something evocative of the fall of man considered as an American event. This sensitive citizen "thought he knew before, thought he had the sense of the degree in which it is his American fate to share the sanctity of his American consciousness, the intimacy of his American patriotism, with the inconceivable alien; but the truth had never come home to him with any such force." He would go around "about ever afterwards with a new look, for those who can see it, in his face, the outward sign of the new chill in his heart."[10] Henry James assumed that "[o]ne's supreme relation, as one had always put it, was one's relation to one's country—a conception made up so largely of one's countrymen and one's countrywomen."[11] At the same time, he knew that the opposing

---

[6] See www.ellisisland.org (Web site). Not all immigration to the United States was through Ellis Island.

[7] It also show that outsiders (the Mormons of chapter 3) can become insiders over time.

[8] Henry James, *The American Scene* (New York: Penguin, 1994), 66.

[9] Ibid.

[10] Ibid.

[11] Ibid., 67. He was, of course, critical of America: But he saw at the same time, its immense possibility. "What you see is the space and the freedom—which at every turn, in America, make one yearn to take other things for granted. The ground is so clear of preoccupation, the air so clear of prejudgment and doubt, that you wonder why the chance shouldn't be as great

concept of the "alien" was not easy to deal with. "Who and what is an alien, when it comes to that, in a country peopled from the first under the jealous eye of history?—peopled, that is, by migrations at once extremely recent, perfectly traceable and urgently required."[12]

Henry James, was of course deeply aware of the difference in national cultures. A cosmopolitan American who lived in England and was finally naturalized in 1915, he wrote fiction that dealt largely with the contrasts between the New and Old Worlds and was based on contrasts between innocence and corruption. His well-known list (1879) of the intellectual and cultural deficiencies of Hawthorne's world left America at a serious disadvantage.[13]

But it might be a mistake to conclude from this that James's primary identification would be defined in national terms. William James said of his brother that he was "a native of the James family and had no other country."[14] And if we move from Henry to William, we find not only the family as a country, but also a complex idea of the self. For William James, the self was social. In a notable discussion, William James referred to a self, even a most private self, as engaged in dialogue with a "deepest judging companion." The interior dialogue is, finally, identified with prayer.[15]

These two comments of William James introduce the next two sections. The "James family" as the country of origin places all individuals in family groups, and these groups have their own frameworks. The following section, on Susanna and the Elders, considers some issues introduced here. The comment that the self is not unitary but dialogic switches the lens, so that we are not looking at a unitary self that is affiliated, but rather a complex self whose internal aspect is made up of others. This is explored through a discussion of names.

---

for the aesthetic revel as for the political and economic, why some great undaunted adventure of the arts, meeting in its path none of the aged lions of prescription, of proscription, of merely jealous tradition, should not take place in conditions unexampled. From the moment it is but a question of some one's, of every one's caring, where was the conceivable quantity of care, where were the means and chances of application, ever so great?" (327).

[12] Ibid., 95.

[13] Henry James, *Hawthorne* (Ithaca, N.Y.: Cornell University Press, 1975), 34–35:

[O]ne might enumerate the items of high civilisation, as it exists in other countries, which are absent from the texture of American life, until it should become a wonder to know what was left. No State, in the European sense of the word, and indeed barely a specific national name. No sovereign, no court, no personal loyalty, no aristocracy, no church, no clergy, no army, no diplomatic service, no country gentlemen, no palaces, no castles, nor manors, nor old country-houses, nor parsonages, nor thatched cottages, nor ivied ruins; no cathedrals, nor abbeys, nor little Norman churches; no great Universities nor public schools—no Oxford, nor Eton, nor Harrow; no literature, no novels, no museums, no pictures, no political society, no sporting class—no Epsom nor Ascot! Some such list as that might be drawn up of the absent things in American life—especially in the American life of forty years ago, the effect of which, upon an English or a French imagination, would probably, as a general thing, be appalling.

[14] Quoted in Jean Strouse, *Alice James: A Biography* (Cambridge: Harvard University Press, 1999), x.

[15] James, "The Consciousness of Self," 315–16.

THE AFFILIATED SELF: SUSANNA AND THE ELDERS

The story of Susanna is familiar. "There once lived in Babylon a man named Joakim. He married a wife named Susanna, the daughter of Hilkiah, a very beautiful and pious woman. Her parents also were upright people and instructed their daughter in the Law of Moses."[16] Two elders of the community were judges who desired Susanna, but she rejected their advances, despite their threat to accuse her of immorality. The elders in fact make this accusation of immorality with a young man.

There is a judicial proceeding in which Susanna insists on her innocence. But the elderly judges are believed, and she is sentenced to death. Susanna appeals to God. "And the Lord heard her cry, and as she was being led away to be put to death, God stirred up the holy spirit of a young man named Daniel, and he loudly shouted, 'I am clear of the blood of this woman.'" Daniel's intervention, focused on the inconsistencies in the testimony of the elders—what kind of tree was it under which the man stood with Susanna?—results in a finding of her innocence.

"And Hilkiah and his wife praised God for their daughter Susanna and so did Joakim her husband and all her relatives, because she had done nothing immodest. And from that day onward, Daniel had a great reputation in the eyes of the people."

Using the story of Susanna and the Elders,[17] we can raise the various responses that individuals in a family might make to a problem, noting the frames in which individuals organize the story, depending on which affiliation they invoke. The text itself contrasts the context of the old men,[18] threatening her within the law, which indeed backs them, with the organizing structures, seen as true, of Daniel, inspired of God. In another frame of reference, Daniel may look like a self-appointed prophet who exerts an illegitimate power over a mass of people cowed by a single voice in a story that becomes one about authoritarianism in action.[19] Or in another frame, the modern feminist version, the story is about rape.

---

[16] *The Apocrypha: An American Translation,* trans. Edgar Goodspeed (New York: Vintage, 1989).

[17] The following discussion uses parts of Weisbrod, "Susanna and the Elders: A Note on the Regulation of Families," originally published in the *Utah Law Review* 1998:271. That essay focused on the questions how big is the family? who governs the family? and what is the subject of family law? The questions here are different.

[18] See R. H. Charles, *The Apocrypha and Pseudepigrapha of the Old Testament in English* (Oxford: Clarendon Press, 1913), 1:647–51. Susanna and the Elders is part of the Apocrypha. The Vulgate offers Susanna as chapter 13 of Daniel (ibid., 639, 647–51). See generally, Robert H. Pfeiffer, *History of New Testament Times* (New York: Harper, 1949), 67 (discussing the history of the stories of Daniel and Susanna).

[19] This reading was suggested to me by Ellen Ash Peters.

Paintings of Susanna and the Elders tell a story about lascivious old men viewing and even moving to rape a beautiful woman, vulnerable and naked at her bath.[20] Through another optic, another frame, it is defined as concerning the sequestration of witnesses.[21] The narrative offered by lawyers focuses on the trial scene, so that we imagine all participants clothed, speaking to each other, asking questions. Helmholz notes, as to the use of the story by canonists, that the story of Susanna and the Elders in the Book of Daniel was seen to vindicate a particular manner of receiving testimony, that is, by private and separate examination of each witness.[22]

But around the couple itself, there are frequently other people with an interest in the questions. These persons support one side or another and may have, by their example and teaching, done one thing or another to frame the issues and influence or even dictate the answers to the questions.

Daniel is not a member of Susanna's family, and he is not a representative of the official legal system surrounding the family. In modern terms, we would say that representing a religion, he was a representative of a *mediating institution,* between the state and the individual. But it is perfectly plain that Daniel does not really, in the story of Susanna, represent anything intermediate to anyone human. Daniel is a divine representative in the Apocrypha. As he would emerge today, Daniel would be less a carrier of the divine voice and more a church official.

As a divine representative, Daniel is not simply a wise judge whose decisions are informed by the religious tradition. Rather, he is someone who has a direct line to Divinity. And thus he knows, in advance, that Susanna is innocent.[23] Generally speaking, this is knowledge we do not have. "[I]t is current doctrine that the age of miracles is past," Karl Llewellyn wrote in *The Bramble Bush*.[24]

Professor John Henry Wigmore tells a secular version of the Susanna story, omitting the references to Susanna's appeal to God and God's ap-

---

[20] The story is a familiar subject in art, in part because of the visual opportunities it presents the artist. For modern feminist commentary, see for example, Mieké Bal, *Reading Rembrandt: Beyond the Word-Image Opposition* (Cambridge: Cambridge University Press, 1991), 148–76; Mary D. Garrard, *Artemisia Gentileschi* (Princeton: Princeton University Press, 1989), 173, 182–209; Kathryn Smith, "Inventing Marital Chastity," *Oxford Art Journal* 16 (1993): 3–24.

[21] See Charles, *Apocrypha and Pseudepigrapha,* 650 (quoting Daniel as saying "put them [the Elders] asunder one far from another and I will examine them").

[22] R. H. Helmholz, "The Bible in the Service of the Canon Law," *Chicago-Kent Law Review* 70 (1995): 1557, 1573 (discussing use of story of Susanna to justify manner of receiving testimony in the *ius commune*).

[23] See Charles, *Apocrypha and Pseudepigrapha,* 650 n. 51b.

[24] K. N. Llewellyn, *The Bramble Bush: On Our Law and Its Study* (New York: Oceana, 1969), 38.

pointment to Daniel altogether.[25] We go from "the assembly believed [the Elders]" to Daniel, "standing in the midst of them, said: . . . 'Are ye such fools?' "[26] This stance makes possible Wigmore's odd interpretation of some of Daniel's speeches. Wigmore was concerned about the "vituperation"[27] and "disconcerting anathema"[28] in the Susanna story, in which Daniel predicts the downfall of the Elders. (Wigmore attributes this to Daniel's "desire to anger and confuse the witness, preventing him from recollecting the details of his story if he had invented one."[29] But Daniel knows that Susanna is innocent and knows therefore that the story is invented. He is more likely, then, to be denouncing the Elders because they deserve denunciation.)[30]

The proposition that a divine will directly regulates the family is linked for some to the problem of the Akeda and the command to Abraham to sacrifice Isaac.[31] And indeed, a broad social-historical approach to the history of the American family might note that at times, as an aspect of the importance of the Bible and religion in the culture generally, we see a direct use of the story of Genesis.[32] Thus, in 1879, Charles Freeman killed his young daughter, Edith, believing that this sacrifice had been divinely commanded, and that the child would rise on the third day.[33] Freeman had consulted his wife and, after some deliberation, had concluded that this was a test, like the test of Abraham, recounted in Genesis.[34] One

---

[25] See Wigmore, *Evidence in Trials at Common Law,* revised by James H. Chadbourne (Boston: Little, Brown, 1976), sec. 1837, 455–56.

[26] Ibid., 455.

[27] Ibid., 456 n. 3.

[28] Ibid., 456 n. 4.

[29] Ibid., 456 n. 3.

[30] See Charles, *Apocrypha and Pseudepigrapha,* 650 n. 51b. I do not mean to suggest that all modern expositions of the Susanna story omit the element of inspiration. Nonetheless, the omission provides a parallel to our modern church-state doctrine in a way that seems worth noting.

[31] See Gen. 22:2. Among recent treatments, see Martha Minow, "Child Endangerment, Parental Sacrifice: A Reading of the Binding of Isaac," in *Beginning Anew: A Woman's Companion to the High Holy Days,* ed. Gail Twersky Reimer and Judith A. Kates (New York: Simon and Schuster, 1997), 145, 145–53; George Steiner, "A Conversation Piece," in *Proofs and Three Parables* (London: Penguin, 1993), 101, 101–14.

[32] It is an aspect of the nineteenth century particularly difficult for a much more secular age to fully appreciate.

[33] See Carol Weisbrod, "Charles Guiteau and the Christian Nation," *Journal of Law and Religion* 7 (1989): 187, 216.

[34] Ibid., 216–21 (citing Folsom, "The Case of Charles F. Freeman of Pocasset, Mass.," *American Journal of Insanity* 40 (1884): 353–63). Freeman was found insane of the basis of a hearing held in 1879 and declared unfit for trial. He was in an institution at the time of the Guiteau trial. Freeman was finally tried in 1883. Following his acquittal, Freeman, though then legally sane, was hospitalized pursuant to the Massachusetts statute of 1873, which provided that a prisoner should be kept in confinement "until it appears to the Governor

hundred years later, it is still true that cases of divine command arise with reference to parents killing children and that the insanity issue is raised.[35]

Divine command is, then, one immense frame. A modified version of the divine command frame arises when we say that the entire family sees itself as under the authority of religious law. All are committed to that regulatory system, which has something to say about who in the family takes precedence on various points. A conventional hierarchy would be husband, wife, child.

Today, as much as in the time of the biblical narrative, the family may submit itself to church sanctions. Sometimes, the submission of the family to the authority of the religion results in a conflict with the state authorities. The divine will is interpreted by religious authorities and linked to strong cultural traditions.[36] But "the family" is in fact individuals. Individuals decide things on the basis of some idea, some value. Thus, we can see the family as a place in which normative orders compete through individuals. Such competition between codes, and the negotiations between individuals that result, may change the question from "Who governs?" to "Who decides what, when, and how?" We recall the joke about decisions in the family to the effect that the husband decides such large questions as who will be president while the wife decides such issues as where the children will go to school.[37]

Our models of family decisions relate to several kinds of decisions and contemplate several kinds of decision-making processes. Thus, we speak of decisions in the family relating to health, education, and the like, in relation to children, and allocate these to parents, or sometimes persons in the place of parents. We distinguish between power and influence when

---

and council that he may be discharged and set at large without danger to others" (Weisbrod, 217 n. 119, quoting *Gleason v. Inhabitants of West Boylston*, 136 Mass. 489, 490 (1884)).

[35] See John Makeig, "Mother Acquitted on Grounds of Insanity in Killing of Child," *Houston Chronicle,* March 11, 1998, A1. The death of children through exorcism is occasionally reported. See Matea Gold, "Women Convicted of Killing Girl in Exorcism," *Los Angeles Times,* October 15, 1997, B1.

In the Jewish tradition, there is an argument that one should not rest one's judgments on divine command. See Izhak Englard, "Majority Decision vs. Individual Truth," *Tradition* 15 (spring–summer 1975): 137. In the story of the Oven of Achnai, the Divine Voice says, "Why do you disagree with Rabbi Eliezar [*sic*]. The Halakhah is always as he says it is" (Englard, 138).

[36] In a fairly recent incident in Nebraska young daughters complained, defining themselves as aggrieved by the traditional rules because they perceived an assimilation option as desirable. See comments of Lawrence Friedman on a comparable issue in "The War of the Worlds: A Few Comments on Law, Culture, and Rights," *Case Western Reserve University Law Review* 47 (1997): 379 (discussing female circumcision).

[37] For some different meanings of *agency* here, see Amartya Sen, *Inequality Reexamined* (Cambridge: Harvard University Press, 1992), 57–58 (distinguishing between an agency that involves participation and an agency that does not).

we say that, for example, someone must be notified of something before it happens. We leave room for judgment and reassessment when we ask for waiting periods before something can be done. Increasingly, we associate family decision making with life-and-death issues. Though the family has always had a critical role in relation to life chances--who is educated, for example, and how--it is apparent that its power in the field of medicine particularly is growing as the choices become simultaneously more complex and more visible.

Susanna is in these groups at least: the couple, the extended family, the household, the religiously ordered political community, the religious community ruled by the divine voice. She might also be in many other groups, involved with their particular "club" law. The groups have a priority in her time and place that is not universal. The relationship between the religious-political community and the divine voice is not, of course a constant. The modern American emphasis on the couple is not found in the Susanna story. The household that is so prominent in her story has all but disappeared in modern life.

But we are as embedded in our groups as Susannah and as caught up in brokering their demands. Pooh-Bah's answer was that each of his incarnations must receive a bribe. Other answers are given.

One answer insists that there is no necessary conflict, since the ordering is clear and the groups are, in effect, often nested in one another. Thus, Durkheim, speaking of only three groups (the family, the nation or the political group, and humanity), asked, "Ought one to commit himself to one of these to the exclusion of others?"[38] No: He concluded that "despite certain simplistic statements that have been made, there is no necessary antagonism between these three loyalties, as if one were only able to be a citizen of his country to the extent that he was alienated from the family, or could not fulfill his obligations as one of mankind except as he forgot his duties as citizen." Durkheim believed that "[f]amily, nation, and humanity represent different phases of our social and moral evolution, stages that prepare for, and build upon, one another." Thus, "[T]hese groups may be superimposed without excluding one another . . . as each with its part to play in historical development" complements the other in the present: each has its function. The function he saw were these: "The family involves the person in an altogether different way, and answers to different moral needs, than does the nation. It is not a matter then of making an exclusive choice among them. Man is morally complete only when governed by the threefold force they exercise on him."[39]

---

[38] Emile Durkheim, *Moral Education: A Study in the Theory and Application of the Sociology of Education,* trans. Everett K. Wilson (New York: Free Press, 1973), 74.

[39] Ibid.

Moreover, Durkheim suggested that the groups "constitute a hierarchy." He thought that "[t]he evidence suggests that familial goals are and should be subordinated to national objectives, if for no other reason than that the nation is a social group at a higher level. Because the family is closer to the individual, it provides less impersonal and, hence, less lofty goals. The circle of familial interests is so restricted that it is in large measure the same as individual interests."[40] But, again, he was thinking of only three groups.

A more complex list of groups is offered by Chester Barnard, who also sees the need for some sort of hierarchical arrangement. In *The Functions of the Executive,* Barnard discusses the function of multiple roles in these terms. Barnard speaks of a man "in Massachusetts, a member of the Baptist Church, having a father and mother living, and a wife and two children, who is an expert machinist employed at a pump station of an important water system."[41] These, however, are only some identifications among many others that the man might have:

> We impute to him several moral codes: Christian ethics, the patriotic code of the citizen, a code of family obligations, a code as an expert machinist, a code derived from the organization engaged in the operation of the water system. He is not aware of these codes. These intellectual abstractions are a part of his "system," ingrained in him by causes, forces, experiences, which he has either forgotten or on the whole never recognized. Just what they are, in fact, can at best only be approximately inferred by his actions, preferably under stress.

Barnard thought that his individual figure "has no idea as to the order of importance of these codes, although, if pressed, what he might say probably would indicate that his religious code is first in importance, either because he has some intellectual comprehension of it, or because it is socially dominant."[42]

Barnard's version of the hierarchy of importance is quite different from Durkheim's. "I shall hazard the guess . . . that their order of importance is as follows: his code as to the support and protection of his own children, his code of obligations to the water system, his code as a skilled artisan, his code with reference to his parents, his religious code, and his code as a citizen . . . It not only takes extraordinary pressure to make him violate any of his codes, but when faced with such pressure he makes great effort

---

[40] Ibid.

[41] Chester I. Barnard, *The Functions of the Executive* (Cambridge: Harvard University Press, 1966), 267.

[42] Ibid.

to find some solution that is compatible with all of them; and because he makes that effort and is capable he has in the past succeeded."[43]

A second point to note here is that Barnard is using a figure who is Everyman. Carl Schmitt, as part of his critique of pluralism, had doubts. It is an empirical mistake, he thought, to suppose that an individual, not a social group, decides. Further, even if this might be true of some people, it was not true of everyone. "Perhaps there exists a nimble and agile individual who can succeed in the feat of maintaining his freedom between social groups, as one might hop from ice-floe to ice-floe. But this kind of freedom-as-balance could not be put forward as the normal ethical duty for the mass of ordinary citizens."[44]

In the real world, different groups try to impose their modes of organizing reality on to individuals. Which is to say that different individuals try to influence each other, to get them to see the world as they do, to behave as they would like.

Some of this happens under the heading *club law,* described by William James, drawing on John Locke,[45] as the pressure of the opinion of one's fellows.

But some individuals seem not to be not much influenced. We regularly see individuals deciding more on the basis of their own positions on certain large issues than on the basis of any group that might claim their loyalty. This may go so far that we begin to speak of antinomianism or anarchism. Mises, for example, projected an antinomian stance when he discussed the genius and marriage. "As a social institution," he wrote, "marriage is an adjustment of the individual to the social order by which a certain field of activity, with all its tasks and requirements, is assigned to him." But still, this could not be a good system for everyone. "Exceptional natures, whose abilities lift them far above the average, cannot support the coercion that such an adjustment to the way of life of the masses must involve. The man who feels within himself the urge to devise and achieve great things, who is prepared to sacrifice his life rather than be false to his mission, will not stifle his urge of the sake of a wife and children." And again: "Even the man of genius whose married life seems to take a normal course, whose attitude to sex does not differ from that of other people, cannot in the long run feel himself bound by marriage without violating his own self."[46]

Susanna and the Elders is used to show individuals in a wide variety of coexisting social contexts. But who is that individual? Are the groups

---

[43] Ibid., 267–68.

[44] Schmitt, "Ethic of State and Pluralistic State," in Mouffe, *Challenge of Carl Schmitt,* 200.

[45] James, "The Consciousness of Self," 295.

[46] Ludwig von Mises, *Socialism,* trans. J. Kahane (New Haven: Yale University Press, 1951), 99. We are accustomed to the image of marriage as a constraint on women. There is also a tradition that sees marriage as a prison for men.

outside the person somehow also inside? Is there a deepest judging companion, as William James suggested? Is the self singular or plural? These issues are explored through a discussion of names.

THE NAMES OF THE COMPLEX SELF

The claim that citizenship is the most important membership in our situation is made from time to time, by philosophers, political theorists, and of course states. This is the observation of Henry James when he suggests the relation to his country was the supreme relation. But other memberships, the memberships of intermediate groups, are also crucial for individuals. This is true because individuals' identity is created in part by these memberships and also because their security depends in good part on these memberships.

D. W. Winnicott wrote of "[a] person as represented by a sphere or circle. Inside the circle is collected all the interplay of forces and objects that constitute the inner reality of the individual at this moment in time."[47] In the collection of the Metropolitan Museum of Art at the Cloisters there is a sixteenth-century wooden rosary bead that is measurable in inches but that opens to reveal a complete and fully articulated scene focused on the Crucifixion. The bead is filled with people and action. The central events take place in a populated world. Using Winnicott's theory, the "self" is something like this bead.

If we say that the self is social, and that our identities include affiliations with many groups, we also feel that we make decisions with which the various groups, all hypothetically making intense and all-encompassing claims,[48] do not agree. Subgroups can easily be seen as subworlds. As to such worlds, William James suggested that they were disconnected, alternative, each "real whilst it is attended to" and "real after its own fashion."[49] We do not try to order, give priorities, to these subworlds until we have to, and we shift frames. "The whole distinction of real and unreal, the whole psychology of belief, disbelief, and doubt, is thus grounded on two mental facts," James wrote, "first, that we are liable to think differently of the same; and second, that when we have done so, we can choose which way of thinking to adhere to and which to disregard."[50]

The claim that the self is social means that the judgment of the individual concerning the ordering of the groups in which he or she is embedded

---

[47] D. W. Winnicott, *Home Is Where We Start From: Essays by a Psychoanalyst*, ed. Clare Winnicott, Ray Shepherd, and Madeleine Davis (New York: Norton, 1986), 75.

[48] Not all groups make such claims in fact.

[49] William James, "Perceptions of Reality," in *Principles of Psychology*, 2:293. Identity issues have to do with reality itself.

[50] James, *Principles of Psychology*.

is made by a complex agent. If the alternate selves of the schizophrenic or dissociative multiple personality are not to be taken as universals, the selves of youth and age can be. Bodies and minds change. This is true despite the fact that we say that one should find oneself, that we take as a motto, "Resolve to be thyself and know that he who finds himself loses his misery."[51] But which self is one looking for?

Various literatures discuss in various ways the self embedded in groups, not as a monolith but as a complex entity. We can quote William James, or modern psychologists'[52] work on transformation.[53] But perhaps by looking at the phenomenon of naming, we can add something to the discussion, since naming illustrates not only recognition of the "sources of the self," as Taylor puts it,[54] but also the fluidity and transformative aspect of the self. The discussion of names is intended to illustrate the ubiquity of the multiple self. It is also intended to open ideas of the role of the outside, whether the state or society.

In a single name we find not self, but selves. That the individual is plural has been clear to poets. Walter Stone has an account of his interior selves in the poem "Brothers," which imagines each year of his life as a separate self, "Each the heir and murderer of the others."[55] Another of Stone's poems sees these selves as poets real or potential ("Keats in me was never born").[56] For Stone, some of the selves are dead, unborn, killed, while others live on. But the Irish novelist Claire Boylan finds them all yet living: "She used to imagine that old age must be awful, the death of everything. But it wasn't so. Nothing died. The child and the young girl and the mother

---

[51] Matthew Arnold, "Self Dependence," in *Poems,* vol. 2 (London: Macmillan, 1903), 98–99.

[52] See, e.g., Robert Lifton, *The Protean Self: Human Resilience in an Age of Fragmentation* (Chicago: University of Chicago Press, 1999).

[53] See discussion in Thomas Morawetz, *Making Faces and Playing God* (Austin: University of Texas Press, 2001). For other accounts of the complex self: F. H. Bradley, quoted in Fox, *The Search for Society,* 80, seeing an anticipation of G. H. Mead.

[54] Charles Taylor, *Sources of the Self: The Making of the Modern Identity* (Cambridge: Harvard University Press, 1989).

[55] Stone, "Brothers." Walter Stone, "Poems, 1955–1958," in *Poets of Today* (New York: Charles Scribner's Sons, 1959).

[56] Stone, "Poeta Nascitur."

We can also see the multiple self in some discussions of the relations between author and character. Thus, D. H. Lawrence provides a description of James Fenimore Cooper, "lying in his Louis Quatorze hotel in Paris, passionately musing about Natty Bumppo and the pathless forest . . . while Mrs Cooper is struggling with her latest gown in the next room and the dejourner was with the countess at eleven." *Studies in Classic American Literature* (London: Penguin, 1977), 54. "Men live by lies," Lawrence writes. But then he analyzes the issue in terms of several realities. "In actuality," Cooper wanted one thing, and then "In another actuality," he wanted something else. Cooper's "actual desire was to be . . . *le grand ecrivain americain,*" yet his "innermost wish was to be Natty Bumppo" (54).

and the middle-aged woman full of rage and grief and dawning wisdom were all there together and she reigned as peacemaker over this tribe."[57] And in Philip Roth's recent version of two selves in *The Dying Animal* (2001), inside each sane rational person there is another, terrified of dying.[58]

As to the naming of individuals, in the West a person commonly has *a* name, in contrast to certain other societies in which the givenness of the fixed name is nowhere near as clear. Sometimes two components are not sufficient to create identity. A middle name or initial may be required. John E. Smith, a philosophy professor at Yale, has said that without his middle initial he is anonymous.[59] In the United States, it is common to assume that people have one name and that the role of the state is limited to facilitating their (parents') choice of that name. However, even in the Unites States, a more directive role for the state is possible, and in some countries state regulation of names is more evident.

We link the name of the person to his or her deepest identity. We react, for example, with serious distress at the injury a parent would cause a child by giving a second child the name as the first. It would be somehow to attack or even replace the first.

Even if the state does not regulate choices of names, it is centrally involved in the possibility of naming. Roscoe Pound in his late encyclopedic work *Jurisprudence* included names and naming practices as part of a discussion of juristic personality and the law of persons. In general, the law of persons —and here he followed the French approach, which differed somewhat from German and English categories—consisted of the law concerning names, patrimony, status, and capacity.[60] James Scott discusses the invention of permanent inherited names as "the last step in establishing the necessary preconditions for [the modern state]. . . . The development of the personal surname (literally, a name added to another name, and not to be confused with a permanent patronym) went hand in hand with the development of written, official documents such as tithe records, manorial dues rolls, marriage registers, censuses, tax records, and land records. They were necessary to the successful conduct of any admin-

[57] From Clare Boylan, *Beloved Stranger* (Washington, D.C.: Counterpoint Press, 2000).

[58] Philip Roth, *The Dying Animal* (Boston: Houghton Mifflin, 2000). See also Jacques Presser, *The Night of Girondist* (London: Harvill/HarperCollins, 1992), for a fictional account of complex self-identification and crisis of an assimilated Dutch Jew who assists the Nazis during the Holocaust. Robert Musil's novel *The Man without Qualities*, trans. Eithne Wilkins and Ernest Kaiser (New York: Perigee Books, G. P. Putnam's Sons, 1980), 1:34, identifies "at least" nine characters for the inhabitants of a country, as well as an inner tenth, still, however, shaped by one social situation. The novel is set in the dying Austro-Hungarian Empire in Vienna, 1913.

[59] Letter to the *New York Times,* March 3, 2001.

[60] Roscoe Pound, *Jurisprudence* (St. Paul: West, 1959). On names as an object of commerce, see Matthew Purdy, "A Boy Named Soup," *New York Times,* August 1, 2001, B1.

istrative exercise involving large numbers of people who had to be individually identified and who were not known personally by the authorities."[61]

If Scott assumes that the state has had a major role in the regularizing of naming, another perspective sees names in the context of patriarchy. The struggle to name oneself—a modern feminist concern—develops out of the centrality of one's name to the expression of oneself. But the self is taken as unitary in these discussions. Omi writes, "One area in which naming and the power to name are particularly important is law. First, both law and naming are intimately related to social control and the distribution of power in society. Second, the primary tool of law is names; that is, words, terms, labels, and language. It follows that if language itself is not neutral, neither is law. Similarly, it can be inferred that if language generally excludes and disempowers women, it is women who will be excluded from the full protection of the law."[62]

Elsdon C. Smith notes, "For most of us, a name is much more than just a tag or a label. It is a symbol which stands for the unique combination of characteristics and attributes that define us as an individual. It is the closest thing that we have to a shorthand for self-concept."[63] As Harold Isaacs pointed out, to be without a name is almost not be.[64] *Through the Looking Glass* plays with names as a philosophical question, and Freud comments on names in a way that suggests that for him, names are similarly important. To manipulate a name or forget a name is to use a kind of weapon.[65]

Certainly the official name has an immense importance. We answer to it. Perhaps even stand alert. "Entendre son nom, cela sent le tribunal" [When one hears one's name, one feels the tribunal]. So Paul Valéry.[66]

[61] James C. Scott, *Seeing Like a State* (New Haven: Yale University Press, 1998), 65–67.

[62] Omi, "The Problem That Has No Name," *Cardozo Women's Law Journal* 4 (1998): 321, 326. The basic difference between names and words is that names confer particular being or individual identity, while words refer generally to beings or identities. Accordingly, all words are derived from names. Perhaps that is why it was understood, as early as 400 B.C., that "the beginning of all instruction is the study of names." Omi continues:

In the realm of law, namelessness and powerlessness to name have far-reaching consequences. For instance, recognition of names in law is required in order for an individual to address a court in the first place—one must be recognized as a "legal personality." Even then, the manner in which the law describes and defines that personality is consequential. In addition, recognition of a legal "cause of action" is a necessary prerequisite for a claim to be made before a court. In order to be redressed, therefore, a harm must possess a name in law.

On the power to name differences see Martha Minow, *Making All the Difference: Inclusion, Exclusion, and American Law* (Ithaca, N.Y.: Cornell University Press, 1990), 113–14.

[63] Quoted in Omi, "Problem."

[64] Isaacs, *Idols of the Tribe.*

[65] Sigmund Freud, "Psychopathology of Everyday Life," in *The Basic Writings of Sigmund Freud,* trans. A. A. Brill (New York: Modern Library 1995), e.g. 28, 48, 49, and the essay "Forgetting of Proper Names" in the same volume.

[66] Paul Valéry, *Lettres à Quelques-Uns,* letter of April 30, 1917, quoted in Nathan Leites, *Rules of the Game in Paris* (different translation), trans. Derek Cultman (Chicago: University of Chicago Press, 1969), 335.

While the name and the individual are deeply linked, we do not think that the name is never to be changed. On the contrary, we assume that there are times when the name must change—thus the biblical changes of name associated with Abraham, Isaac, and Sarah. To begin with, individuals have different names in the course of their lives. Most obviously, women have traditionally adopted married names, and people often take a new name upon the assumption of a new status, entry into a religious order perhaps, or immigration to another country. The new name is not merely a convenience, but the mark of the new relation. These names are conceived ordinarily as sequential, representing new and old.

But another practice even in the West[67] is that people have different names in different concurrent relationships. They may retain pet or family names throughout their lives in relation to certain people who knew them when those names were first used. Helen Lynd notes that "[w]ithin a family or other close relation of intimacy, the use of banter or joking nicknames may serve a . . . function of recall, or of expressing and at the same time veiling tenderness, which might for some persons involve a kind of shame if expressed more directly."[68] We read that Picasso renamed at least some of his friends and that President George Bush, for example, gives nicknames to friends and associates.[69] None, we might say, is official, but they are all used.

If we look for names in the work of anthropologists, we immediately locate the complex naming system of Bali described by Clifford Geertz. Geertz's description indicates that in this system names have little to do with a private sense of self. Rather, they are rooted in the public context, the stage. "All Balinese receive what might be called birth-order names," Geertz notes. "There are four of these, 'first-born,' 'second-born,' 'third-born,' 'fourth-born,' after which they recycle, so that the fifth-born child is called again 'first-born,' the sixth 'second-born,' and so on."

"Further," Geertz reports, "these names are bestowed independently of the fates of the children. Dead children, even stillborn ones, count, so that in fact, in this still high-birthrate, high-mortality society, the names do not really tell you anything very reliable about the birth-order relations of concrete individuals." In short, "the birth-order naming system does not identify individuals as individuals," rather it suggests that "for all procreating couples, births form a circular succession of 'firsts,' 'seconds,' 'thirds,' and 'fourths,' an endless four-stage replication of an imperishable form."

---

[67] The question of the self cross-culturally opens the possibility that common Western understandings of the self may be very different from non-Western understandings. See Janet Ainsworth, "Categories and Culture," *Cornell Law Review* 82 (1996): 19, on the Chinese self as fluid and constantly created and re-created.

[68] Helen Merrell Lynd, *On Shame and the Search for Identity* (New York: Harcourt Brace, 1958), 249.

[69] *New York Times*, February 18, 2001, on nicknames bestowed by President Bush.

But in the West we also have a sense of the world as stage, and the issue may be of degree, not kind.[70]

While it is possible that the current interest in identity is a sign of the decline of community,[71] it is also possible to suggest another kind of connection between these phenomena, made visible through naming, since naming is not only an assertion of a claim of individuality, but an expressive aspect of identity that insists on public recognition of the specific individual in the group. The name is a public signal of membership, complex memberships, in communities. Thus in Woody Allen's film *Mighty Aphrodite,* a couple adopts a child. The adoption itself is a mark of the deliberate creation of community, the family, by an act of will, in the absence of a biological nexus. The choosing of a name by the parents suggests various community involvements. The father's name is Weinreb. He is a sports writer. Before settling on *Max* for the child, the parents consider the problem. Some of these names, it is suggested, would be more appropriately joined to the mother's (gentile? ordinary American?) name. After the patriarchal/matriarchal issue is settled, the parents test the names against professional titles, *judge, doctor.* Class signals are also involved in naming.[72]

It is common to find citations to an attitude toward names that reflects the idea that naming is not an individual right but rather a policing institution.[73] A judge once argued that "a person's surname was his most manifestly public feature, . . . and it cannot be claimed that this element of identification is part of an individual's private life." Moreover, "[P]rivate life ends when the individual comes into contact with public life."[74] There is a good deal of writing on state policies and naming practices.[75]

---

[70] In response to the Geertz account, Richard Sweder noted that child psychologists, who purport to be describing human development in general and across cultures, see the development of individuality at a certain early age. This being so, Sweder asks, possibly we should ask of the Balinese case, at what point is the ordinary human development of individuality reversed. *Culture Theory: Essays on Mind, Self, and Emotion* (Cambridge: Cambridge University Press, 1984), 13.

[71] "[N]ever was the word 'community' used more indiscriminately and emptily than in the decades when communities in the sociological sense became hard to find in real life." Hobsbawm, quoted in Zygmunt Bauman, *Community: Seeking Safety in an Insecure World* (Cambridge: Polity, 2001), 15.

[72] Other movies provide material on names. In the movie *Galaxy Quest*—the characters in the movie are actors in a television series —one actor insists that lack of the definition of his fictional television character is signaled by the absence of a last name.

[73] E.g. Ralph Slovenko, "Names and the Law," *Names* 32 (1984): 107, 108.

[74] Quoted by Aeyal Gross, "Rights and Normalization: A Critical Study of European Human Rights Case Law on the Choice and Change of Name," *Harvard Human Rights Journal* 9 (1996): 272.

[75] See, for example, Roderick Munday, "The Girl They Name Manhattan: The Law of Forenames in France and England," *Legal Studies* 5 (1985): 331. See on the Nazi name decrees, Robert Rennick, "The Nazi Name Decrees of the Nineteen Thirties," *Names* 18

As to the primacy of the state role, some states at least take a considerable interest in the naming of individuals. France until very recently required children's names to be taken from an approved list of classical or historical names. Germany also regulated the names of citizens, and the decrees of the Nazis, requiring Jews to take specifically Jewish names, were from this point of view an aspect of a more general interest of the state in names, here designed to differentiate subgroups. In the American stance also there is an active role for the state, though there is considerable room for individual choice. (In the French and German context the regulation takes hold at birth. A typical American controversy arises in the context of divorce, where the issues are resumption of a maiden name, or the decision about a child's name postdivorce.)

Religious groups present complex issues of naming. For example, Jews may have names that are entirely different from their legal names. Joseph Roth in *The Wandering Jews* writes, "Once in America everyone is automatically issued with a new name and new papers. Don't be surprised at the Jews' lack of attachment to their names. They will change their names with alacrity, and the names of their fathers, even though those particular sounds, to the European sensibility, are charged with emotional weight. For Jews their names have no value because they are not their names. Jews, Eastern Jews, have no names. They have compulsory aliases. Their true name is the one by which they are summoned to the Torah on the Sabbath."[76]

Accurate in details or not,[77] the description conveys the complexity of the name in the community and the name in the state. The official name is the "compulsory alias."[78] Along the same line, Maxine Hong Kingston writes, "The Chinese I know hide their names; sojourners take new names when their lives change and guard their real names with silence."[79] The "real" name is the original Chinese name. The new one is false. But is the new name not real and true in another world? And finally, as assimilation proceeds, it may be the original real name that will seem secondary to the present self.

(1990): 65–85. See also Gunther Stent, *Nazis, Women, and Molecular Biology: Memoirs of a Lucky Self-Hater* (Kensington, Calif.: Briones, 1998), 109.

[76] Joseph Roth, *The Wandering Jews,* trans. Michael Hofmann (New York: Norton, 2001), 99.

[77] Ibid., 58.

[78] Official and unofficial naming is nothing new. "In those days Mattahias, the son of John, the son of Simeon, a priest of the descendants of Joarib, removed from Jerusalem, and settled in Modin. He had five sons, John, surnamed Gaddi, Simon, called Thassi, Judas, called Maccabeus, Eleazar, called Avaran, and Jonathan, called Apphus" (1 Macc. 2).

[79] Maxine Hong Kingston, "No Name Woman," in *The Best American Essays of the Century,* ed. Joyce Carol Oates (Boston: Houghton Mifflin, 2000), 385.

Names associated with titles, whether the title is professional or familial, *judge* or *uncle,* are insisted upon by some group in relation to an individual; if the individual accepts it, the name reflects one of his or her selves, since that name defines a role that the person has, by accepting the name, agreed to perform. Some name changes are associated with a drive to singularity (Pierre Louis to Pierre Louys). Some involve changes of codes for gender (Marianne Evans to George Eliot).[80] Some have to do with languages. But for the bearers of the names, it is clear that the fact that there are various names and that they can be changed is evidence and reinforcement of the point that the self is fluid, potential. Each particular name is fixed. The change of name is a kind of escape, as it is of course in the context of divorce. And the individual private names (like the private name of the cat in Eliot's poem) suggest the complexity of the individual subject.

It seems quixotic to say that people may reject their official names and refuse to answer. But perhaps there are examples. The Prisoner in the libertarian cult television program of the 1960s refused to answer to his numeric name (Number 6): "I am not a number."[81] (A softer approach to a number as a name is offered in Charles Schultz's *Peanuts,* in the person of the little boy who has a numeric first name and the family name 95472, with the accent on the 4.)[82]

If in a drama like *The Prisoner* we see an ideal of refusal and rejection, we also see in popular material the secret name, parallel, it seems, to a secret self. The name of the quirky Inspector Morse (Endeavor) is not disclosed throughout many years of his work as a detective in Oxford; he is simply Morse.

Henry James referred to the "cauldron" in which the nation, America, would receive aliens.[83] And we recall the melting pot. But we also recall the critique of the melting pot.[84] Names may be a signal of both the drive

---

[80] See Jan Morris, *Conundrum: An Extraordinary Narrative of Transsexualism* (New York: Henry Holt, 1986), 121–22 (name change from *James Morris*). Of course gender itself may be changed, and then the name also. Or the gender issue may be reflected in an alter ego *(Tootsie; Victor, Victoria).*

[81] E.g., Yevgeng Zamyatin, *We,* trans. Mirra Ginsberg (New York: Avon, 1999); Ayn Rand, *Anthem* (New York: New American Library, 1995), and *"The Prisoner" Official Companion,* ed. Matthew White and Jaffer Ali (New York: Werner Books, 1988).

[82] Charles Schulz, *Peanuts Treasury* (New York, Holt Rinehart and Winston, 1968), n.p. Some number/name questions raise First Amendment issues where the government requires use of a social security number as part of a procedure for receiving licenses or benefits. See *Tennessee v. Loudon,* 857 S.W.2d 878 (1993) (social security number as "mark of the beast"); *Bowen et al. v. Roy,* 476 U.S. 693 (1986) (Native American belief that social security number would rob child of her spirit) (both claims denied).

[83] Henry James, *The American Scene* (New York: Penguin, 1994), 92.

[84] "Israel Zangwill was guilty of a great mischief," Louis Marshall wrote, "when he spoke of the melting pot, and indicated that in it he found the solution of the Jewish prob-

to assimilation and the drive to maintenance of a public connection. Names may skip a generation or more. Names then, of course, reach deeply into the past, as much as reject the past. One may have several names simultaneously, containing within oneself the contradiction of identity. As Henry Adams observed, "[C]ontradictory qualities are the law, not the exception."[85]

Useful comments on the problem have been offered by Jeremy Waldron: "If we live the cosmopolitan life, we draw our allegiances from here, there, and everywhere. Bits of cultures come into our lives from different sources, and there is no guarantee that they will all fit together. . . . [T]he self constituted under the auspices of a multiplicity of cultures might strike us as chaotic, confused, even schizophrenic."[86] Waldron notes the communitarian critique of this idea of an independent self, which functions as a "manager, standing back a little from each of the items on the smorgasbord of its personality." Waldron points out that Michael Sandel "quite properly has raised the question whether this is really the way that we want to view our personality and our character."

Waldron's solution to this problem is to reopen the question of identity: "So long as we think that the management of the self is like the personal governance of a community or a corporation, we will be driven to ask embarrassing questions about the specific character of the 'I' in its capacity as manager. But suppose we think instead about personal identity, not in terms of hierarchical management, but in terms of the democratic self-government of a pluralistic population. Maybe the person is nothing but a set of commitments and involvements, and maybe the governance of the self is just the more or less comfortable (or at times more or less chaotic) coexistence of these elements." There is a threat, schizophrenia,[87] but it

---

lem." Clearly, Marshall wrote, "Zangwill is not a metallurgist or else he would know that in the art of metallurgy the great effort made by those concerned in it, by electrolytic powers, is that the various elements composing the melting pot shall be separated into their constituent parts, so that the copper shall be fused with the copper, the silver with the silver, and the gold with the gold." Charles Reznikoff, ed., vol. 2, *Louis Marshall, Champion of Liberty* (Philadelphia: Jewish Publication Society, 1957), 809.

[85] Ira Nadel, introduction to *The Education of Henry Adams* (Oxford: Oxford University Press, 1999), xii.

[86] Jeremy Waldron, "Minority Cultures and the Cosmopolitan Alternative," *Michigan Journal of Law Reform* 25 (1992): 751.

[87] Ibid., 789. The "schizophrenia" in Jeremy Waldron's comments suggests that our idea of psychological health relates basically to the integrated personality that D. W. Winnicott referred to as the "unit self." Where, Winnicott asked, could the unconscious be? But the idea of real self and false self, true self and constructed self, has a resonance with the argument that we are members of different communities and construct ourselves with reference to those communities. In fact, those are often the contexts of the alternative selves. See, on the multiple self, Ian Hacking, *Rewriting the Soul: Multiple Personality and the Science of Memory* (Princeton: Princeton University Press, 1995; and Ralph Slovenko, "The Multiple Personality and Criminal Law," *Medicine and Law* 12 (1993): 329–40.

"may be better understood as radical conflict or dissonance rather than mere unregulated plurality."

Waldron is cautious about his speculations. They need to be matched more closely to the "empirical psychology of personality." But he has hopes for his "cosmopolitan vision."

THE COMPLEX SELF AND THE WORLD

The individual presents himself or herself as something finite, closed, and defined—like a medieval rosary bead. As seen from the outside, the individual is one person, with a name, an intention, a profession, a context. But we know that this is only a partial truth. What shall we do with what we know? This question has two parts. First, what shall we as individuals do with—or how should we respond to—what collectively is called "the law," or the state? Second, what shall we, as collectively something called "the law," do with what we know of the complex self?

The Portuguese poet Fernando Pessoa describes a position toward law that distances the speaker entirely from responsibility for its compromises and inadequacies.[88]

Obey the law, whether it's wrong or you are.
Man can do little against the outer life.
Let injustice be.
Nothing you change changes.

But this position is available to the poet and his many selves fundamentally because of his all-but-total isolation from the world of events and of human beings. He disdained action; he wrote and tried not to act. So what could the state want of him?[89]

The difficulty with Pessoa's conclusion (at least as presented by his heteronym Ricardo Reis, the Epicurean doctor) is that it does not address the issues of life in a world of others at all. All selves withdraw from contact with the world, with church and state, with other people. Pessoa's commitments are absolutes—"relatively possible" even in this world. But Pessoa's stance has attached to it a critical social condition. Capital punishment is finished, he writes, and so the most the state can do is harass me. If things got worse, he says, he would retreat further into his dreams.[90]

---

[88] Pessoa's many heteronyms left poems and prose after his death in 1935. See the introduction to *Fernando Pessoa and Co.,* trans. Richard Zenith (New York: Grove Press, 1999).

[89] Some whose selves were also complex did not take this position. Carl Jung, another famous example of a divided self, found joy in his family. See Jung's autobiography *Memories, Dreams, and Reflections* (New York: Vintage, 1989).

[90] Fernando Pessoa, *The Book of Disquiet,* trans. Richard Zenith (Riverdale on Hudson: Sheep Meadow Press, 1996). This kind of life, as Fernando Pessoa said, was impossible in

The American transcendentalist Ralph Waldo Emerson offered a more moderate stance. In his essay "Experience,"[91] he suggested that while major issues had to be settled and would ultimately be settled, it might take years or centuries, and that life meanwhile went on, the buying and selling, the writing, the work. In effect, he would stand aside and watch. When Emerson did intervene in public debate, as in his essay on the Fugitive Slave Law, he began with an apology for stepping out of the scholarly role. This position, which emphasizes the individual and the interior life—Emerson does not confuse, he says, his life in the city and on the farm with his thinking—does not reject a public role when it is necessary. Clearly, however, this role must be adopted as a part of a moral imperative, and a focus on the individual.[92]

Emerson's politics are not newly observed. The eleventh edition of the Encyclopedia Britannica published a long article on Emerson explaining that "the America that he loved and admired was the ideal, the potential America. For the actual conditions of social and political life in his own time he had a fine scorn. He was an intellectual Brahmin. His principles were democratic, his tastes aristocratic. He did not like crowds, streets, hotels—'the people who fill them oppress me with their excessive civility.' Humanity was his hero. He loved man, but he was not fond of men."[93]

The central problem in relation to Emerson is the possible tension between individualist self-reliance and a collective reformist politics. George Kateb formulates the problem in terms of stoicism. It is easy to imagine Emerson as a late Roman stoic, standing by, watching, self-enclosed, acting when necessary. More activist orientations are easy to imagine. Scarlett Pimpernels are the extreme cases.

But what can law do with the complex self?

Allan Farnsworth's recent discussion of the issue is a good place to begin.

He refers to the "beguiling notion that over time a person may evolve into a 'later self'—a distinct individual with different preferences that pro-

---

absolute terms: "But . . . not impossible relatively" (139). Pessoa is, in effect, living parasitically on someone else's political effort. One may note that in some places, capital punishment is not finished.

[91] Ralph Waldo Emerson, "Experience," in *The Portable Emerson,* ed. Carl Bodie and Malcolm Cowley (New York: Penguin, 1981), 266.

[92] See T. Gregory Garvery, ed., *The Emerson Dilemma: Essays on Emerson and Social Reform* (Athens: University of Georgia Press, 2001). See also George Kateb, *Emerson and Self-Reliance* (Lanham, Md.: Rowman & Littlefield Publishing, 1994).

[93] "He had grave doubts about universal suffrage. He took a sincere interest in social and political reform, but towards specific 'reforms' his attitude was somewhat remote and visionary. On the subject of temperance he held aloof from the intemperate methods of the violent prohibitionist. He was a believer in woman's rights, but he was lukewarm towards conventions in favour of woman suffrage. Even in regard to slavery he had serious hesitations about the ways of the abolitionists, and for a long time refused to be identified with them" (*Encyclopedia Britannica,* 11th ed., s.v. "Ralph Waldo Emerson").

duce regret." He quotes Alice to the caterpillar: "I know who I *was* when I got up this morning, but I think I must have changed several times since then," and then La Rochefoucauld: "We are sometimes as different from ourselves as from other people."

"Although this recognition of personal development has found favor among some legal scholars, it has had no significant impact on courts," Farnsworth notes. Country music star Willie Nelson, when asked about his four marriages, replied, "I've changed. I'm not the same guy that was married to this person or that person . . . . [E]ach of my wives [*sic*] have been married to a different person." As Professor Farnsworth's account makes plain, contract law does not take this view. "Feeling like a different person may bring relief in one's own mind, but it will not bring relief from one's promises. As a prominent jurist concluded, for the purpose of 'evaluating a proposal to allow elderly people to repudiate obligations made when they were young, it is more fruitful to think of the present and the future self as one person.' "[94]

This is true, one suspects, because each of our plural selves lives in a world of other people. We may be in, but not of, our various worlds.[95] But other people may rely on us in our relationships, connections, and contexts. It is true that the law may allow the Jekyll-Hyde phenomenon to be treated as insanity so as to excuse using the insanity defense. Similarly, avoidance for a capacity problem might be possible for an extreme case of multiplicity that was, again, something like mental illness. But in the ordinary case, the complexity of the human subject is assumed by law but flattened into someone simply considered an actor, or contracting party, or A in the A-B hypothetical. The issue of the younger and other self is subsumed in capacity issues, minority at one end and senility at the other. The attack on a thin notion of the human being in law is sometimes expressed in terms of criticisms of the A and B of, for example, the Restatements of Law, or the law-and-economics figure of the self-interested actor.[96] John Noonan, in *Persons and Masks of the Law*, approaches the subject through an analysis of the rejection of the individual and the individuals narrative in a judicial opinion, particularly that of Cardozo in the famous Palsgraf case. Noonan asks, Who, aside from the injured person, was Mrs. Palsgraf?[97] An American woman, we would say, to begin with.

[94] E. Allan Farnsworth, *Changing Your Mind: The Law of Regretted Decisions* (New Haven: Yale University Press, 1998), 26–27.

[95] Cf. John 17:16.

[96] Anne C. Dailey, "The Hidden Economy of the Unconscious," *Chicago-Kent Law Review* 74 (2000): 1599.

[97] John Noonan, *Persons and Masks of the Law* (New York: Farrar, Straus and Giroux, 1977).

But going to another body of material, we find that some approaches to the issue of selves distinguish not between, say, France and the United States, or Bali and America, but between "hunter-gatherer" societies and industrial societies. On the basis of such a distinction, Edward Wilson[98] notes that in hunter-gatherer societies roles are few, while in industrial societies they are many. It is no wonder then that we see role confusion in modern Western life. He goes on to quote Goffman, on the consequent difficulty in the modern world of distinguishing between roles and self.

In law, one answer turns to the history of the law of persons and goes back to systems in which one role is chosen by the law to be the dominant one, and all rights and duties are attached to that role.[99]

Another answer looks to those instances--I am citing American law now—in which particular relations are identified as having specific character.: Husband-wife, parent-child; principle-agent; merchant-nonmerchant. Some of these currently or historically implicated legal capacity and thus are linked to the law of persons (married women; children), but others are understood to be a role definition that is partial. One is not only a merchant, debtor, trustee. That is merely a way of talking about one's role in a particular transaction. The larger descriptions—reflected in and enforced by rules of status and capacity—make a greater claim to "be" the individual.

The law's position is parallel to the position that Jung identified as that of "society." Jung's discussion of the individual and society suggests the important point here: no matter how complex the inner life in fact, society insists that individuals perform one role, and in effect "be" one thing. If one wants to get on, Jung says, one must behave as though this fiction were the truth.[100] And this split is not a matter of individual pathology for Jung. Everyone creates an artificial personality. "Society expects, and indeed must expect, every individual to play the part assigned to him as perfectly as possible, so that a man who is a parson must not only carry out his official functions objectively, but must at all times and in all circumstances play the role of parson in a flawless manner." The fact that one carries several alternate selves—or even that one's self is nothing more, on some views, than a collection of multiple roles, does not change the law's view any more than the common understanding that a person may have both religious memberships and club memberships. However rich the interior life of the actor, in law he is simply the A who did some-

---

[98] Edward O. Wilson, *On Human Nature* (Cambridge: Harvard University Press, 1978).

[99] For overview, see Pound, *Jurisprudence*.

[100] Carl Jung, "Ego and the Unconscious," in *Basic Writings of Jung* (New York: Modern Library, 1959). It is this fiction that underlies for example, Nigel Dennis, *Cards of Identity* (New York: Vanguard Press, 1955).

thing of which law takes cognizance. It is nothing more than the recognition that we talk about intention as if it were real, and as if we could know. But we know of course that it isn't and that we can't. These are among the great "as ifs" of law.

In summary, this chapter has made the following points. We often argue, following liberal political theory, that groups result from the choices of individuals, each group created by a fictional social contract, each role (another way of talking about a relational issue, or a membership issue) assumed by a deliberate act or choice.

We also feel, however, that the groups were there first, and that the roles we assume are somehow there first. Sometimes we feel that they are natural or innate. We can perhaps say both at the same time: individuals create groups and groups create individuals; individuals chose roles, and roles constrain those who chose them. While some accounts discuss individuals and groups as if those individuals were affiliated with only one group, more likely individuals are part of many groups and assume many roles. We are surrounded by groups with which we have affiliations, and we internalize the values and stances of many groups as part of our identities.

This book has tried in general to illustrate the connections among individuals, groups, and the state with a variety of histories, some at the macro, or international or legal, level, some at the level of individual narrative. The book has used material from many sources, academic and popular, theoretical and historical, legal and cultural, to make visible and real the complexity of interactions that are too often treated flatly. We live in culture and we live in law. We live in communities of people who are different from each other, and, as this chapter has urged, we are even plural in ourselves, operating in different groups with their associated roles, contexts, frameworks, and belief systems. This book has not attempted to propose a solution to the questions it has raised. The attempt rather has been to join the conversation on pluralism by reviewing the complexities of the problems.

Conclusion

✦ An emblem book on pluralism might contain this description by Benjamin Rush of an eighteenth-century parade in Philadelphia. "In eighty-fourth place"—after the "gentlemen of the bar" but before "the college of physicians"—marched seventeen clergymen. They "formed a very agreeable part of the procession," Rush notes. "Pains were taken to connect Ministers of the most dissimilar religious principles together, thereby to show the influence of a free government in promoting Christian charity. The Rabbi of the Jews, locked in the arms of two ministers of the gospel, was a most delightful sight. There could not have been a more happy emblem contrived, [of a nation?] which opens all its power and offices alike, not only to every sect of christians, but to worthy men of *every* religion."[1]

On January 1, 2000, the government of Sweden and the Lutheran Church officially divorced. Until then, Sweden had one of the last fully established churches in the West. Simultaneously, there were notable efforts in the Islamic world to develop a scheme of economic arrangements that would respect the rules of Islamic law and also meet the general expectations of modern economic life. Both of these developments represent aspects of the relation between religion and law. The Swedish disestablishment is the end of a process of secularization and modernization signaled by the Philadelphia parade. The Islamic efforts are characteristic of regimes attempting both to build the state on religious law, and to accommodate requirements of the modern world—an effort in a different direction.

Not all states in our world are liberal or based on the value of individual rights. But for those that are, a significant problem is how to acknowledge the group presence.[2] Religious opinions are not merely background preferences, to be seen as forming voter opinion in the same way that all other background preferences form opinion. Churches, for example, have institutional relations with other groups, political and religious, and an awareness of groups is needed for analysis of these relations. The respect to be paid to group life involves serious questions for any political society. We focus on the issues of conflict of standards not so much because these

[1] Benjamin Rush quoted in Borden, *Jews, Turks, and Infidels*, 5.
[2] See generally Soifer, *Company We Keep*.

conflicts occur frequently, but because they "stick out."[3] (The language gets close to raising the issue of deviance.) But we do best, I think, discussing groups with an eye on both positive and negative aspects of group life. And we cannot, as Martha Minow suggested in another context, end with the implication that hard problems would go away if we all behaved well toward each other.[4]

Some two hundred years later, after the Philadelphia parade, the American Anthropological Association meeting in Philadelphia found it necessary to issue a resolution repudiating theories of racial inferiority and concluding that "all races possess the ability to participate fully in the democratic way of life and in modern technological civilization."[5] The story ran on the same page as an article carrying the headline "Freedom Riders Lose on Appeal: 4 Whites and 7 Negroes Get Jail in Montgomery."

The unresolved tensions in America were not unique. The twentieth century witnessed slaughter on a scale beyond understanding. The century began with the murder of millions of Congolese, proceeded through the European Holocaust, and continued through the catastrophes of Cambodia and Rwanda. In the new century, issues of violence in state and nonstate context are intense. The issues of framework and structure, to both accommodate and contain difference, remain as critical as ever.[6] We are living with violence by states and groups; sometimes that violence is called war, sometimes called terrorism.

This book has taken as a foundational point the idea that law functions in relation to something outside itself (culture, society,) shaping it and being shaped by it. It has used some overviews of groups and states and has addressed some relations between the state and groups within the state. The argument of the book is, in effect, that the last sentence could be written differently. One could, for example, play with capitalization to signal reinforcement or resistance to hierarchy: The State and groups within The State. Or: The State and Groups within The State. Or even: the state and Groups within the state. We could introduce quotation marks: The "State" and other groups (Groups?) within "the State." Perhaps one could somehow produce a text (hypertext?) in which the words showed their interpretations and overlaps, so that individuals who are the officials of the state are also members of groups, while the members of

[3] See G. D. H. Cole, "Loyalties," *Proceedings of the Aristotelian Society* (1926): 151, 155.

[4] Martha Minow, "Speaking and Writing against Hate," *Cardozo Law Review* 11 (1990): 1393, 1402.

[5] Resolution adopted by the Council of the American Anthropological Association, at its annual meeting in Philadelphia, November 1961, *New York Times,* November 21, 1961, 29.

[6] And issues of reconciliation begin. See Minow, *Between Vengeance and Forgiveness.*

groups are also citizens of the state. The book has argued that the individuals have multiple affiliations and plural selves. Henry Adams said of Gladstone "in him, as in most people, there are two or three or a dozen men."[7] These perspectives may resonate with certain ideas that are called postmodern, but that body of writing is not the source of this way of looking at the world. It is more likely that these perspectives are visible throughout history.[8]

An American theorist once observed on the issue of groups, individuals, and the state that she was "advocating throughout the group principle, but not the group as the political unit. We do not need to swing forever between the individual and the group. We must devise some method of using both at the same time."[9] Mary Parker Follett's sense of what was needed holds true still. We must think about groups and individuals at the same time. The discussion throughout has suggested some ways of doing that, and suggested also that there are serious limits on the law's capacity to reflect the full complexity of the identity of a single human being, precisely because the law speaks for the community of human beings.[10]

For individuals, citizenship and membership are issues of meaning, and of how people make sense of what they do by setting their activities within frames.[11] Taking the individual as the basic unit means more than concentrating on an individual vote (though it may also mean that). It also seems to require acknowledgment of the importance of the ongoing adjustment and interpretation of frameworks in social and political interactions beneath the level of the issues on which we vote. That adjustment—individual and also social—defines those issues that can be voted upon, discussed, or even spoken about, in the political world.

The English philosopher Leonard Hobhouse remarks, "Essentially political freedom does not consist in like-mindedness, but in the toleration of differences; or, positively, in the acceptance of differences as contribut-

---

[7] *Education of Henry Adams*, introduction.

[8] See Umberto Eco, *The Name of the Rose* (San Diego: Harvest, 1994), postscript, suggesting that as the label *postmodern* is applied to earlier and earlier figures, Homer might one day be called postmodern.

[9] Follett, *The New State*, 92. Parts of this discussion have drawn on Weisbrod, "Practical Polyphony: Theories of the State and Feminist Jurisprudence," *Georgia Law Review* 24 (1990): 985.

[10] Mary Parker Follett wrote, "My relation to the state is always as an individual. The group is a method merely" (*The New State*, 292). And also: "[N]o one group can enfold me, because of my multiple nature. . . . But also no number of groups can enfold me. This is the reason why the individual must always be the unit of politics, as group organization must be its method" (295).

[11] Clifford Geertz, *Local Knowledge: Further Essays in Interpretive Anthropology* (New York: Basic Books, 1983), 23. See generally, Goffman, *Frame Analysis*.

ing to richer life than uniformity."[12] For Hobhouse, difference is dealt with as an aspect of individualism. The emphasis on individual rather than collective rights is justified by its focus on experience rather than form, he says. Individuals, of course, relate to communities, and individuals are not eternally self-separated, and egoism is not the truth of the world. But, as Hobhouse indicates, the focus on individuals is a recognition of the human situation. The focus on individuals

> is . . . an effort to go back from institutions, laws and forms, to the real life that lay behind them, insisting that this was a life of individual men and women with souls to be saved, with personalities to be respected, or simply with capacity for feeling anguish or enjoying their brief span of life.[13]

Individualism can also reappear in the idea that one's interest in group life and in the diversity of group life and even its sovereignty has its roots in individual autonomy. There is, on the individual level, an analogue of the point that Acton made as to the growth of political liberty. Civil liberty for the individual, Acton argued, was a result of the conflict over centuries between church and state.[14] So too, one might say that the claims of groups to normative authority over individuals result in the freedom of those individuals to evaluate and finally to choose between those normative claims.[15]

As to the individuals whose choices underlying the state and all other associations, this book has also been an attempt to complicate our assumptions of the unit-self. Using this sense of self, the book has attempted to present a view of individuals and groups in which individuals stand in various relations to groups, creating them, operating as members within them, and finally having the groups operating, in a way, within them.

As to the state, the discussion argues that there is no single sense of the state over time and in all countries, and that possibilities for individuals in relation to the state will be highly various. Montaigne could write of

---

[12] Leonard T. Hobhouse, *The Metaphysical Theory of the State* (Westport, Conn.: Greenwood Press, 1984), 60. On Hobhouse, see generally Jan G. Deutsch, *Selling the People's Cadillac: The Edsel and Corporate Responsibility* (New Haven: Yale University Press, 1976).

[13] Hobhouse, *Metaphysical Theory*, 26. He also notes that the danger exists that an emphasis on individual personality can be exaggerated "to the point of depreciating the common life" and that "criticism might degenerate into anarchy" (26–27).

[14] Acton, "The History of Freedom in Christianity," in *Essays on Freedom and Power* (Boston: Beacon Press, 1948), 58, 62.

[15] Another emphasis sees the value of pluralism in the richness it brings to society. See Gutmann, *Democratic Education*.

the French nobleman, "In truth, our laws are free enough, and the weight of sovereignty scarcely touches a French nobleman twice in his life."[16] Clearly that freedom from control was not available to everyone. Montaigne was talking about nobility. By the time Thoreau said that he spent little time under government, there is more of a sense that this stance, a stance removed from the state, was available to people more generally, across classes. But by now, in an age of the expansion of state responsibility, we may have lost the idea that anyone can be free of the state. But we can still ask, following Thoreau, how much time we spend under a government, how much time in the state, and how much in society.

This book has assumed that law is not distinct from culture but is part of larger social context, a point often now associated with the work of Clifford Geertz, and his notable formulation, Law is a "distinctive manner of imagining the real."[17] That way of imagining the real has a good deal of social importance, both reflecting and deflecting society,[18] as the realist Karl Llewellyn put it. Law at different levels is important in shaping the life of subgroups within the larger society as well as the identity of individuals who are citizens of the state and members of the groups.

A *Dictionary of Global Culture,* by Kwame Anthony Appiah and Henry Louis Gates Jr., stresses that we live in a world that is not only local or national. That book presents the material that Americans living in that global culture ought to know. Law is, as it should be, included. *Brown v. Board of Education,* for example, is given a place in the story.[19] Law figures also in an entry that might be used to illustrate a problem of the limits of tolerance as well as the limits of law. Sati, in the *Dictionary of Global Culture,* is described as an Indian cultural practice. The entry refers to the law of the Brahmin, the Indian government, the English government, and, finally, the tenacity of the practice itself.[20] We see that law alone will not change such an embedded practice. We see also that toleration does not mean that all things must be tolerated. The questions, of course, are which will or will not be, and who will decide, and what will combine with law to bring about change.

[16] Montaigne continued, "The real and essential subjection is only for those among us who go seeking it and who like to gain honors and riches by such service; for anyone who wants to ensconce himself by his hearth, and who can manage his house without quarrels and lawsuits, is as free as the Doge of Venice." *Complete Essays of Montaigne,* trans. Donald Frame (Stanford: Stanford University Press, 1989), 195.

[17] Geertz, *Local Knowledge,* 173.

[18] Karl N. Llewellyn, "Behind the Law of Divorce," *Columbia Law Review* 1 (1932): 1281, 1283: "Law deflects society but society is reflected in the law."

[19] *Dictionary of Global Culture,* ed. Kwame Anthony Appiah and Henry Louis Gates Jr. (New York: Knopf, 1997).

[20] Ibid., s.v. "Sati."

If, as James Clifford has told us, culture is "contested, temporal and emergent,"[21] we can say similar things about law. Justice Oliver Wendell Holmes said that is "always approaching, but never reaching, consistency."[22] Grant Gilmore said, more recently, "Law is an unstable mass of material in precarious equilibrium."[23] Related ideas were powerfully summarized in 1937 by Arthur Corbin: "Since the evolution of law is struggle and compromise, no system of law can ever be static or definitely knowable," he wrote. "The struggle is a continuing struggle; the compromise is constantly renewed. Legislatures as well as courts constantly take a hand in constructing new lines and distinctions. The practices of business, and even the fundamental *mores* that are the source of our notions of 'right and wrong' are in constant process of evolution. Our beliefs as to what general welfare and 'public policy' require are confused and inharmonious."[24] Law becomes one of the cultural sites in which these social uncertainties are negotiated and compromised.

It is possible that the visual images used in this book, the emblems, are inadequate for the future we want, in part because they are too static. Musical metaphors may go deeper.

Plato argued in *The Laws* for unison, urging that training in music should result in a situation in which the whole community may come to voice always one and the same sentiment in song, story, and speech.[25] We have tended to move away from unison as a goal toward something called harmony. We even want to be in harmony with some committed to the goal of unity. Thus, we speak sometimes of wanting a pluralism that will tolerate some who are themselves not tolerant of plural approaches. Both the Platonic and the pluralist ideas are expressed as musical metaphors, Plato's "unison," our "harmony." To the extent that uniformity, or musical unison, is required, the folk culture, taken as the deviant culture, will tend to be ignored, or suppressed. But if some recognition is to be accorded the subculture, we still have a question as to the degree and form of the recognition. One metaphor some have invoked recently is polyphony, which becomes particularly apt when one stresses the pluralist interpretations of law.

[21] James Clifford, *The Predicament of Culture: Twentieth Century Ethnography, Literature, and Art* (Cambridge: Harvard University Press, 1988), 19.

[22] Oliver Wendell Holmes, *The Common Law* (New York: Dover Press, 1991).

[23] Grant Gilmore, *Ages of American Law* (New Haven: Yale University Press, 1978), 53.

[24] Arthur Corbin, "Recent Developments in the Law of Contracts," *Harvard Law Review* 50 (1937): 445, 475. These perceptions are, broadly speaking, associated with American legal realism. It should be noted that ideas of law, legal functions, and legal possibilities are themselves culturally specific.

[25] Plato, *The Laws*, trans. Trevor J. Saunders (New York: Penguin, 1986), 664a II 4–7.

The feeling for pluralism reduces itself more to a stance, or a mind-set, than it does to an agenda or an answer. It becomes a preoccupation more than a thesis, relating to horizontal rather than vertical relations. The attempt here has been to illuminate certain interactions to the end of complicating a political conversation on pluralism that goes on in different places. Some of the conversation on these points goes on within the official state law. Some of it goes in the interaction between the unofficial law of the internal group and the law of the surrounding state. Some goes on in our heads, as we position ourselves with reference to a variety of frames. The state hierarchy is not perfectly controlling, even at its strongest. In this sense, the Erastus Field painting is perhaps like M. C. Escher's Belvedere, a building that cannot exist in fact. And as to the Hicks paintings of the peaceable kingdom, perhaps the most serious point we can take from these efforts is that there are so many of them, continuing attempts to give physical form to the prophetic vision.

Index

Minorities Treaties of the League of Nations (1919–1920), 118–37; and affirmative action, 132; vs. American approach to minorities, 151–53, 151n, 152nn.67–68; Arendton, 149n.57; on categories and relevance of memberships, 124; and estates/privileges, 132–33; failures of, 122–24, 123n.14; and family autonomy, 134–35, 134n.60; on funding, 135n.61; government parties to, 119–20, 119n.2, 123n.14; on group life, importance of, 128; on Julian Huxley's universalism, 140; and identities of groups, 9–10; influence of, 123, 123n.13, 133; limitations of, 127–28; on loyalty to the state, 123n.13; on membership in a group, 124; on minority schools, 10, 130–31, 131nn.46,49, 133–35, 135n.61, 140, 155; Mises on, 149n.57; on nondiscrimination, 131–32; on oppression of minorities, 120, 120n.4; political objectives of, 120, 120n.4; on political units, 124; purposes of, 119, 120; renunciation of rights by Turkish Jews, 128–29n.37, 158–59n.5; and state monopoly on education, 10; vs. United Nations human rights materials, 123, 134–35

Minow, Martha, 172, 184n.30, 204
Mises, Ludwig von, 3, 3n.8, 140, 188
Moberg, David O., 106n.28
Modern Times community, 37n.30
Mohammedan Law, 126n.27
monogamy, 56
Monroe, James, 22, 23
Montaigne, Michel Eyquem de, 5, 103, 206–7, 207n.16
Montesquieu, Charles de Secondat, Baron de la Brède et de, 5–6
Moore, Sally Falk, 94n.55
Morgan, Edmund, 114n.63
Mormon Church v. United States, 56
Mormons, 46–64; on adoption, 62; assimilation/retrenchment of, 59–60, 60n.59; birth/death rate among, 57; children's removal from their families, 163; as churchlike vs. sectlike, 60–61, 60n.59; on church/state separation, 50–60, 57–58; communitarianism of, 57; and constitutionalism as a framework or set of folkways, 61; on the Constitution as divinely inspired, 54; Ellis Island archives of, 179n.5; family values of, 58; on Gentiles, 57n.38; health of, 57; insiders vs. outsiders, 179n.6; and law vs. religion, history of, 46–49, 48n.3, 49nn.6–7; in literature/film, 63–64, 63–64nn.68–70; majority/influence in Utah, 57–58, 57n.38,

57n.40, 61–62; migration to Utah/persecution of, 49, 50–51, 64, 92; on political change, 51n.11; and the polygamy dispute, 8, 49, 50n.8, 54n.26, 175 (*see also* polygamy; *Reynolds v. United States*); polygamy officially abandoned by, 53–54, 54n.25, 56, 59, 60, 63; and the state, modes of relations with, 62–63; theocracy of, 159n.8; and Utah, modes of relations with, 61–62; and Utah's state constitution, 49–50; Word of Wisdom of, 57

Morrill Act (1862), 51, 51n.13, 52
Morse, Inspector (fictional character), 196
Morse, Samuel, 13
Mortara case (Mortara, Edgardo), 10, 159, 160–63, 160n.10, 161n.14, 169n.45, 170n.52, 171, 177
Mozert v. Hawkins County Bd. of Ed., 138n.2
Musil, Robert: *The Man without Qualities,* 191n.57
Musser, Joseph, 59, 59n.49
Mussolini, Benito, 90, 128n.35

Nabokov, Vladimir, 83n.17
names of the complex self, 188–98; and assimilation, 197; Bali naming system, 193, 194n.69; and class, 194; definition of the complex self, 178; and identity, 189nn.47–48, 191, 197; inherited names, 191; and law, 192, 192n.61; and membership in communities, 194, 194n.71; multiple names/nicknames, 193; multiple selves, 189–91, 190n.55, 191n.57, 197–98, 197n.86; name changes, 192–93, 196; rejection of, 196; and religious groups, 195, 195n.77; self as social, 188; state's role in naming, 191–92, 194–95; and titles, 196; and transformation, 190; Western vs. non-Western view of, 193n.66

Napoleon Bonaparte, 81
national identity, and religion/ethnicity, 48
Native Americans. *See* Indian tribes
natural law, 37–38, 38–39n.37
Nazis, 91, 163–64, 195
Nelson, Willie, 200
New Deal, 107n, 128n.35
New Harmony (Indiana), 7, 21–22, 23–24, 26–27, 27n.54, 28n.58
New Lanark (Scotland), 18, 22, 27n.54
Newton, Sir Isaac, 45
New York City, 87
Nicholls, Anthony H., 113–14
The Night of Girondist (Presser), 191n.57